Reviews

"When life throws a curve ball most people duck, but Jane Albanese catches it and throws it back. *Whoa! I'm Walking on Water* is a compelling and inspirational story about love, loss and the ability to hang in there. It keeps your interest to the last page. Jane takes us on her personal journey through the good times and the bad, and shows us what hard work and perseverance can accomplish. This is a must read for anyone wondering how to get through this thing called life." — *Barbara Donaldson*

"This is a fascinating story of a woman who had it all. Then betrayal took her down and nearly did her in. It made me wonder why it all happened. Eventually, after traveling numerous roads seeking satisfaction in her own life, she realized her need to do something meaningful to help others in need. Then, utilizing her many talents, she makes a difference in the lives of many who had nowhere else to turn. It's a brave portrayal of honest emotions and experiences told in a sometimes light and other times graphic way. I found myself getting emotionally involved and didn't want to put it down." — *Alicia B. Taylor*

"Jane Albanese provides us with a spirited glimpse into a bygone era, as a member of a prominent Bergen County family—when family and friends lasted a lifetime, as did their stories and antics.

Then after a life-shattering episode delivers her a crushing blow, Albanese picks herself up, draws upon her inner strength and goes on to do great things."

— *R. Bennett Radol, BBA, MS, MSED, MPBA, JD*

In the end,

When I asked my editor, Barry Sheinkopf, his opinion of the book, without hesitation he replied, "In all of the years I've been doing this work, I have edited hundreds if not thousands of stories about families, but never one like this.

Whoa!

I'm Walking On Water

Whoa!

I'm Walking On Water

Rising From A Life Shattered

D. Jane Chagaris Albanese

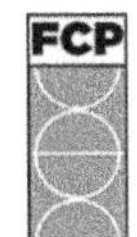

Full Court Press
Englewood Cliffs, New Jersey

First Edition

Published in the United States of America
by Full Court Press
601 Palisade Avenue
Englewood Cliffs, NJ 07632
www.fullcourtpress.com

visit us at www.whoaimwalkingonwater.com

ISBN 978-1-946989-28-4
Library of Congress No. 2019931565

Edited by Barry Sheinkopf and proofread by Christopher Chaberski
A special thanks to Barbara Donaldson, Kimberly Naphegyi & Roger B. Radol, esq.

Book design, cover art, and photo enhancements by
D. Jane Chagaris Albanese

Colophon by Liz Sedlack

I dedicate this book to my dad Peter Chagaris,
my first love,
and to the other wonderful men who have graced my life,
loving me just as I am.

A special dedication to Sam Vaughn,
– President, publisher, and editor-in-chief of Doubleday Books –
I had the great pleasure of spending many informative
and fun filled hours with
Sam in the year just prior to his death.

Contents

Book Three

The Rising

Foreword

With unparalleled honesty, Jane Albanese shares her at once heartwarming and heartbreaking story of family, love, loss, reinvention, and redemption. Written in three parts, we first witness an idyllic childhood. As a young woman Jane was surrounded by love, warmth, laughter, and the richness of family and friends. She paints vivid and lifelike portraits of debutante balls, encounters with old Hollywood legends, meeting the Pope, and the glamour and glitz of growing up privileged.

In book two we see the family dynamic change. The bliss enjoyed during her extraordinary younger years comes to a screeching halt. Family dysfunction, alcoholism, violence, illicit love, and secrecy all played key roles in Jane's life.

Faith gives her the will to become the person she is today. The woman we find in book three is no longer flying too close to the flames. We witness her growth as a spiritual person on a quest to live her best life by putting herself in the service of others. Inspired by an Oprah Winfrey program, she establishes a non-profit organization that has changed the lives of thousands of people for the better.

Whoa! I'm Walking on Water, told with a spiritual poignancy and hard-earned wisdom, is for anyone who has been brought to their knees by love, loss, or despair. It is a true testament of survival, hope, and rising to a new life. Most importantly, Jane finally arrives at a place of forgiveness.

— *Kimberly Naphegyi*

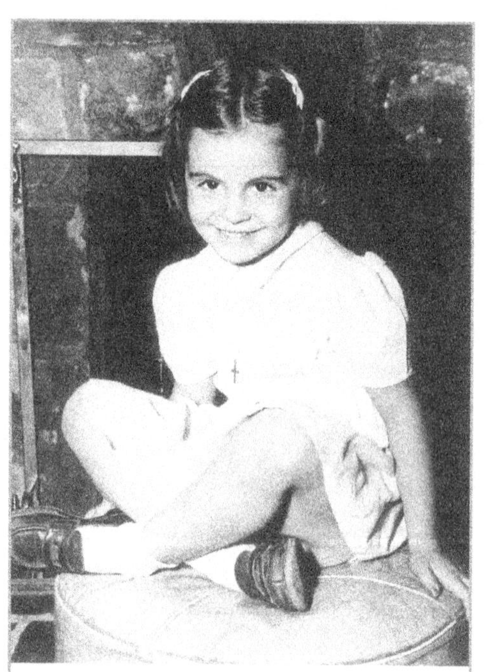

Me at age five in my penny loafers

Introduction

I FELT AS IF A BOMB HAD RIPPED my world apart when my family tried to snuff me out for the second time. What they didn't know, though, was that the Man upstairs wasn't finished with me yet. Had I been clever enough to foresee His plan for my life, I might have been able to circumvent the resulting pain.

Nonetheless, I have come through these experiences to learn many valuable life lessons about courage, survival, faith, and hope. Regrettably, I have also unveiled a great deal of gripping information about betrayal and greed, and their abounding consequences.

Although my journey has been a difficult one to comprehend, the lessons I have learned can be of great value to others. My life story can, I think, positively influence the lives of many who are going through their own agonizing trauma by showing how my faith has always picked me up, setting me back on the right path.

Given my dyslexic tendencies, I wonder how this book was written at all. It is, however, a story of great love, bursting with loads of joy and laughter, and pierced with excruciating, seemingly endless pain. Written solely from my own perspective, the book intends to explore the true spirit of love, the importance of family and good friends, and the truth.

As I've recounted the blessed if paradoxical trek that I have been on and cling to my cherished memories, I have questioned and studied my fate and my faith.

Like a pendulum on steroids, life's twists and turns have taken me from a place of great privilege to one I hope never to visit again—not quite as I had envisioned it. I've been happier than a songbird in spring and sadder than anyone should be allowed to be. I've been deeply in love, safe, and financially secure. And I've been cold-heartedly thrown away, abandoned, and betrayed—fueled by anger and dysfunction. At times I have also been hungry and terribly frightened.

These experiences have taught me how fragile we are, and why we must always be there for one another in order to sustain life.

I hope that this story will help others recognize the precious value of human interaction and the priceless bond of family, as I believe our Creator intended.

Forever present in the crevices of my mind, as if a guiding light of life, are these marvelous words of wisdom often shared by my late husband Dom: "Every human being possesses three distinct characteristics:

"First there are inherited characteristics—the things we receive from our gene pool, like our looks, the color of our eyes, and our ethnic background.

"Then there are environmental characteristics—the things in our surroundings that guide and direct the course of our lives, such as where we live or go to school, our religious training or lack thereof, the friends with whom we associate, and the neighborhood where we grow up.

"Finally, and perhaps the most important, are the individual characteristics. These are the traits that are uniquely ours and offer us the ability to find our own way, to make better choices, to learn dignity of self and the nobility of spirit—giving us the strength to improve upon or change the things of which we disapprove."

How liberating the possibilities!

My heart goes out to all who may never have experienced the joy of a loving home or the gift of a happy childhood. Mine were deliriously happy, although not without a hiccup or two along the way.

Did I say hiccup?

Actually, that depends on the vantage point from which you are viewing my life—sometimes there was a little hiccup or bump in the road, sometimes a smack on the head.

Having enjoyed an abundance of great blessings and then the reversal of that good fortune, I have come to know that, without our consent, our goals and dreams can be extinguished in a nanosecond. With the reality of that sobering thought, my knees buckled and my heart shriveled, as everything for me was lost yet again! I would never have thought that experience possible, given the charmed life that we had lived. The feelings of isolation and desperation consumed my every thought, and I became despondent—resigned to giving up.

Then, as a broken-winged angel rises anew from the ashes of yet another devastating blow, an Oprah Winfrey program, and the memory of a family's estrangement and their reunion in the opening chapter, once again reignited my spirit and redirected my path. It caused me to make a transformative decision—one to do something meaningful to help others.

Although unsteady at times, I was not terribly surprised when my calling to a new endeavor became evident. Convinced that God has a master plan, I forged ahead. With this new venture came its own set of ambitious goals and pitfalls, and yet, no matter how challenging or perplexing, I have walked with a confident stride—my determination never faltering.

Then one day, as I turned sixty-five, while working as the

creative director in a verbally abusive situation in which stealing from my paycheck *was not* an uncommon practice—I quit.

As in the fourth watch of the night, *(Matthew 14:25-32)* I placed one foot outside the office, raised my eyes to heaven, and, in one great act of trust, said, "Lord, I'm going to walk on water to You, for I know not what else to do."

I have since come to fully trust in God's promises, albeit sometimes with a heavy heart. As difficult as my challenges have been, I am certain that I've been chosen to serve, and that my trials and tribulations have been set before me to demonstrate the divine power of faith. There have been times, however, when I've struggled to remain buoyant, especially when negative comments flowed freely from naysayers. Luckily, I knew that *they* do not know God's plan for my life!

I have heard His voice whispering through the crashing of the waves, saying, *Come, rest in the warmth of my embrace. Know that I will never leave you or forsake you.*

While seeking calm through the pounding of the stormy seas, I knew instinctively, that I must keep my faith strong and be encouraged that all will be well. I have since kept my eyes trained on Him, and thus far, only my sandals are wet.

It is my fervent hope that through my witness, and by your faith, that you, too, will arise from the depths of your valleys.

Book One

The Oddness of a Happy Youth

1

THE REUNION

LIFE WAS AS CLOSE TO BEING PERFECT as it could get, and to me that wasn't odd at all. I had every reason to believe that it would last forever. We had a loving and happy family with a fabulous circle of friends, all of whom helped fill our side-splittingly funny and colorful life.

But then it happened.

Life got turned inside out, filled with turmoil and sadness. Unable to get the answers I needed to comprehend why I was at the center of great conflict, I had to find a way to survive and to heal. You and I may never know exactly what transpired next, and why; so let me take you on this journey, and then perhaps we can both draw our own conclusions.

While trying to find some semblance of understanding, I attended a self-help seminar in Tampa. There I met a man who reappeared in my memory several times over the course of my life.

As we began to settle in the first evening, the din of the crowd had a detached eeriness to it. We smiled awkwardly at one another, in an effort to get comfortable on the frigid gray metal folding chairs. A microphone, a clean blackboard, and an empty platform in a stark and annoyingly cold conference room set the stage as the three hundred or so ordinary, nameless people were instructed to take their seats.

Then, in walked David Cunningham, our coach. He began by bellowing, "Hi, everyone, welcome! Those of you who are here for the first time can expect a breakthrough this weekend. We're going to have some fun, and we'll explore what makes the human species tick."

Although I was looking for some kind of sign or direction in my life, I hadn't the faintest idea what the coach had in mind, but I was ready.

As the weekend progressed, David asked some audience members to approach the mics that were strategically placed around the room. He asked, "Why are you here, and in what areas of your life do you need a breakthrough?"

Some of the stories they told had us cracking up; others were remarkably sad and we wept for them as we quietly shared their pain.

At first, everyone was nervous, but David's wildly infectious laugh quickly put us at ease. We played some funny mind games and listened to stories of why these people had chosen to spend their weekend at the Landmark Forum.

I had been through a lot and I wasn't quite ready to spill my guts to a group of strangers, so I stayed clear of the mics for the first few days.

We were told not to leave our seats until we had a scheduled break, and, after each break, we were to sit next to someone new.

The second day, I sat next to a man who looked to be in his late eighties. Curious why someone of his age would be at a seminar of this kind, I waited for an opportunity to ask him.

His reply took my breath away. I could fully sympathize with him, not only because of his obvious pain, but also because of a similar situation in my own life.

He was Jon Shepard, from Easton, Pennsylvania, and his first words were "I haven't seen my son in twenty-five years, and I'm dying."

His skin was pale as cream. With a furrowed brow, he looked at me pleadingly; tears filled his sad eyes.

Without hesitation and before he could continue, I raised the palm of my hand to him and said, "Wait! You must find your son. I'm going to help you find him."

What are ya, nuts? I said to myself. How the hell am I going to do that? I'd almost wished I could suck the words right back into my mouth. How had it happened that I'd sat next to *this* particular man?

The thought of possibly helping him find his son came from the joy and gratitude still fresh in my mind from having just been reunited with my own family, after an eight-year estrangement.

Jon went on to say, "My wife and daughter are here at the seminar. I'll introduce you during the next break."

When I asked him what had caused the rift, he replied, "He'd been smoking pot and, thinking I was being a good father, I told him not to come home until he stopped smoking it.

"He never came home!"

Jon's voice began to crack. "I didn't mean it," he said, "if only I could take those words back! Short of hiring a private investigator, we've tried everything to find him over the years but have had no luck at all. God, we've got to find him, please. I don't want to leave this earth without being able to tell him how sorry I am."

As his tired eyes welled up again, I tried to offer him a glimmer of hope in an effort to comfort him when I said, "I'll do everything I can to help find your son."

I'd committed to giving the search my best effort, because I wanted so badly to reunite them, yet I knew that I was likely only kidding myself.

Having that conversation with Jon Shepard would years later alter the course of my own life. Although our stories are similar and we are reluctant members of the same club, our outcomes have been very different. Estrangement has not been a stranger in my life.

Jon Jr.'s last known address was somewhere in Florida, which gave me an edge since I was living in Daytona Beach at the time.

When I got home, I went to the new library on City Island, figuring I could begin my search the old-fashioned way—looking through phone books for Jon Shepard, Jonathan Shepard, J. Shepard Jr. I could have gone online, but I prefer the tactile feel of paper, and I thought it would be much easier that way.

The bindings of the musty-smelling old phone books cracked open, pages had been torn out, earmarked, and scribbled on, but I quickly scanned a few counties, looking for his name. As I jotted the numbers down, I was surprised that there weren't as many as I had expected.

The first day I found only six. I thought they would be as good a place as any to begin and could hardly wait to make the first call.

When a man answered, I said, "Hi, my name is Jane Albanese and I'm looking for a Jonathan Shepard from Easton, Pennsylvania."

"Sorry," he said, "that's not me. I'm from Ann Arbor, Michigan."

I thanked him and then dialed the next number. This Jon Shepard was in a nursing home in Jacksonville, but he, too, was unrelated to the family.

I was beginning to realize the process might be a long and arduous one, and hoped I wouldn't give up too easily.

I dialed the third number.

The man on the other end asked, "Who are you, what do you want, and what business is it of yours anyway?"

I explained, "I'd just sat next to a man with the same name at a seminar in Tampa, who's looking for his son. I'm a friend just trying to help. Are you from Easton, Pennsylvania?"

There was a split second of silence on the line.

Again he inquired, "Who are you?"

I retold my story, suddenly realizing that I might have hit the jackpot.

"Give me your phone number," he said gruffly, "and I'll call you back in a little while."

My goodness, he wasn't very pleasant, I thought. In that instant, I went from elation to deflation. If this was Jon Jr., maybe he didn't want to be found. It was as if I had hooked the big fish and, just as I was reeling him into the boat, the line broke and icy seawater drenched my face, stinging my eyes—and he'd gotten away.

What on earth was I going to tell Jon and his family? What if I never heard from this man again? What if he didn't want to see them?

My heart ached, and my mind was racing.

After what seemed like an awfully long fifteen or twenty minutes, the phone rang. Still excited, yet dumbfounded by the possibility of this miraculous stroke of luck, I answered. I didn't know who was more shocked, he or I. Again he asked, "Who are you, and what's this call all about?"

"As I told you earlier, I'm trying to help a man find his son. Are you from Easton?"

"I–I'm embarrassed, and almost ashamed to tell you this, but when you called me earlier, I was sitting on the edge of my bed sobbing—missing my family."

My heart skipped a beat. My eyes got misty, and a quiet came over us both, as if embracing each other. There was a long pause.

I never saw the house where Jon Jr. lived, but in my mind's eye, as if in a movie, I could see the Key West style tin roof, leaning slightly to the south, rusted and curling with age, Spanish moss dripping from its eaves. The old wood-frame house seemed tired and worn. Broken-down rocking chairs adorned the weathered front porch; they were in need of a fresh coat of paint, and they creaked in the wind as though beckoning family and friends. An occasional breeze stirred the mist, and cotton-like clouds floated high above. It was early afternoon, the sun high in the sky, the air heavy with moisture, and it was hot!

I pictured the camera panning to the inside of the half-opened casement window of his bedroom. There, I imagined a somewhat disheveled middle-aged man sitting on the edge of his bed, bent over—his head in his hands. He'd been crying. He rubbed his eyes, then ran his fingers through his thinning gray hair.

As he reached for the phone, a bubbly voice on the other end said, "Hi, I'm Jane Albanese, and I'm looking for a man named Jonathan Shepard from Easton, Pennsylvania."

Calling from my den in Daytona Beach, his split second of silence had startled me. As if finding a needle in a haystack, I knew that I had found the man I was looking for! How could this be? For twenty-five years his family had tried to locate him with more passion and desperation than I. Why was I the one who'd found him? It was a question that, many years later, I have finally been able to answer. I had been given a gift, without knowing at the time how I was to use it. This realization was the breakthrough that David Cunningham, from the Landmark Forum, had promised—slightly delayed in its delivery, however, and far more formidable than I could have imagined, as you will see.

Still reeling with emotion, quite choked up, he asked about his mom and dad. His sister, now thirty-eight, had been only thirteen the last time he saw her.

Of course, I had to tell him, "Your dad is not well, and he needs to see you. Are you willing to meet with them?"

Anxious, excited, and a bit afraid, he said, "I need some time to sort this all out, but yes, I will consider meeting with them."

His pain was palpable, God's timing impeccable.

I wish I could say I can't begin to imagine how he must have been feeling, but that wouldn't really be accurate. I believe I knew exactly how he was feeling.

Overcome by my own recollections of my family reunion just weeks earlier, my hands were trembling as I picked up the receiver again to make the next call. Tears were blurring my vision. I dialed his father's number.

When Jon answered, I quickly said, "Hi Jon, it's Jane Albanese. How are you?" Before allowing him to respond, I asked, "Can you get Mary on the extension?"

"Mary, get on the phone!"

When I heard her pick up the line, I announced, "I've found your son!"

Their shrills and shrieks were ear-piercing.

"Where is he? How is he? When can we see him?" they screamed.

Was this one of the happiest and proudest moments of my life, or what?

"He's in Lakeland, Florida, just miles from where we first met," I said, "and he's fine, but he needs some time to take this all in. He misses you, and he's eager to see you."

Within weeks, the Shepard family was reunited. I was happy for them and wished I could have been there. They spoke of how they had embraced, sharing their regrets and family photos, and they forgave one another.

Jon Jr. had never married, but his sister, Mariah, had two girls and a boy she had named Jonathan, III.

Over the next several months, I enjoyed hearing about how they'd created precious new memories. We kept in close contact for a while, and I believe my new friend Jon was finally at peace when he passed away later that year.

Whoever coined the old childhood adage "Sticks and stones may break my bones, but words will never hurt me" was dead wrong. This real-life story is proof of that. Not only can words shatter the human spirit, they can unravel a family unit, bringing it to near extinction.

2

A Hallmark Family

Heading for the land of opportunity, my grandparents and their young family immigrated to America in 1914.

After crossing the Mediterranean and the Atlantic on a very small vessel for more than forty days and nights, they reached Ellis Island from the tiny little town of Kalamata, Greece.

They were a family with a pioneering spirit. Dad, his parents, and two older brothers, Felix and John, and my grandmother's two sisters Olga and Anna, endured the trip after contracting dysentery and seasickness from the rough, wind-blown high seas. Uncle Jim was born in this country. My grandmother, Theodora, passed away, unfortunately, shortly after Jim's birth.

Although Thea Olga and Thea Anna never quite mastered the English language, they had quick wits and discerning wisdom, and were great fun to be with.

While seeking to secure a new life after bringing his family here, my grandfather invested his meager savings in a small luncheonette in Hoboken, New Jersey. My father worked there after completing only fourth grade in grammar school. His three brothers went on to college, and Dad, although he worked hard, enjoyed reading whatever he could lay his hands on—from The Wall Street Journal and Barron's to The Christian Science Monitor. He became a successful, self-educated businessman and a self-taught master chef.

As the family matured in its new homeland, Gramps opened a second small eatery in Jersey City called The Bar-B-Que. By then Uncle John and Uncle Jim were also involved in the daily operations of the two restaurants.

The twenty-four-hour, truck-stop-type luncheonettes were right out of a Norman Rockwell painting. They had open griddles, Formica countertops, and swivel stools mounted to the floor—one with pink marbleized plastic seat covers, the other with yellow. There were half a dozen round tables with old-fashioned ice-cream-parlor-style chairs—pretty high fashion back then, I suppose.

Uncle Felix became a student and teacher of history, and a very successful entrepreneur in his own right. He sold homemade pies, made at our restaurants, from street carts in Jersey City. He later purchased and then sold the majestic and historic Fairmont Hotel, which was often visited by U. S. Presidents, to Father Divine of The Peace Center Church and Home and The Palace Mission, two non-profit corporations under the Peace Mission Movement. The sale took place in February 1962 for four-hundred-thousand dollars in cash, an extraordinary sum for the day.

Felix was different from his brothers. His dark, deep-set eyes, bushy black eyebrows, and crooked smile used to scare me. It seemed like those eyes followed me as I moved around the room. Fortunately, we never saw that much of him. My last, lingering memory of him is as he lay dying in a large, zippered plastic oxygen tent in Margaret Hague Hospital, the place of my birth. His eyes were intent on mine, and it felt creepy.

Dad's eyes, on the other hand, always had a twinkle in them. He was blessed with a set of native strengths that influenced the course of his life. For him, cooking and laughing were like breathing.

A prankster at heart, he usually worked the graveyard shift. As I think of him, still missing his loving ways, I'm reminded of a joke he often played on some of his regular customers. The same tired, burly truck drivers came to roost at the counter around three in the morning and ordered the usual, ham or bacon and eggs, with toast, and a hot cup of coffee. On more than one occasion, they placed their order and rested their weary heads on the counter to take a snooze while my father slaved over the hot stove. During the course of many years, they became good friends, so no one was offended when Dad decided to crumple up a paper napkin and place someone else's dirty plate in front of the sleeping driver.

When he awoke, Dad said, "You owe me a buck and a quarter!"

The driver was puzzled and scratched his head. "Golly, I don't even remember eating that."

My father collected the money and said, "Now, get the hell out of here!"

But the driver said, "Geez, I'm still hungry."

Unable to keep from laughing, Dad was caught red-handed, and I'm sure he was pelted with the crumpled-up napkin and probably a saltshaker or two. It was all in good fun, and it was how this man endeared himself to his guests.

Entertaining himself often while peeling carrots in the yard behind the restaurant, Dad would throw one or two over the fence to where Emily Moseman lived. Sometimes it was a potato or even a ham sandwich. A unique way of wooing your girl, I thought. However, laughter being his driving force, and with that sparkle in his eye, they began courting, and as he put it, "I've been feeding her ever since."

Mom's heritage was strongest on her father's side. Born in this country, my maternal grandfather was half-German and half-American Indian—Mohawk, I think, from upstate New York. As I look back, that may explain a lot.

An Irish stepmother, who never quite measured up to the role in my mother's eyes, raised her. My mother often quipped, "She was cold and indifferent, and she was un-nurturing."

Mom's natural birth mother was also Irish. Sadly, she died two years after my mother's sixteen-pound birth.

My mother had a brother named Valentine, who married our sweet Aunt Philomena. I used to call them Uncle Phil and Aunt Val, and they had two daughters, Margaret and Beverly.

Aunt Phil was Italian, and that side of the family was different from my father's in a playful kind of way. The simple things in life were important to them, and they constantly made us laugh.

Aunt Phil, in her flowery, misbuttoned housedress and sensible shoes, invariably did a little soft-shoe for us on the landing going up the stairs in our home on West Clinton. She would recite a riddle called "The Horsey." She'd curtsey and say, "The horsey has one, two"—then looking rather bashful and shy, not remembering the words, she would bow and start all over again, "The horsey has one, two, three legs." Then she'd sort of kick the ground with her right foot and say, "Aw, shucks," and curtsey again. "The horsey..."

I can't remember how many legs that damn horsey had, but I do remember the beautiful spirit of my Aunt Phil. She filled our home with love and laughter, and I miss the joy she brought to us when our families were together.

Uncle Val and my mother were very close. He was there in the background, and I sensed she felt, at times, that he was her only ally. He was a slight man and typically had a cigarette hanging from the side of his mouth. His shiny, straight black hair was worn in a crew cut, and he had a bunch of teeth missing. We teased him relentlessly about looking like Rudolph with his nose so bright. Yes, he did enjoy the health benefits of his father-in-law's homemade Italian (guinea red) wine.

I never knew we had an Uncle Harold until many years later, when he died. I heard my mother crying in her room.

"Mom, what's wrong?"

"My brother died," she said.

"Uncle Val died?"

"No, Uncle Harold."

"Who the hell's Uncle Harold?"

She told me the story of their estrangement—there's that ugly word again.

"Why didn't you ever tell us about him? I would have loved to have another uncle. Did he have a family?"

"Yes, he was married to Aunt Cora, and they had two girls."

"What happened to cause the breakup?"

"Harold was my stepmother's son. When she died, just thirteen days before your grandfather, Harold and I had an argument over her will. She had left me her one-thousand dollar fortune, and Harold was upset," she explained. "After all, I took care of her at the end of her life. He didn't."

I suppose my mother felt justified in not sharing the money with Uncle Harold, or Uncle Val for that matter, although I'm sure Uncle Val would have sided with her; he always looked up to her.

Uncle Harold went on with his life, but they never spoke again. In my curiosity, I wondered why Mom was crying when she heard of his death five decades later. There seemed to be no love lost between them. She was never able to articulate her feelings about it. Perhaps she felt some guilt or had a strong brotherly bond, feelings she only realized after years apart. Regrettably, we never did get to meet Aunt Cora or their girls either.

I WAS JUST THREE WHEN OUR FAMILY MOVED from a three-story walkup in Hoboken to my parents' dream home in the quaint little village of Tenafly, New Jersey.

Tommy, my older brother, who is three and a half years older than I, and my younger sister, Linda, three and a half years younger, both resemble our mother's side of the family in coloring and personality.

Mom was a pretty lady with hazel eyes and a button nose. She had a great complexion and a beautiful head of hair. She stood about five-foot-one-inch tall and was rather voluptuous, and she dressed impeccably. I often said that she reminded me of Queen Elizabeth, but for some reason she didn't like that; apparently she didn't appreciate the Queen's looks.

I take after, and closely resemble, Dad's Greek heritage, with dark eyes and an olive complexion. I love the Greek culture, Greek food, and Greek dancing, and have a particularly strong sense of family.

Tenafly extends through the valley between the western slope of the Palisades and the Hackensack meadows of northeast New Jersey. An important commercial enterprise in its early years was a wampum factory where local currency was made from clamshells.

Tenafly played an important role in 1776, when George Washington and his small army crossed into New Jersey to prevent Generals Howe and Cornwallis from capturing Philadelphia.

Up north, a picturesque tavern stood alongside the road on the site of what is now the Clinton Inn Hotel and Event Center, and General Washington paused there in his hurried travels for a bit of libation and refreshment.

At the turn of the twentieth century, the old inn burned to the ground, but it was later restored as a red-and-white colonial-frame structure with a charming posted front porch.

Just after purchasing our adorable new home, Dad, who was always looking for a challenge, inquired whether that old colonial building in the heart of town was for sale. Unbelievably, it had just been sold. Dad and his friend Scotty continued on their afternoon drive before returning to Hoboken, and they came upon another old frame building in Hackensack called the Red Lion Inn. They stopped in for a cocktail to check the place out. It had more of an old English charm.

Dad said to Scotty, "This place is beautiful, too. Let's see if it's for sale." They inquired, but it was not.

As luck would have it, though, two weeks later, Garry Felter, our realtor, called and said, "Are you still interested in that old Inn in Tenafly? The other deal has fallen apart."

"Yes, absolutely," Dad said.

So once again, the family expanded its business. On July 31, 1948, my grandfather, Dad, and my two uncles bought the Clinton Inn Restaurant, just five minutes north of the George Washington Bridge and thirty minutes from downtown Manhattan. Dad ran it alone in the beginning, until the other two restaurants could be sold and everyone could move to Tenafly.

The Inn was a bustling and pleasant local eatery, with ten guest rooms on the second floor and two full baths down the handsomely wallpapered hall. If those walls could speak, I'm sure they'd reveal tidbits of Americana, plus many a tale of local gossip during the years we owned it from the late 1940s through 1998.

There was also a lovely old white-frame guest house we called "the annex" at the rear of the parking lot, with eight additional guest rooms, each with a private bath. Next to that sat a bank of twelve white garages that were used for storage and some guest cars. They made for perfect hiding spots when we played hide-and-go-seek with our cousins and friends.

The Inn's distinctive facade stood catty-cornered across from the historic stone train station. Around the holidays, we decorated the exterior with two enormous, thirty-foot live-lighted Christmas wreaths that hung from the double-gambreled roof, facing town. They could be seen from the other side of town and all the way up the railroad tracks.

Blue lights defined the crisp architectural lines of the old train station, and a life-sized crèche sat among the towering maples and oaks of Huyler Park, creating a picture-perfect postcard.

Sunday mornings, while the wives and kids were across the street at Our Lady of Mt. Carmel, the men enjoyed a "Whiskey Sour Mass," as they called it, at the end of the bar. The Grill Room with its elegant, high-backed Windsor chairs was paneled in pickled-oak, and the ceiling was adorned with embossed plum-colored tin tiles. A beautiful colonial hand-painted mural, ornately framed, proudly stood behind a richly oiled rosewood bar, and on it appeared these words: "A thousand welcomes you'll find here before you, the oftener you come, the more we'll adore you."

Everyone agreed the spirits were fine, the food was superb, and the atmosphere was warm, friendly, and delightfully cozy. Our entire menu was made from scratch. We butchered our own prime meats, sold the rendered fat trimmings to soap factories, made soups from homemade stock, and even produced our own ice cream and salad dressings. My father's first cousin, Stamatis, also baked all of the luscious pies and pastries, everything from Napoleons to honeybuns. The house specialties were the Clinton Inn sliced steak sandwich, the likes of which I have yet to find anywhere else; pot roast and potato pancakes every Saturday; corned beef and cabbage every Thursday; and homemade pecan pie that we served with a dollop of vanilla ice cream. With his innate culinary expertise, Dad often said, "You eat with your eyes first, and when you've finished you should want just one more bite."

Not even five years later, our family, all settled in Tenafly, purchased the Red Lion Inn in Hackensack.

The sparkling-clean stainless steel and tiled kitchens could be observed from the lobbies through large glass-paneled doors. In the early 1960s, the kitchens were fully air-conditioned, a practice still unheard of in the restaurant industry today.

Aside from the inviting ambiance, the Inns offered a man whom everyone loved—he was as much a draw as the food and the reason the guests returned again and again. They called him Mr. Pete. Gracious every hour of every day, he was the life of the party.

Women enjoyed being with him, men wanted *to be* him.

He was my dad.

3

To Thine Own Self Be True

One warm, stormy Saturday morning in August of 1951, the rain kept us inside. The windows of our new home were cracked open, and in the dampness the smell of burning cotton permeated the air. My mother was standing in the dining room, ironing my father's dress shirts. She always used a spray bottle of water to get the wrinkles out. That smell still conjures up a potpourri of happy memories, although ironing doesn't get done much anymore these days. It's a familiar and comfortable smell of home, and reminds me of our early idyllic family life. Waves of flavor hung in the air as Dad was in the kitchen, making my favorite French toast.

What happened next wasn't monumental at all but has been the compass guiding the rest of my life.

Tommy and Linda were tickling each other and rolling around

on the living room floor, laughing.

It was raining really hard, I remember, as I sat tucked in our big, orange-tweed barrel chair, looking out the window. My legs were stretched out straight, because I wasn't quite seven years old, which probably put me at a height of about three-foot-eight.

I had to squiggle and squirm to get out of the chair in order to join them on the floor.

In unison, they began to scream, "Mommy, tell her to go away."

Mom's knee-jerk reaction was, "Jane, leave them alone—they were playing so nice."

How could a little statement like that alter the course of my life? Although I couldn't put a label on it, I intuitively knew that I was different. I felt like an outsider or somehow unworthy of joining them.

I've never forgotten that moment and have always worked hard to gain my mother's love and respect, and to be accepted by her.

Tommy and Linda were having so much fun, and I never knew why I wasn't good enough to play with them.

Looking back now, intellectually I understand no harm was intended—at least that's what I chose to believe. Emotionally, however, I was hurt; but I loved my family so much, I felt it didn't matter. We had a life I still wish I could return to.

It wasn't until many years later that I heard about the "middle-child syndrome" and stories of others who felt like the black sheep of their family.

That was the explanation I was looking for: middle-child black sheep! *It had a name*, I thought to myself. At that moment, I knew it was part of this complicated phenomenon called *family*.

I remember Tommy saying, "We're such a close-knit family."

I looked at him and said, "No, we're not."

"That's because of you," he said.

Well, were we or weren't we?

Was that a hint of what was to come?

From then on, perhaps unknowingly at times, my guard was up. If people didn't readily accept me into their fold, I would stand alone. I'd be fine, but I would stand alone. It became my defense mechanism as I steeled myself against rejection. The irony of it was that it also created in me a deep, lifelong sense of loneliness on one hand, yet inevitably, on the other, fed a driving force to excel in whatever I chose to do.

It's been said that the black sheep is often more sensitive to the energy and dynamics of the rest of the family, and that therefore, he or she is considered weird, different, even an embarrassment. I have come to learn from that incident that each of us is different, and that we must find our unique nobility of spirit and be true to ourselves.

These days, I've noticed that some people seem to feel threatened by, even a bit envious of, my convictions in that regard. I'm aware that, although I'm a people lover, I don't bend easily to the will of others. My dream has always been to have everyone I love all together in the same place, at the same time. I used to fantasize about it. *Maybe that's heaven.*

Some forty years later, when my mother and I were having an in-depth conversation about my childhood, I mentioned how that one experience made me feel rejected by her.

Defensively, she replied, "I don't believe that a little comment like that could do you any harm." She went on to say, "When you were in a baby carriage down the shore one summer, I caught Tommy trying to overturn your carriage. I sent him to his room and I took you to the beach, leaving him home alone with Mrs. Mertz for several hours to punish him. So how can you say I singled you out?"

If I was still in a baby carriage, Tommy must have been about four or five years old. Could he have felt the same kind of rejection then? Why was he trying to overturn my carriage in the first place? Being the firstborn, he had been the only child in a very loving family for three and a half years before my arrival. Perhaps he was resentful of my mere existence.

Growing up as one of the few girls in the neighborhood, I remember he would often say to my mother, "Why does she have to hang around with us?"

We were just kids, and I believed that it was a simple case of sibling rivalry. So when Linda came along, though she was a girl, I'm sure he felt he had an ally in her.

Thinking back, I can't ever recall having had a pleasant, heartfelt conversation with Tommy, although we did spend a great deal of time together.

Here's one very funny incident I remember about Tommy. Our parents often went out for the evening, and one night our usual babysitter couldn't make it, so she sent a friend as a replacement. The poor soul was missing a few teeth and had a large hooknose with a big wart on the side and long straggly hair black as ink. I swear if she'd had a witch's hat, she'd have been the real deal. It was about six in the evening when Tommy caught a glimpse of her, and before my parents could get out the door, he said, "Mommy, can I go to bed now?" Trying not to laugh, they quickly escaped after telling him he had to have his dinner first. I think we all went to bed early that night. She was scary! The next morning, they promised to never leave us alone with her again.

Born under the October sky, I'm a true Libra. I tend to analyze both sides of every situation, to understand why people act as they do. Some may call that being arrogant or an unbearable perfectionist. I prefer words like astute, confident, and detail-oriented.

As I matured and was becoming more aware of my own intuition and sensitivities, my love for my family was boundless.

Someone once said of me, "You are blessed with a wisdom beyond your youth and cursed with a fine-tuned sense of awareness." I didn't know if it had been meant as a compliment or just another confusing explanation of why I didn't fit in. Some may have perceived my stand alone inclination as being snobbish or aloof. In fact, in the process of protecting myself from harm, I was also stretching my knowledge and studying the behavior of others with great curiosity.

I needed assurance that we were a normal, healthy, happy-go-lucky clan, blessed with an interesting and joy-filled life. We were living the American dream.

As our family grew, soon there were ten cousins among us. Athena and Arthur belonged to Uncle John and Aunt Helen, and Uncle Jim and Aunt Sophie had Tom, Ted, and Diana, and there was Margaret and Beverly, who came from Mom's side. Thea Olga and Thea Anna lived well into their nineties, and each had one son.

The elders kept us entertained with the beauty of their love and their heritage, especially on Greek holidays, birthdays, and name days. Both of our great uncles died very young, and as is traditional in Greek culture, the aunts remained dressed in black the rest of their lives. When they turned ninety, I found it so comical that, together, they stopped dying their hair, which had always been worn up in a bun on top of their heads. Soon there was an inch of white at their foreheads and temples, then two inches, and before you knew it, their heads were entirely white and just the bun was black. We teased them unmercifully, but they were good sports about it.

Each year, after going to the three-hour Easter mass at the Greek Orthodox Church in Fairview, New Jersey, Uncle John, the eldest, hosted a midnight feast at his home. The elders fasted for forty days and nights, so they looked forward to our traditional meal with great enthusiasm. The stars of the menu were egg-and-lemon magiritsa soup, made with chicken broth and the innards of a chicken, and there were lamb brains (I never quite got up the nerve to try them) accompanied by roast leg of lamb with pan-roasted potatoes, which I still love.

Aunt Helen dyed the brightly colored red and blue Easter eggs, which she never seemed to time quite right. We were going for hard-boiled, and she apparently preferred soft-boiled. Before the meal was served, we each took an egg; holding one end up in our hands, we went around the table cracking each other's eggs, saying, Christós anésti—Christ is risen. Sometimes we wondered if she actually cooked them at all, because all of a sudden the sticky, gooey, uncooked yolk would run down our arms to our elbows. Her quiet and subtly devious sense of humor had us in stitches. At the end of that ritual, the lucky one with the unbroken egg was assured good fortune for the rest of the year.

I have come to understand that the life I considered to be ordinary was, instead, rather extraordinary—we *all* had good fortune, and family was everything to me.

Living in Tenafly was like living in the Garden of Eden. During the summers, if we weren't traveling the world for six or eight weeks at a time, we vacationed at the Jersey Shore, spending months in the surf and sand. Either way, we returned to school bronzed and golden brown, with tales of our summer break. We also managed to squeeze in a trip or two to Palisades Amusement Park before school started again.

There, off in the distance, a monstrous creature arose from the rocks of the Palisades. It looked as though zillions of Popsicle sticks had been glued together in a helter-skelter fashion, creating gigantic mountains and valleys, and lazy, crazy curves high in the sky.

Clackety-clack-clack went the roller-coaster cars as they slowly ascended to the heavens, up to the pinnacle of a rickety frame structure aptly named The Cyclone. It whipped you through the air as if you were in the center of a vortex. You have to be nuts to ride that thing, I thought—*and they call this amusement!* Even the thrill-seekers screamed 'til their tonsils jumped from their throats. Their eyeballs seemed to leave their sockets as the Cyclone cars plummeted straight down into the depths of the valleys and then gradually climbed back up—just to do it all over again.

Brightly colored carousel horses galloped in place on their rotating platforms. Clowns with large, protruding red noses laughed and teased little kids with animal-shaped balloons, and the gaiety of carnival music filled the air. Tommy and I went from ride to ride. Although he was game for almost anything, I wanted to remain firmly connected to the ground—a thread woven throughout my personality.

As a spirited tomboy, I was ready to try rock climbing and bumper cars, but you wouldn't catch me on that Cyclone.

Although it wasn't the scariest ride at Palisades Amusement Park, it was up there on my list of things *not* to do in my lifetime.

Tommy's favorite ride was the Hell Hole, which consisted of a very large barrel with one door allowing the "crazies" to enter and stand against the wall, unattached to anything. It began to spin faster and faster, until their bodies became a blur, they were pinned to the wall by the centrifugal force of the rotation.

Spectators could watch from high above. Then suddenly, the bottom of the barrel would drop out from under them—and there they were, suspended and squished. It was frightening just to watch. As the barrel slowed, the floor would return. The totally dazed and disoriented people were soon back on their feet. They staggered out of control until their equilibrium caught up with them, and even then they were barely able to find their way to the exit. How could having your brains scrambled like that be fun? And how they kept down the cotton candy, soda pop, and pizza was a feat I will never understand.

It's been nearly fifty years since that old park was torn down in the name of progress, making room for high-rise condominiums with one of the most spectacular views in the world—the New York Harbor and its skyline.

I can still evoke memories of the sights, sounds, and smells of that fantastically whimsical place, and I'm grateful for my recollections.

4

THE RIGGERMAJIGGER MACHINE

ONE SATURDAY AFTERNOON, DAD SAID, "Pack your things everyone. We're going away to Blairstown for the weekend."

"What's in Blairstown?" I asked. "I don't wanna go."

"Oh, you'll have a good time. Some friends from Hackensack have invited us up to their lake."

"No, I'm not going, and that's all there is to it," bristled the ten-year-old me.

As we headed out Route 46 to Route 23, then down the long and winding stretch of Route 94 over the hills and dales, I sat in the back seat of our woody with my arms tightly crossed in defiance. I moaned and kvetched, but it did no good—we were almost there.

I was hoping he'd get lost, but Dad seemed to know exactly which little side roads to take. I could hardly wait to leave before we had even arrived. It was Labor Day weekend, and I had better things to do at home with my friends.

Up the rocky driveway as we made our way to their home, I noticed there was a life-sized replica of what seemed to be an old schoolhouse, sitting high on a huge bed of rock guarding the entrance, with a big bell on the roof. I could see a couple of dogs in pens off to the left, and Linda said, with surprise in her voice, "Look, there are chickens over there!"

It was beginning to look interesting, but I didn't want to admit that I might have been wrong. Truth was, all I had left behind soon paled in comparison to that magical place. I learned never to question my father's judgment again.

Our hosts for the weekend were Marjory and Emil Wulster. They welcomed us and were warm, loud, and funny, so I gave some thought to at least unlocking my arms, trying to be polite.

The Eldridges had gotten there before us with their two sons, Bryce and Jimmy, and just as we all got out of our cars, the Law family pulled up right behind us. We'd never met any of them before, but their daughter Melissa was Linda's age and Sheila and Cathy were close to mine. We got along surprisingly well—they were tomboys like me and loved to explore. Tommy had stayed behind and was at a friend's sleepover. Bryce was the oldest; I think he was in high school.

The Wulsters' home was an old stone gristmill, which they had disassembled on the other side of the lake—stone by stone and beam by beam—then reassembled it on a perfect piece of land nestled among clusters of tall pines, maples, and oaks about fifty or sixty feet up the hill from Cedar Lake.

Dogs were barking with delight, and everyone was talking as we greeted one another like long-lost friends.

Surprisingly, the weekend was beginning to display great promise, and my attitude perked right up. Within minutes of our arrival, after the introductions had been made, we felt like one big, happy family.

Emil and his wife, "Bunny," had two sons—Wayne, who stood six-foot-six, and Greg, who was a hunk and easy on the eyes, the spitting image of Marjory with her beautiful blue eyes and thinning blonde hair. She had been a raving beauty and a model when she was young, and although she had gained a great deal of weight, she was still beautiful, and they were a lovely-looking family.

My eyes popped when we entered their home. A well-worn Western saddle was perched on the end of the banister, a hand-painted upright player piano tucked beneath the stairwell. An enormous stone fireplace was ablaze and took up the whole wall across the room, flanked by two huge copper kettles that contained the firewood. I had never known a world like that existed, but I sensed that I was right in my element.

There were mammoth carved beams holding up the second floor and oversized matching sofas covered in a comfortable, put-your-feet-up kind of plaid fabric. Paintings of horses, chickens, and cows decorated the walls, along with dozens of family photos and pictures of the guys on hunting trips.

As we entered Marjory's kitchen, the first thing I noticed was another beautiful fireplace. This one was different: blue-and-white German tiles surrounded the firebox, and it had a more delicate wooden mantle. In the bay of the window sat an oblong wooden table and ten comfortable ladder-back chairs overlooking the lake.

On the far side of that large kitchen stood a cream-colored porcelain-and-polished-chrome stove next to a matching double sink. The counters were deeply grooved butcher block. You could tell this was her favorite room. Every little nook and cranny was filled with Hummel figurines. Her brightly colored pots and pans were artfully displayed, and carved beams braced the ceiling. When the windows were opened, a breeze off the lake filled the room with the scent of pine and fresh lake air.

Picture this: Off the kitchen lay a substantial screened porch, sixteen feet wide and a good twenty feet long, overlooking the lake. In addition to an octagonal table and chairs, there were two supersized triple-wide lounges. I had never seen anything quite like them; clearly they had been custom designed. The frames were made of wrought iron and very sturdy. They were about eight feet wide and possibly also eight feet long. Each was covered with thick cushions and handmade quilts. Three or four of us kids could lie on each of them with room for Wendy, the house dog, to snuggle in and cuddle up about our toes. There was a bearskin rug in the middle of the porch floor, and a few rifles and a moose head hanging on the wall. The view of the lake from the porch was tranquil and awe-inspiring.

Back in the house, a large elongated dining room extended well past the porch. All fifteen of us could fit quite nicely around it with Marjory at one end and Emil at the other. Mom and the other ladies set the table as Dad prepared a sumptuous meal.

The men hung around the kitchen, sipping cocktails, telling dirty jokes, and laughing out loud.

Before dinner was served, the seven of us kids took off on an expedition. We went down to the lake, where they docked their canoes and the riggermajigger machine. How cool was that? Wayne Wulster, their eldest son, had built a contraption with two large yellow vinyl seats atop a platform that straddled a set of aluminum pontoons, which he had salvaged from a seaplane at the local airport. He'd recycled some old bicycle pedals that turned the shaft and propelled the craft forward. He had an oversized set of handlebars to steer the rudder; it all looked like something out of Willie Wonka's chocolate factory. We peddled our way around the lake, exploring each little cove and beach, and then jumped into the water to cool off and give someone else a chance to peddle. The rest of us swam back to the dock. By the end of the day we were well worn out, ready to rest by the fire with a hot chocolate and some homemade German butter cookies.

They also had a beautiful old mahogany in-board motorboat moored there, which they kept covered under canvas. Her finish was like a mirror, and she seated four, with a steering wheel on the right. Her sleek dashboard had a bunch of dials, and the windshield framed in brass, glistened in the sun. She was a beauty! I could hardly wait to go for a ride.

In the late afternoon of that first day, a large school bell rang to call us all back to the house, so we could be assigned our beds. It was like being at camp. The adults all had rooms in the main house, and all of the kids, Bryce and Jimmy included, got to sleep in the bunkhouse that doubled as Emil's workshop.

During the days that followed, as the sun rose over the surrounding peaks, it warmed the lake. Good thing, because Dick Law would be the first one up in the morning, before sunrise, and he became our alarm clock as he ran down to the water stark naked with a hand towel covering his private parts, screaming, "Everyone up! Let's get into the pool!"

We were not quite as courageous as he, but, as if at his command, we scrambled to get into our bathing suits. We were in co-ed living quarters, so we had to hide behind beach towels and blankets as we removed our pajamas and pulled on our suits. Finally we tiptoed down to the lake to stick our toes into the chilly water. We relished the fun of watching the other men join Dick. They were buck-naked too, so heave-ho, they just ran and jumped in. We laughed, filled with embarrassment. Fortunately, Dad wasn't one of them. He was up in the kitchen preparing breakfast for everyone with our big, healthy fresh-air appetites.

Wendy, who was part collie and part shepherd, with a long curled-up bushy tail, became our constant companion. She was a great swimmer, and whenever we got into the water, we'd yell, "Help, Wendy, help!" She dropped whatever she was doing, scrambled down the mossy stone walkway and then leapt from the end of the dock to save us. She licked our faces and turned in circles until we grabbed her tail so she could pull us to safety. She seemed to know we were just teasing, yet she never tired of rescuing us.

The days soon began to show signs of autumn, and the evenings could get rather nippy, so we looked forward to the warmth of the fireplace as we cuddled under comforters and quilts. The fire felt good on our cheeks after an exhausting day on the water. High above the lake you could see the silhouette of the trees against the cool, deep blue of the horizon. Long after sunset, before the moon popped up over the hills, there were more stars than I had ever seen, dazzling like diamonds in the velvety blackness. Lightning bugs danced among the trees by the thousands. We had been blessed and felt as though we had discovered paradise.

Emil was a handsome lawyer whom I hardly recognized when I saw him again back home in his three-piece navy pinstripe suit. He was clean-shaven, his curly hair neatly combed. He had been legal counsel to the Vanderbilts and the Rockefellers, but the mountain man we had met at the lake wore an old sweat-stained brown fedora with a bullet hole right through it, two different boots, and a red-plaid flannel hunting shirt buttoned kind of cockeyed. His laugh was contagious and his pants were baggy, but his heart was solid gold.

Evening fell, and a stillness spread over the woods, broken only by the sound of a million crickets and deep-throated frogs. The soft glow of the moon illuminated the lake, and we gathered around the fireplace to listen to how they had moved the mill from the one side to the other. Emil was an ingenious and animated storyteller and kept us intrigued.

That beautifully peaceful spot took my breath away, and the warmth and love of our hosts enriched and enlarged my heart. Many years later, when the movie *On Golden Pond* won several

Academy Awards, I felt as though I had been in that very place, and that the little brat who didn't want to be there was me.

Although Katharine Hepburn and Henry Fonda looked nothing like Marjory and Emil, it was as if a cameraman had been hiding in the bramble bushes behind us all those years before the film's debut. Emil taught us how to fish and water ski, and he didn't let up on me until I mastered the back flip off the dock. I was the only one crazy enough to try it.

Down the road a piece from the main house stood a very large whitewashed two-story barn that housed Emil's collection of antique cars, a Conestoga wagon, an authentic stagecoach, and an 1886 Blairstown fire engine.

Daisy the mule lived there with Elsie the cow, and Aunt Elsie, Emil's older sister, who lived up the road, came by daily to feed and groom them along with Sunshine and Bucket, their two ponies.

Emil laughed as he told hunting stories and at night took us up into the woods and through the fields in his old army Jeep to go snipe hunting. Deer roamed the fields as if they owned the place, and off in the distance we could hear wolves from the Lakota Wolf Preserve.

A love was born in me that weekend unlike anything I could have ever imagined. Each year, as summer came to a close, we looked forward to our Blairstown retreat no matter where we had spent our vacation. All fifteen of us met there on Labor Day weekend until Bryce Jr. went off to college.

We didn't see much of one another throughout the year, except when Marjory and Emil came for dinner at the Inn. Dick and Dottie Law used to frequent the Red Lion Inn, as they lived on the other side of the county. Bryce and Mary Lou Eldridge lived out west of Bergen County, but we never missed the opportunity to spend our memorable weekends with the Wulsters in Blairstown.

On that brightly lit and warm Monday morning at just about nine o'clock, Emil had us cracking up because he knew none of us

Margory and Emil Wulster

wanted to leave. He called his office and told his secretary to cancel all of his appointments for the day, telling her that we were snowed-in and he couldn't get to work. It was Labor Day, and there was no snow falling in Blairstown, but in our child-like glee we were sure he had convinced her.

Later that afternoon, as our first weekend retreat came to an end, Dad struggled to pry my fingers from the banister to get me to leave with them. I had found a home away from home and a bunch of people I loved like my own family, only their home was cooler than ours. So I was pulling another no-I'm-not-going-and-that's-all-there-is-to-it routine. But eventually Dad convinced me that all good things must come to an end.

As the years passed and I got my driver's license, I spent every Labor Day weekend with Marjory and Emil, hoping to truly get snowed-in one day in Blairstown, so that we couldn't leave our little slice of heaven. They welcomed me and adopted me as surrogate grandparents would, and I relished my time with them.

My mother never quite understood why I spent so much time there. I think she may have felt that I loved them more than I loved her. Not true, but they were more fun to be with than she was, and they were old enough to be my grandparents. They seemed to enjoy my company as well, having had only two boys. I was playful, inquisitive, and respectful, and they became wonderfully loving confidants.

5

KNUTE ROCKNE

JUST AS I WAS ABOUT TO TURN SIXTEEN, I heard that one of the most famous actors of his time, Pat O'Brien, and his wife, Eloise, were coming to stay in the annex of the Inn for a month or so while they were appearing at the Fort Lee Playhouse in *Father of the Bride*.

I had such a crush on this man that my knees would knock just thinking about meeting him. I ran to the Inn from school the day they were scheduled to arrive, only to hear they had been delayed. After the third delay, I was convinced that the staff was just pulling my leg and they weren't really coming at all.

Still hoping for the possibility, on the fourth day, out of breath again as I got to the Inn, they said, "He's here!"

I was terrified!

The O'Briens were in their room in the annex and would be

joining us for dinner. My heart was jumping out of my chest as I waited for what seemed an eternity. Finally, around 6:30 p.m., I heard someone say, "There he is."

I looked through the big glass of the kitchen doors and saw him. His breath-takingly beautiful blue eyes and familiar grin were the first things I noticed, as he shook hands with everyone in the kitchen.

As fast as my feet would carry me, I ran into the corridor behind the old bar where the liquor was stored and where my father had his small office, and locked myself in. Dad's secretary had already gone home for the day. I hoped they wouldn't find me there. With all of the commotion and the excitement, I heard Walter, the bartender, say, "The owner's daughter, Jane, has been dying to meet you. Now she's locked herself in her father's office, and she won't come out."

I couldn't believe it. My knees got like jelly; I leaned against the post and slithered to the floor feeling as though my cover had been blown. Somehow they got Pat O'Brien to stand there coaxing me to come out. "Hi, Jane," he said. "I'm eager to meet you. Come on out."

"I'm so scared. Why do you want to meet me?"

"I have two daughters of my own, and you can call me Uncle Pat. Please come out. Don't be afraid."

Grateful for his persistence, I timidly unlocked the door, leaving the chain still attached.

He was gorgeous—and I was speechless! My secret love was standing there in the flesh with a warm and loving smile, like an uncle.

I finally unlatched the chain. He embraced me with the biggest hug and said, in his Irish brogue, "See, that wasn't so bad, was it?"

Had I not come out of that office that day, I might have missed getting to know that marvelous human being.

Uncle Pat was most famous for playing Knute Rockne, the Notre Dame football coach, in *Knute Rockne, All American*, alongside Ronald Reagan. He was a constant companion to James Cagney and Spencer Tracy, often playing a priest in their many films. He also starred opposite Marilyn Monroe, Jack Lemmon, and George Raft in *Some Like It Hot*.

During Uncle Pat and Aunt Eloise's four-week stay, we became very close friends. They celebrated their thirtieth wedding anniversary, and his sixtieth birthday, with us.

My father, experienced in how to throw a great party, filled the entire dining room, which held about three hundred people. He invited all of our friends and customers to celebrate the anniversary. On each table sat a huge Cattleya orchid plant with a dozen or more blossoms the size of baseball mitts—some in shades of lavender and pink, others in deep velvety purple and magenta, or lily white with yellow flourishes. They filled the room with a delicate fragrance and pomp. Comedians and dancers entertained us, and a few of our talented friends played the piano as we sang along. Pat was captivating as he performed a scene from *Knute Rockne*, inspiring his team to victory after having tragically lost one of their own, a guy they called "The Gipper," played by Ronald Reagan.

Eloise was slender and quite attractive, with dark hair, high cheekbones, and bright stars in her eyes. They were a handsome couple. It seemed, though, that she was not quite as comfortable in her own skin as he. She was heavily made up and warmly reserved, and she had a cigarette-smoker's nervous tic in her hands. Although a good actor in her own right, she always appeared to be onstage.

We celebrated my Sweet Sixteen party and Pat's sixtieth at our sprawling home on the east hill. After chasing me around the living room and the dining room table, he was the first to kiss me on that special day. That same evening, our longtime family friend Dom

Albanese was the second.

The O'Briens said, "In all our travels, we have never felt so at home. We are overwhelmed by your hospitality and hope to keep in touch with all of you."

A few nights later, twenty of us went to see them perform at the Playhouse. In one scene Uncle Pat was commiserating with a friend when he said, "I just bumped into my friend, Pete Chagaris. Poor guy, he has two daughters to marry off—one is bad enough!" We were shocked and felt as though everyone in the theater knew that we were there! I was stunned that he would go off-script like that, and thrilled beyond words.

After their visit to the Inn, we often surprised them backstage at one of their performances all over the country as we traveled and they toured with their entourage.

Their lovely Beverly Hills mansion, with its four Corinthian columns resembling those of the White House, welcomed us, and we got to know three of their four children—Sean, Terry, and Bridget. Mavoureen was away at college.

In their poolside-cabana studio, brimming with memorabilia of old Hollywood, they shared their family movies and a gigantic photo album, which filled the entire pool table when opened. I was struck by how normal they were, given their fame.

One evening they took us to the Beverly Hills Hotel for dinner. As we entered the understated, elegant foyer, the maître d' said, "Good evening, Mr. O'Brien. We have your table waiting."

Elizabeth Taylor, who was living at the hotel for an extended stay while her home was being renovated, was sitting at a table just behind a sago palm off to my right. I couldn't stop staring between the fronds. She was the most gorgeous woman I had laid my eyes on. I hoped she hadn't noticed my stare.

We visited the secluded gardens and the beautifully landscaped pool, where Lana Turner, Grace Kelly, Fred Astaire, and all the studio regulars came to spend their weekend retreats.

That evening Uncle Pat took us for a ride through the gated and private drives of Beverly Hills to show us where Lucille Ball and Desi Arnez lived. Up the winding road a piece were the homes of Milton Berle, Dinah Shore, and Bob Hope. There was an island of flowering hot-pink oleanders among the towering royal palms reaching for the sky, standing straight as soldiers. Many homes had shrubs sculpted in the shapes of elephants and giraffes. Others had large stone lions standing guard at the entrance to their circular drives.

The next day he took us to see Rodeo Drive, one of the world's richest shopping streets, lined with Rolls-Royces and Bentleys, and there I sat in the front seat of Pat O'Brien's Cadillac, between Dad and Uncle Pat, secretly pinching myself in disbelief.

We parked and walked for a while, window-shopping and people-watching. As we were crossing one of the streets, I thought I recognized a man waiting to cross from the other side. I was sure I knew him from the Inn, or Tenafly, he looked so familiar. The light changed, but I still couldn't place him. As we approached each other, our eyes met, and I had a supercharged, light-bulb moment—my mouth dropped, I gasped, and can only imagine that my facial expression was something to behold when I realized the face was that of actor, Lee Marvin. We were in Beverly Hills, after all. He started to laugh and was probably thinking, there goes another crazy fan.

I said to Linda, "Did you see Lee Marvin?"

Her glance had been off in another direction, and she had missed the experience.

We left the O'Briens home with tears, hugs, and hopes of seeing one another again.

More than twenty years later, when I drove a friend to the

Tampa airport, I noticed Pat O'Brien's name on the marquee of the Showboat Dinner Theater. *Could it be?* I thought.

I immediately called my father, "Dad, would you believe Pat O'Brien is here at the Dinner Theater?"

He said, "Call the theater and leave him a message."

"Oh, sure, they won't believe that I know him."

"Well, you have nothing to lose, so give it a try."

"Okay."

I called the theater, feeling like that sixteen-year-old girl of many years ago, and said, "I'd like to leave a message for Mr. O'Brien. Could you please tell him that Jane Chagaris lives right up the street from the theater and would love to see him again?" Then I shrugged my shoulders expecting that he would never get the message.

Late one Sunday afternoon my phone rang, and the man on the other end said, "Where the hell have you been?"

"Who the hell is this? " I said.

"It's me, Pat O'Brien. I've been trying to reach you for weeks. Don't you ever stay home?"

"Oh, my God! Is it really you?" I screamed.

"'Tis I," he said. "How are your parents?"

"They're both well. I can't wait to tell them I've spoken with you. How's Aunt Eloise?"

"She's fine, in fact Eloise and Bridget are here with me."

I said, "You must come for dinner one evening."

"We're just here a few more days, I wish I had reached you sooner."

"Me, too. Please give everyone my love."

I immediately called my parents and told them how exciting it was to speak with him again, and that he actually called *me*.

It had never occurred to me that I might be able to get some friends together and go to the show. They didn't believe that I really knew him, but agreed to go nevertheless. I got tickets and the four of us went to his final performance. Our seats were great, right in the center on the third parterre only about forty feet from the stage. Dinner was served buffet-style, but being overjoyed with excitement, I could barely eat. Just after dessert, the announcer said in his boisterous stage voice, "Ladies and gentlemen, please welcome Pat O'Brien, his wife Eloise and their daughter Bridget."

The curtains rose—the stage lights were set—and *there he was*, walking on stage with a cane in the opening scene. I was trembling, tear streaming down my face. His unforgettable blue eyes were still full of life, his hair was white and much thinner, and my heart was doing flips. I think I expected him to look the same as the last time we'd met. I could feel my girlfriends watching me as the curtains opened; they wanted to see my reaction. Finally they believed that I did, in fact, know him and they patiently waited with me to go back stage afterwards. The Showboat was a small theater and many Irish lads and lassies were in his dressing room, also thrilled to meet him.

Shaking like a leaf, I stood in the background waiting my turn; my friends had their cameras ready. After signing autographs and greeting the other ladies and gents, he looked up through the crowd, then looked away and quickly back up again—*he recognized me*. He stood and held out his arms. The crowd parted and I overheard someone saying, "Who is she?"

Then as if in slow motion, we walked toward each other and embraced. Tears messed up my makeup, but he patted them dry with his handkerchief as we sat arm-in-arm and reminisced. It was one of the most priceless moments of my lifetime.

Pat O'Brien and me –1981

James Cagney and Pat O'Brien in Angels With Dirty Faces – 1938

6

The Traveling Chagarises

Over the years, the success of the two inns offered us a larger-than-life, life. We were always on the go and flew or sailed from one part of the world to the other. We soon earned a reputation as the Traveling Chagarises.

Uncle Jim was a world-renowned fisherman with the New York Athletic Club—one year he caught the second largest fish at the world championship. Actually, he caught both the largest and the second largest. However, when you're in a competition, and you get two bites at the same time, you must call over another boat, so you can hand off one of the lines to a different angler. Much to his dismay that day, Uncle Jim discovered at the end of the tournament that the woman he gave his line to had caught the largest fish in the competition.

Time and again, Uncle John took his family—including his

aunts, Olga and Anna—back to Greece and all around Europe. What a thrill it must have been for the two of them to return to their homeland after many years of living in America. Life in Greece was behind the times on many levels, which only added to the charm of the country.

During Easter break in 1954, we traveled to Las Vegas, Los Angeles, and San Francisco. The glitz and glamour of the Vegas strip took my breath away long before the Eiffel Tower and the gondolas of Venice were recreated there. We stayed at the Sands Hotel, Frank Sinatra's home base. Dad knew Frank's mother from his years in Hoboken. The rough-and-tumble Dolly Sinatra used to stop in at our New Jersey restaurant for breakfast once in a while. He often told us stories of her character and their frequent political debates over a cup of coffee and a doughnut. Thanks to that connection, we had great seats at Frank's performance. When he sang "My Way" it became clear as to why he had been named The Chairman of the Board.

One of the special highlights of that trip for me, however, took place in Los Angeles. There were seats waiting for us at a taping of an original Amos 'n Andy radio episode. The theater was dark, dank, and musty-smelling. We arrived just seconds before the curtains rose, and there was a hush as we tiptoed down to where five deep red velvet seats had been roped off for us in the front row.

Everyone knew Amos 'n Andy, the number-one radio show of its time. Their blackface slapstick humor was clean and corny, and hilarious—but much to my amazement, Amos and Andy were as Caucasian as we. Their down-home southern stage accents had me fooled.

They taped the show in front of a live audience. The two men stood on an empty stage. The curtains rose, exposing the rafters and ropes that made everything work. Large, old-fashioned microphones stood there, naked, waiting for them to read from their paper scripts and banter with each other. Their best friend, Kingfish, soon joined them. It felt as if we were all standing on the street corner with them.

After the show, we were invited backstage by Charles Correll, the voice of Andy. It was such a kick to meet him. The warmth of his smile melted my heart. His hair was wavy and pure white, like snow frozen in the ripple of the wind. He was handsome as the dickens too, with a beautiful smile, and we quickly became dear friends.

Somewhere tucked away in my treasure chest, I still have the original paper script Correll gave me from that show, taped on March 7, 1954.

He took us for dinner that night to the original Brown Derby in his brand new baby blue Cadillac convertible.

At the end of the week, Dad drove us up the Pacific Coast Highway, where we wandered through the Hearst Castle and on to the quaint Danish village of Solvang, which richly displays the architecture and atmosphere of a time long ago. I could almost imagine dressing in the costume of the day and living as the Danes had back then.

Heading north, we stayed four nights at the uniquely designed Madonna Inn in San Luis Obispo. Mr. Madonna was in construction, and he and my father struck up a friendship. Dad helped him with his menu items, and he often joined us at the dinner table with stories of his partner, John Wayne, and of their plans for that one-of-a-kind hotel.

Linda and I nestled into the Paddle Wheel Room, where an actual paddle wheel was embedded in the shower door and the motif was right out of Mark Twain. Tommy's room was called the Caveman Suite, appropriate for him, and Mom and Dad's suite was called the Kona Rock Room, with a natural outdoor rock waterfall as their shower. This place was fascinating to see and, I was told, had been very expensive to build. The hotel has grown from twelve uniquely decorated rooms when we were first there to its present one hundred ten, each with its own exotic decor.

The main dining room was called the Gold Rush Steak House, and it had hand-carved columns imported from Italy, encircled with grapes and vines in bas-relief. The dining room was done in hot pink and gold. Up a few steps to the left stood the hand-hammered copper breakfast bar, with wire-backed chairs and a carousel-type canopy. Their food was wonderful, too. I especially remember the Monte Cristo sandwiches and the giant slices of chocolate cream pie for which they were famous—and who doesn't enjoy a good piece of chocolate cream pie?

After a bite at the breakfast bar, I was immersed in the scenic backdrop of pastures adjacent to the hotel, where a herd of wild buffalo roamed freely. I was in my glory, a photographer's dream, come true.

Over the years we returned to the Madonna for more such memories. It remains a tourist attraction honoring Mr. Madonna, who passed away in the late 1990s, shortly after Mom and I visited with him once again.

From there, our travels took us up the coast to Big Sur and the Tickle Pink Motor Inn on the outskirts of Carmel-by-the-Sea. The wild surf crashing on the rocks below and the sizzling sunsets in a rainbow of vibrant hues were visible from our balconies. The lens of my 35-millimeter camera couldn't capture the grandeur of that beautiful place.

Eventually we reached San Francisco with its rickety cable cars, frighteningly steep hills, and Fisherman's Wharf. We sampled the rare delicacy of abalone steak, a jewel of the sea, and stayed at the St. Francis Hotel on Union Square, with its lavishly appointed rooms. Tommy, Linda, and I, hopped on and off cable cars like toads on lily pads. Up and down the hills we went, challenging the conductors to teach us how they were able to stop to pick up more passengers, as the cars were perched at such a steep angle.

North of the city, our side trips took us to where the tallest living creatures grow: the enchanted, fog-shrouded giant redwoods, and Sequoia National Park. Butterflies danced in the mist rising from the streams as shards of sunlight pierced the shadows. Long before the movie *Honey, I Shrunk the Kids*, the parade of trees dwarfed us. Straight as arrows, they soared upward, the girth of their circumferences spanning from sixteen to eighteen feet, and possibly even more. The tallest trees there stand about three-hundred-seventy feet in the air, some six or seven stories higher than the Statue of Liberty. Their majesty leaves you speechless, and looking up at them puts a crick in your neck.

Not far from there, my parents sampled the offerings of Napa Valley's wine country. The air was crisp, yet warm and fragrant. Lush vineyards blanketed the valleys as far as the eye could see. We took a few tours of several wineries, to see how the grapes were cleaned and prepared for processing. I was too young to drink but found the area fascinating. I couldn't help but recall the scene from I Love Lucy, when Lucy got in the barrel to stomp on the grapes with a happy old winemaker.

THE SUMMER OF THE FOLLOWING YEAR, we spent eight weeks in Hawaii and the Pacific Northwest.

Arriving in Honolulu, beautiful Hawaiian women dressed in traditional muumuus, welcomed us with an "Aloha" and dozens of dendrobium and plumeria leis piled so high I could barely see over them. Their delicate fragrances made my nose twitch.

During our month-long stay on the islands, Tommy and I learned to surf on Waikiki Beach with eight-foot surfboards, and we could ride the waves standing up. Linda was a little too small, but we all got to try outrigger canoes. Even Mom and Dad came along.

Eating with our fingers, we dined at a traditional luau pig-roast, and we did the hukilau at night under the starlight, dragging in nets filled with hundreds of tiny fish.

In the cool of the evening, after a fiery sunset danced on the western horizon before melting into the sea, dozens of people gathered around a bonfire, playing songs and singing 'til midnight. I fell in love with Charlie, our beach attendant, who personally taught me how to play the ukulele and sing "Beyond the Reef." The warmth of the people, and the bouquet of those islands, permeates my senses to this day.

A dear friend from Tenafly, Harold Patterson, was the Orchid King of the World. He had provided the orchid plants for the O'Briens' anniversary party at the Inn, and he introduced us to Mr. Nakimoto, his partner on the Islands, who with his wife invited us for dinner at their Japanese-style mansion high above Honolulu. They had crisp white silk kimonos prepared especially for each of us, and as we entered their luxurious home, we were given foot sandals to wear inside the house, which were ours to keep. Sitting on the floor to dine was a whole new experience. Their warm hospitality and delicious but distinctly different food perfectly complemented our stay. Many years later I had the good fortune of returning to the Islands several times during my career in the travel business.

From there, we spent four more weeks driven by chauffeured limousine from Portland, Oregon—home to the world's most beautiful rose gardens—to Seattle, Washington, with its lush mountain views. We passed through Vancouver, British Columbia, where we ran into the Johnsons, a family we had met in Hawaii; their itinerary closely followed ours through the Pacific Northwest. We had three staterooms on a steamship that took us overnight to Victoria, where we were stunned to discover that the Johnsons, who had left the following day on a four-hour day cruise, had reached Victoria at the same time we did. It was a shock to discover that we must have been cruising around in circles all night long.

Victoria was the prettiest city I had ever seen. We stayed at the Empress Hotel, which sits at the mouth of the inner harbor and is aglow with thousands of tiny lights in the evening. Each antique street lantern was adorned with two enormous hanging flower baskets—and there were flowers everywhere. The aromas from the many local bakeshops danced in our senses. Each night along the esplanade across from the hotel, people strolled along the water's edge listening to the music of the night, as some showed up with a guitar or saxophone to entertain.

After visiting Butchart Gardens and swimming in the pool at Saanich Commonwealth Place, we took a scenic railway ride to Banff. The grandeur of the Banff Springs Hotel, modeled after a Scottish castle, is often pictured on postcards highlighting the best of British Columbia.

The downtown streets of Banff seemed to flow right out of the towering pines of the Canadian Rockies, and oozed with charm. As we window-shopped along the main street, we came upon a local eatery called Gus's Restaurant. Gus was Greek, so Dad was right at home. On the cover of the menu was a picture of Gus in his prime, playing the bouzouki. *Opa!*

Every night when we arrived for dinner, Gus entertained the whole house on the bouzouki. Dad once asked him, "What will your other customers think?"

Gus replied, "I didn't ask them to come here. If they don't like it, they can go next door."

As we made our way a week or so later to Lake Louise, past the majestic icy-blue mountains of the Canadian Pacific Highway, Dad noticed that a few cars had pulled off to the side of the road. Curious, he also pulled over. Sitting there, just on the fringe of the highway, was a little black bear—cute, yes, but I really wouldn't call him little.

"Dad," I said, "let me get out of the car to take his picture."

Before he could say, "No, honey, that's not a good idea," I was off and running, camera in hand. I'd almost gotten right up to the bear when he turned, stood up on his hind legs, and chased me right back to the car. We all screamed as I dove through the window on Dad's side of the car—my feet sticking out.

Fortunately, Tommy somehow distracted the bear with a Ritz cracker on the other side of the car, but he accidentally dropped the cracker inside the back seat.

The bear's enormous head, with its sloppy jowls and razor-sharp fangs, came in the window searching for the cracker. We screamed louder and peed in our pants. My father was laughing so hard, he couldn't have helped us if he tried—and besides, he had my young butt right in his face. Finally regaining his composure, he leaned on the horn and began driving away as my mother pulled me into the front seat. Other cars pulling up behind us distracted the bear.

After composing ourselves and changing into clean underwear, we continued on our journey.

Our next stop was the Chateau Lake Louise. It even sounds pretty, doesn't it? Off in the distance, God alone could have painted such vivid and dazzling snow-covered glaciers. Each dining table at the Chateau had its own panoramic view of the frigid, crystal-blue water through the high-arched cathedral windows. The cold wind would blow through the valley where the Chateau sits like a jewel at the mouth of Banff National Park.

I don't believe I have ever seen anything more breathtaking. Our suite of rooms was opulent, with high-vaulted ceilings, chandeliers, crown and dentil moldings, and heavenly views of the snow-capped mountains.

Even in mid-summer the weather was grippingly cold, so we

hardly ventured out except for a quick kayak ride or two, followed by a foaming cup of hot cocoa. The hotel had enough indoor activities to keep us very busy, and we were enjoying one another's company. It also gave us a pause before heading home.

On the final leg of our journey, we spent a few more days in the old western city of Calgary, home of the Calgary Stampede and Rodeo. Though the season was over and the city was calm and quiet, we managed to buy some cowboy duds and were feeling pretty cool. I thought I looked just like Annie Oakley in my boots, chaps, and cowboy hat.

On our return home, Tommy and I participated in every sporting event available. He played football and baseball, wrestled, and ran track. I played softball, field hockey, lacrosse, and basketball. Linda wasn't athletic at all, so she tagged along and kept busy with her friends.

OVER THE NEXT FEW YEARS, Mom and Dad and several members of the gang rented homes at the Jersey Shore so we could all summer there. I learned to swim and dive from the three-foot springboard and ten-meter platform at Jenkinson's Olympic-sized salt-water pool in Point Pleasant. After we crisped in the sun and dove through the sand-crushing waves of the Atlantic, it was time for another fabulous weekend in Blairstown, my favorite place on this planet.

Everyone in the pool!

Life could not have been more perfect.

In celebration of my parents, I want to express my gratitude for the fabulous upbringing they bestowed upon us. They filled our days with the warmth and love of family, the richness and comfort of home, and the love and laughter of great friends. And they gave us an education far greater than anything we could have learned in a classroom.

7

Ordinary Times

There was nothing ordinary about our ordinary times. My parents' friends had become my superheroes, and our bonds of friendship have lasted a lifetime. Aside from the freedom of their extravagant, entrepreneurial lifestyles, I was drawn to the wealth of their wisdom, their innate kindness, and their copious amounts of humor.

Our family's "gang," as we referred to them, were the most exciting and eclectic group of people I've ever known. They were what some may call party animals, and they certainly knew how to strike up the band.

Four or five times a week, after the men had put in a hard day's work building their empires, the couples would get together. The men were magnetic, one-of-a-kind business tycoons. There was a painting contractor, a surgeon, a haberdasher, a lawyer, Joe was in the lumber business, and Jim and Paul were in construction. Harold was in advertising, and Leo was in the meat-packing business. Tom Barrett was an undertaker, and Joe Squillace was the City Manager of Hackensack and he also owned the Wellington Hall nursing home. The serious nature of their businesses did not keep them from being hilariously funny.

They ate and drank, danced and laughed, and they loved one another deeply. "Without laughter," they often said, "the world would be a dull and silent place. And we'll have none of that."

Some of the gang

Leading by example, they entertained us with good, clean fun, and they showed us how to live life, not to merely exist.

They were welcoming and a lot more fun to be with than any of my peers; it was as though I had become their social equal, which I think my mother might have resented. She'd often say, "Why can't you go be with your own friends?"

Truth was, I had few friends of my own. My life was different than that of my peers, and the older generation made me feel safe and comfortable. I believe, that deep down I am an old soul.

In seventh and eighth grade, I attended Dwight School for Girls in Englewood. I loved it there but I struggled with reading. Although my parents had gotten tutors for me, my severe dyslexia went undiagnosed, and that brought me back to Tenafly High School, where I spent the next four years.

I didn't seem to fit in with my classmates, since all of the cliques had been formed during my two-year absence. Sports had filled the giant void in my life, but when I wasn't on a team, I felt isolated and alone. I walked to the Inn by myself every day to be with my dad, he was always there for me.

Whenever I went to where my mother was playing bridge, she'd ask, "What are *you* doing here?"

I always felt unwanted by her, although her female friends had welcomed me. I longed for my mother's acceptance, but I don't think she understood that I simply wanted to be with her and to be loved by her.

My parents' friends began to take the place of my classmates, and they included me in their antics, which exposed me to a world I could not have entered with anyone of my own age. They needed no excuse to have a party; the mere fact that it was Tuesday or Friday was good enough for them.

One such party stands out in my mind. It was the worst winter storm of our lives, and to our delight, Dad couldn't get out of the garage to go to work. What a treat! As I'm sure you know, the restaurant business is a seven-day-a-week job, and he was there every day. But that day the winds had driven the snow so high, it looked as if you could walk right off our kitchen balcony, across the driveway, and down the street. The drifts were at least ten feet high, and the trees were heavily laden and drooped right into the snow. Tommy, Linda, Mom, and I were in our glory, because it felt like Christmas, but Dad was never home on Christmas, so the day was a very special gift to us all. He made us a luscious breakfast, and we enjoyed our private family time, hoping to play Monopoly or canasta and stay in our PJs.

Then the prankster in him kicked into high gear, and he had what he thought was a brilliant idea: "Why don't we call everyone and invite them up to the house for a party?"

Knowing that they couldn't get out of their homes either, he made the calls. He laughed himself silly, his left eye half-closed, slapping his knee as he so often did. He figured he had really pulled one over on them. My mother was right there with him, and a good sport. Our home was always impeccably clean because she never knew when Dad would call and say, "Can I bring so and so up for dinner?" or "I'd like you to meet someone—we'll be right up."

We did stay in our pajamas that day, playing cards and watching TV, talking and kidding with one another.

Then, as dusk arrived, off in the distance we saw a vision, like a mirage in the desert. The snow clouds had grown dark and ominous, though it was only around four in the afternoon. Suddenly, we saw red and yellow blinking lights glittering off the now deep-purple snowdrifts. It appeared to be some sort of a snowplow.

Intrigued by how it was going to make it up the hill, we stood mesmerized, leaning on one another's shoulders and peering down the street from our kitchen bay window.

It was the biggest plow we had ever seen.

It was, in fact, a super-sized, industrial orange Caterpillar, not the local DPW plow. It looked like something out of Star Wars.

Dad said, "Look, are there people hanging on the edge of the platform?" We scratched our heads, rubbed our eyes, and thought we were dreaming.

"Who are they?" Mom said.

As the huge creature drew near, the snow seemed to part like the waters of the Red Sea. Suddenly, it emerged under the lamp light at the edge of our driveway.

"Dad, look! Tommy said, "Is that Mr. D'Agostino driving that crazy thing?"

I said, "Is that Mrs. Barrett on the left? What are they doing? What's she holding?" Mrs. Barrett was the wife of Tom, the undertaker. Tom was hanging off the back of the Caterpillar, clutching a bottle of Dewar's.

They had gotten my father's call, called each other, and figured they would call his bluff. There were eight or nine of them. One had a turkey under her arm, another a bottle of wine, yet another a bottle of vodka and a ham, and they were bundled up like Eskimos. As they pulled into our driveway and climbed off the platform, they landed in snow at least waist-deep. The drifts were so high they needed to get on all fours as they literally began crawling up our outside steps. That must have taken twenty or thirty minutes, not necessarily because they couldn't make it through the snow, although that was a challenge—but because they were laughing so hard that they could barely move.

Still in our pajamas, we laughed with them, too stunned to do anything else. Laughter being such a unifying spiritual force, we could have built a cathedral.

Mr. D'Agostino was the most dapper of businessmen. Who'd have thought, even though he was in construction, that he could drive one of those forty-foot monster machines? He'd plowed our friends out, and then plowed his way up the hill to our house. We howled for months about it each time we saw one another. That was a party to top all parties.

Life was different during the decades of American prosperity. It seemed pure and safe, and for us it was spectacular.

Every New Year's Day, we had the ritual of putting Garry Felter in the trunk of our car. He would sit cross-legged, guarding a large punch bowl filled with eggnog. He wore a Luftwaffe helmet to protect his head from the bouncing lid of the trunk. That in itself was hysterical. The caravan started at the Inn and stopped at everyone's home. We ate whatever they had prepared, and then, using their eggs and brandy, my father made a new batch of eggnog, after which that family joined the caravan to the next house.

At the end of the evening, we returned to the Inn for dinner. Dinner? Who could eat another bite? We laughed and cackled and drank some more. What we laughed about never seemed to matter. We simply enjoyed being together.

One afternoon in early spring, my mother saw a man pull up in his pickup and park in front of our house. We lived on a dead-end, and as she watched the man get out of his truck, she wondered what he was doing there. She went outside and said to him, "Can I help you?"

He replied, "You're probably going to think I'm nuts, but I'm working in construction around the corner, and yesterday I came here and sat on this rock to have my lunch. All of a sudden I saw a large gorilla right over there. I apparently frightened him and he lumbered away. Then I was wondering if I had been hallucinating," he said. "So I came back today to see if he was here again."

My mother looked at him in disbelief. "A gorilla?"

"Yeah, he was really big, probably as big as me, and I kept rubbing my eyes, thinking I was seeing things."

Mom went back inside, called the Tenafly police, and told the officer about the man in the pickup. "I wondered what he was doing there and he told me that he had seen a gorilla the day before."

"A gorilla?" The detective said.

"Yes, that's what he said."

"Let me do some checking, and I'll send a car up. I'll call you back, Mrs. Chagaris, and let you know what I find."

When Dad came home, he found my mother napping. Then the phone rang. He picked it up and heard, "Mr. Chagaris, this is the Tenafly police calling about the gorilla your wife called about."

"What! A gorilla? Call the men in the white coats, she's finally lost her mind!"

"No, she hasn't," the officer replied with a chuckle. "We wanted to let her know that there is a gorilla on the loose. He escaped from a circus in Jersey City, and he's trained to open doors, so please be careful."

When Mom got up, he told her, and they cracked up laughing. Then, of course, the gang heard the story and teased her endlessly.

ANOTHER TIME, THE WHOLE CROWD was invited to Dr. Ed's home in Brooklyn, about forty minutes away. My father rented a bus, and they all dressed up like accident victims, since they were going to the "doctor's" house. One of them was on crutches with a bandage over one eye, another had his head wrapped and his arm in a sling, and someone else was in a nurse's uniform. One of the men had a plaster cast on his leg; others looked like they were bleeding and limping in pain.

They had enema bags (new ones of course), hanging from the bus's handrails, filled with whisky sours and martinis. The Clinton Inn supplied the hors d'oeuvres for the bus ride, and Betty Mackey, one of our longtime waitresses, accompanied them.

At Dr. Ed's home, there was no place for the bus to park on the street, so the men got out, lifted up a Volkswagen that was taking up two spots, and moved it a spot or two away so the bus would fit. As the "patients" got out, passers-by asked if there had been an accident. Struck by a crowd of people who looked like they had been through a war but couldn't stop laughing, when they heard the story, they wanted to join the party.

Fortunately, they had rented the bus in case any of them had gotten a little too tipsy to drive home. I'm not sure of their condition at the end of the evening, but I do believe that none of them could have driven in any case—they were laughing so hard, tears would have blurred their vision.

When my parents got home that night, they woke us and tried telling us the story but could barely get the words out. They were bent over laughing so hard they couldn't catch their breath. We tried to find out what was so funny, gave up, and went back to bed. The next morning, they still couldn't stop laughing. I don't believe we ever did get the whole picture. It must have been *one heck* of a party.

Recently, when I asked Angie Bracconeri, one of the last remaining members of the gang, to describe in her own words how the friendships had lasted a lifetime, she said, "In my ninety-eight years, I have yet to encounter a group of individuals that could even begin to measure up to the zaniness of these incredibly fun-loving people."

Angie reminded me of when my father kiddingly complained about having to mow the lawn at our new home up on the east hill (which of course, he never did), and her brother Tino had the solution. We had been out at a wedding, and when we returned Dad hit the garage door opener. As he tried to pull in, he noticed a large barrel right in his way. "Who left the barrel there? Jane, get out and move it."

So I got out and grabbed the barrel with one hand, but before it moved an inch, I looked down and saw four eyes, like brightly lit marbles, looking back up at me. I jumped back and let out a scream. Then I heard a baaaa, baaaa. "Dad, come quick!"

Tino was in the meat business, and had apparently jimmied the lock to the side door and left these two beautiful baby lambs, so Dad "wouldn't have to mow the lawn." We named them Porgy and

Bess, and kept them as pets. They were precious.

Angie went on to say, "Whenever I've tried to explain to others some of the things we did, and the shenanigans we played on one another over the course of fifty years, people respond with a blank look of disbelief and a half-crooked smile, figuring I must be exaggerating...*I'm not!*"

8

FROM THE FOLIES TO THE POPE

IN THE SUMMER OF MY SIXTEENTH YEAR, we went to Europe and to my father's homeland—for him, his first visit in forty-five years. We sailed aboard the S.S. Independence, in seven days, not the forty it had taken my father so many years earlier when he came to America.

A few weeks before, at a party at our house, I asked him, "Can Leo come to Europe with us?"

"Ask his mother," he said, "If it's okay with her, it's okay with me." Leo was Angie Bracconeri's son and my best friend.

You'd have thought I was asking if he could come to dinner with us. At sixteen, I didn't realize how complicated that might be. He needed a passport, and all of the accommodations and plane reservations had to be adjusted, but his mother did consent. Fortunately, Leo was able to share the rooms with Tommy.

Our new extended family from the Red Lion Inn, along with the gang from Tenafly, attended the bon voyage party the day we sailed.

Eileen Felter and Jack Kelly played the piano, and Dick Law accompanied them on a homemade Pogo cello, with a honker horn, cymbal, cowbell, bass string, and a washboard. Deep into his rendition of the "Good Ship Titanic," he had his eyes closed, and passers-by thought he was blind. They took over the ship, entertaining the other passengers as well. They danced and sang "East Side, West Side," "New York, New York," and many other old standards. Mrs. Barrett did a little soft shoe on top of the bar. They were having a blast, and I thoroughly enjoyed watching them.

As our guests disembarked, they continued the tomfoolery on the dock below until the ship pulled out of port. During the voyage, passengers came up to us to ask if we had been with that poor blind man playing the boom bass.

Within minutes, we sailed past Lady Liberty and, with the excitement building, we began to settle in.

After getting into our life jackets for the safety drills, Mom and Dad returned to their cabin, and the four of us kids checked out every nook and cubbyhole of the huge vessel. When we were able to find our way back to our cabins, we knew we were on the adventure of a lifetime.

In those days, most ships had three classes of service—Tourist, Cabin, and First. Through Dad's business relationship with the Cunard Line, we had special access to all three classes. It seemed that, everywhere we went, doors were literally opened to us that were closed to ordinary vacationers. It was a great privilege to travel that way.

We participated in every activity the ship had to offer. Dad entered and won the crazy-hat contest in First Class as "The Hawaiian Eye." Tommy (deservedly, I must admit) took first place in Cabin Class for his rendition of "Pennies From Heaven." Mom won at Bingo, and Linda, Leo, and I won the dance and limbo contests.

The captain, dressed in his starched navy whites, was a handsome, rugged-looking yet gentle and gracious man, with a full head of shiny, white, neatly combed hair. We dined at his table several times during the voyage.

Our first port-of-call was Gibraltar, which we had been studying in class before we left. We flew from there to Madrid and stayed at the Castellano Hilton the first week. Each night the waiters prepared a Caesar salad tableside for us in a massive hand-carved wooden bowl. When you're in the restaurant business, good food is the first thing you remember about your travels. We toured the city and shopped till the moon rose over the red barrel roofs.

While in Madrid, we went to see a drama-packed bullfight. It was riveting and gory but spellbinding. Adorned in costumes of red and gold, or purple and silver, matadors armed only with swords and red capes had to prove their courage and artistry in the ring. They taunted and stabbed the raging bulls. It was a fight to the death.

I watched the entire performance through the lens of an 8-millimeter movie camera from my front row seat. In his excitement, Leo kept grabbing my arm to say, "Jane, look!" Needless to say, those pictures didn't come out too well. I was beginning to wonder about my photographic prowess.

Then the unthinkable happened. A wounded bull jumped the fence right in front of us. We screamed and scrambled to get out of the way. The horsemen and several matadors came charging over the rails of the bullring as we ran up the steps. The enraged animal was contained and killed within minutes, and we were safe. I'm grateful for that experience, but I don't know that I'd ever want to repeat it.

The following week we left for Paris and a seven-day stay at the Plaza Athénée. The second night there, we attended the Folies-Bergère; our box seats were just off stage left. Leo was so close that when he turned around at one point, he nearly got a mouthful of plumage as the performers were preparing for their first act. The show lasted four hours with the most astonishing entertainment we had ever seen; it was sexy and sensual, with a forty-piece orchestra, acrobats, comedians, jugglers, and a dog act. Then an old lady playing the accordion came on stage, and we wondered what she could possibly have to offer—everyone else had been so entertaining and funny. Much to our surprise, she was an absolute stitch.

The music was amazing. The girls were naked.

"*Naked*," I said.

Linda, Leo, and I were, of course, under age, and Tommy was nineteen. Stunned and embarrassed, we giggled and pointed.

For the fourth act, the showgirls, dressed in elegant Cinderella-type costumes at a dinner table, levitated off the stage and tilted, creating the illusion that we were levitating above them, as if on a magic carpet ride. It was dizzying. I still haven't figured out how they did that.

In the next scene they were naked again, with sweeping feathered fans and strategically placed tassels covering the bare essentials.

After the beauty of Paris, with its shopping and fine dining, we left for a week in Venice, one of the most charming and unusual places I've ever visited. We swam in the Adriatic Sea and saw all the landmark sights as we familiarized ourselves with the canals of the city and St. Mark's Square. It's hard to imagine the ingenuity of how a water city like Venice could have been conceived. The buildings rise from the sea on a group of small islands separated by canals and linked by bridges. There was no visible land beneath them, and instead of garages most homes had boathouses.

Back home, I had seen a lifelike glass puppy from the island of Murano, Italy, at my Aunt Sophie's house and wanted one for myself. Murano glass had been made famous by some of the finest glass artisans in the world. I love watching things being crafted by hand.

The weather was misty and smelled like the sea. As we were about to board the water taxi, I must have accidently bumped into Tommy. He got angry, and smacked me on the head with his heavy gold signet ring. It raised a lump the size of an egg that stayed with me for a week. He pushed his way past me and jumped onto the boat. Just then, the wake from a passing watercraft splashed onto the boat, and as I threw my precious camera at him from the dock, the boat rocked, he ducked, and I missed.

The camera remains at the bottom of Venice's Grand Canal. Luckily, the film I had already taken was back at the hotel. Dad hadn't seen Tommy hit me, just me throwing the camera at him. He wasn't too happy with me, so they left me standing there, alone, as the taxi pulled away.

I cried, my head hurt, and I was heartsick; Murano was the one place I had been looking forward to, and I was being left behind. I found my way back to the hotel and pouted until they returned. In my anger and frustration, I took all of Tommy's clothes, wadded them up into a ball, and threw them onto the rooftop below his window. I thought he had been unnecessarily mean. He knew how badly I wanted to go to the glass factories.

I realized then—for the first time—that the character of our family was changing, and it upset me. Tommy was grown up now, and I didn't understand his cockiness and lack of compassion.

When they returned to the hotel, I cried out to Dad and said, "Why did you do that and leave me there? You all knew how badly I wanted to go to Murano. I was scared. Tommy hit me first. Why did you punish me?"

"What do you mean? You threw the camera at him."

"Yes, but only after he hit me. Look at this." I showed Dad the lump on my head.

When Dad realized that he had been wrong, he apologized and held me tight. "I'll make it up to you, honey," he said. I don't recall if he scolded Tommy or not, but he should have.

It also became apparent to me around that time that, although the restaurant business gave us a magical life, it had an unfortunate detrimental side. We rarely sat down to the dinner table as a family, and, therefore, I believe we missed precious moments of truly getting to know and understand one another. We didn't have the opportunity to share our dreams, our goals, and our fears. We were never taught that, *no matter what*, we were to stand united. Sadly, lost were the values of the emotional bonding that family members should have toward one another.

FLORENCE WAS OUR NEXT STOP. The hotel had a rooftop pool and all the comforts of home. The museums, the aromas, the cobblestone streets, the shopping—in each city, I bought a gold charm for my bracelet—a matador in Spain, the Eiffel Tower in Paris, a gondola in Venice, and a golden globe in Rome. Shopping for gold on the Ponte Vecchio Bridge was exciting but challenging, because there were so many alluring jewelry shops to choose from, all next to one another—there must have been a hundred of them. I did buy a couple of braided gold necklaces and a bracelet there, too. Florence was also known for its leather goods. Mom bought a dozen pairs of leather gloves as gifts for her friends back home.

The satiny finish of Michelangelo's David gave us another startling lesson in human anatomy. We hadn't been exposed to nudity back home.

The aroma of garlic, tomatoes, and fresh Italian herbs filled our senses. Our mouths watered for a slice of freshly made mozzarella on a hard-crusted roll, drizzled with virgin olive oil and fresh basil. The food was *bellisimo!* The charm and elegance of Florence exceeded my expectations.

In Rome, Leo's uncle, Dominick Maglione, met us at the Grande Hotel Plaza and became our tour guide. Our suites at the hotel were lovely and came with trays of canapés, Champagne, strawberries, and Coke for us kids.

Each night we left our shoes out in the hall and the next morning they were returned with mirror-like spit-shines and a tray of Italian cookies.

As we were waiting to check into our rooms, Dad—Mr. Personality, who seemed to bump into someone he knew wherever we went—recognized the voice of one of our customers from the Inn. We overheard him saying, "What I wouldn't do for a Clinton Inn steak sandwich!"

We laughed as Dad snuck around the sofa and the huge centerpiece to surprise him, and then we adjourned to the bar, where Dad bought everyone a drink.

A monsignor friend of my father's arranged for a semi-private papal audience with Pope John XXIII. Not being Catholic, I didn't know what to expect. Reverence for the Holy Father, however, conjured up images of respect, silent prayer, and dignity.

We arrived at the Pope's summer residence, Castel Gandolfo, an hour outside of Rome, on Greek time—late! The Swiss Guards saw our tickets and frantically began scrambling, running all around to get us into the hall where we were to meet the Pontiff.

Our heads covered with lace out of respect, I was confused and unsure what was happening. I thought maybe we were being arrested or something. Finally, they opened a gate, and we entered an enormous hall, a hundred yards long or so, filled to capacity with excited spectators.

Kids were standing on their parents' shoulders; people were

squished together on the large windowsills. Perhaps ten thousand nuns, Boy Scouts, Girl Scouts, soldiers, priests, and ordinary people had crowded into that huge space, with its fifty-foot-high ceiling.

Our seats were to have been on the altar, with the dignitaries from all cultures and faiths; even the Greek archbishop was there. Since we were late, there was no room left for us on the altar, so the Swiss Guards quickly made six people in the front row move from their Prussian-blue velvet seats, where they had most likely been sitting for hours and for which they had probably paid a premium. They had to squeeze into the crowd, and the guards insisted we stay right there on the aisle. I was so embarrassed at that awkward moment, and I hoped that we hadn't ruined their visit with the Pope.

At that very moment a loud roar arose from the audience. It startled me. The huge doors at the back of the great hall had parted, and in came Pope John, carried on a richly adorned silk-covered armchair called a sedia gestatoria. My eyes stung with tears; it was as if God Himself were appearing.

The crowd went wild, and Pope John seemed to relish every moment. He took off his zucchetto and waved it with great joy. The noise was deafening; chills ran up and down my spine.

They eventually lowered him right next to my mother, and she kissed his ring as he made his way up onto the altar. He was a round and jovial, yet ordinary-looking man. Speaking in seven languages, he addressed each group individually, and they screamed and whistled, yelling, "Viva il Papa." I was awestruck. He spoke to us in English, talked about the Yankees, and was very funny. We had purchased rosary beads and key chains with his likeness on them, and he asked everyone to hold them up as he blessed us all.

Dominick Maglione, with his charismatic Italian charm, was waiting for us back at the hotel. We spent the entire week seeing Rome and the surrounding areas with him. It was great to see it from a native's perspective. We also traveled with him by train to Pompeii and Naples, visiting the Appian Way and other historic sites along the railway. He whistled a lovely tune the whole way there, and I was spellbound. Dominick, with his deep-set gentle eyes, his warm, slightly crooked smile, and his receding hairline was a man I found very attractive. He and I were developing a special connection, and I was in love with Rome and falling "in love" with Dominick, who seemed to favor me, too.

We toured the sites of the ancient cities and broke bread with the locals. As we parted at the end of the week, heading for Greece, I didn't want to leave—I didn't want to leave Dominick. He came to the hotel to say goodbye and kissed everyone but me. *Why not me?* I wondered.

Then with the twinkle and a wink, he said in his beautiful Italian accent, "Pete, can I take Jane downstairs for a moment?"

My heart was a-flutter when Dad agreed.

Dominick took me by the hand. We left the hotel and rounded the corner to a local chocolatier. There, he bought me a huge, five-pound heart-shaped box of chocolates, in a bright red-velvet box with a crimson ribbon and said, "Per la mia bella, Jane." *Wow!* That more than made up for the disappointment of not getting a kiss and not getting to see Murano.

He was a much older man than I, but I'll never forget the special connection we shared. In fact, I have secretly tucked that treasured gift away—not the chocolates, of course, I ate those—but the strikingly beautiful box is still intact.

9

NON-MATCHING FOLDING CHAIRS

I KNEW THAT ATHENS, DAD'S HOMELAND, would be a thrill for him. At times he would be quiet, deep in thought, which was very unlike him. At other times he'd tease my mother, saying, "Be careful, you're in my country now."

Mr. and Mrs. John Baker and Dr. Pappas, friends from home who were also vacationing there, greeted us, and we met several distant relatives I never knew we had.

The Grand Britannia Hotel, with its open-sky rooftop restaurant, lies adjacent to Constitution Square, where the Evzones perform the changing of the guard twice a day. We spent a month in Athens dancing and dining and enjoying Greek delicacies. We also spent many a day at the beach at Vouliagmeni, on the outskirts of the city, with friends and family.

Like arms outstretched to God, rising hundreds of feet above the city, stand the ruins of the Parthenon. Climbing the hill to the Acropolis was a worthwhile challenge. It is considered the most perfect of buildings—but I wondered why they put it way up there? It can be seen from miles around. Though scientists have been studying it for centuries, they are still unsure how its architectural precision was achieved.

We sailed to several of the Grecian islands; the whitewashed buildings and blue-tiled roofs glistened in the sun as they rose from the sparkling azure sea.

Before long, Dad was eager to get to his hometown, so we flew south to Kalamata. The airport was the size of a shoebox, and the Rex Hotel had an old-fashioned wrought-iron elevator. You had to crank yourself up in the cage with a large, ornate iron wheel to get to the second floor. Three people and two suitcases were all that would fit. We turned the big round crank until our muscles ached, but that didn't stop us from playing elevator operator for other guests.

On the cobblestoned streets downtown, we came upon a side road. "I remember this!" Dad said excitedly. "The church used to be right over there, by the courtyard, and we lived in that red building on the right. Looks like the church has been torn down."

We later discovered that it had burned down a few years earlier. He had hoped to get a copy of his baptismal certificate there.

Hesitating for a moment, he went up the three steps and knocked on the door of his old home. There was no answer, so, craning his neck and leaning over the rail, he peered in a window. I watched him closely as he stood there for a moment, wondering what he must have been feeling. I could see that he was fighting to keep his emotions in check. Then he shook his head as if to clear it. I could never imagine leaving my homeland. He'd been just a boy when he left.

The next day Dad arranged for a taxi to take us to the outskirts of town, to visit cousins he hadn't seen in forty-five years.

Back in the States, we had just moved into our new home on the hill in Tenafly that had all the bells and whistles—an intercom system, electric garage door openers, and in my parents' room were master light-switch panels for the whole house. We had a three-car garage, a finished basement with shuffleboard courts, and train sets—a great party room for us teenagers.

The view of the Ramapo Mountains from our thirty-by-forty-foot den was stunning. The focal point at the far end of the room, across its entire width, was a thick Georgia-pink marble fireplace, with a wide marble hearth that we used to pile high with big fluffy pillows to lie on. Sixteen feet of the sidewall opened on full-length piano hinges into our dining and living rooms, giving us nearly a hundred feet of party space. It was an ingenious idea that provided room to entertain large crowds, which, as I have noted, my parents did on a regular basis.

We left the paved streets of Kalamata for dirt roads and drove several miles before making a right turn into a cornfield. Our cabbie was a proud man. Through his short-cropped hair you could see he was balding; he was also a little stout. Although he was missing a few teeth, he grinned from ear to ear. He kept honking the horn, as if to say, "Here I am, look at me!"

Under the dashboard of his cab was a remarkable invention; a floating 45-rpm record player mounted on a spring-type mechanism that never skipped a beat while playing Elvis Presley's "Love Me Tender" as we traversed the bumpy roadways. I was intrigued by its ingenuity.

Continuing down another narrow, muddy, pot-holed road, we came upon a tiny, two-story, whitewashed building off to our left. The taxi stopped. It was our destination, the home of Dad's cousin Maria. It had been built out of cow manure, apparently, in the absence of good stone or wood. I couldn't imagine what it smelled like on a hot, rainy day. I was embarrassed and almost ashamed of the way we lived in America.

When we drove down those bouncy roads, all you could see for miles in either direction were low-growing crops. The land was flat but apparently fertile. There didn't seem to be any trees, and it was quiet—no tractor noise. The air felt light and warm, and you could smell the earth.

The excitement on Dad's face was unmistakable. He leapt from the taxi to greet his cousins, with great jubilation, in Greek. This was his family. They welcomed us warmly and invited us into an open courtyard. There sat five or six rusty, non-matching folding chairs, and a couple of dirt mounds on the ground they used for stools.

At home, the elegant maple stools in our brand new kitchen were comfortable, sturdy, and even swiveled. I wondered how these people could really be living like that in the twentieth century. The entire farmhouse, including the courtyard, could easily have fit into our den.

We were introduced to the family of six, and there were also some neighbors who remembered my father and his family, and wanted to say hello.

Maria was petite, with delicate features. She had a very pretty embroidered collar that looked like she probably made it herself. It framed her face on top of her black dress. She had been widowed for many years, and I guessed she was close to my father's age. Her hair was dyed black as the ace of spades. Her smile went across her entire face, and you could feel her love. My mother was about the same size, and although Mom didn't speak Greek, they seemed to communicate quite nicely.

The kids ranged in age from about eleven to eighteen. Niko was the oldest. Anna was next in line, and she was so pretty—kind of different-looking with a light complexion and blue eyes. She wore her sandy-colored hair in a graceful braid. She was Linda's age. Then came the twins, Sofia and Ellie. Sofia was shy and hid behind Maria's apron, while Ellie sat with us, trying to pay attention, but then got restless and ran around the yard outside the courtyard. Little Angelo, the youngest, disappeared into the house. They seemed to be much like us, but though they were close to our ages and polite, we were unable to speak their language, which made it difficult to communicate. All the while I sat there in utter disbelief, taking in the extreme contrasts of our lifestyles. Maria offered us a sweet homemade preserve called a glyko.

To this day, I'll never forget when she walked over to an old green garden hose sticking through the mud wall that was tied in a knot. She grabbed a large glass pitcher and, having unknotted the hose, filled the pitcher with water that looked like the muddy Mississippi. What's she going to do with that? I wondered. Then, Niko brought tall glasses for each of us and filled them. Niko was himself a tall drink of water. He was a good-looking boy with his mother's eyes and curly black hair, but it was clear that he hadn't been to the dentist in a while. As he handed us the glasses, we looked at my father, who looked back and said, "Drink it."

"But, Dad," we whimpered.

Quietly, with a big grin on his face, he repeated, "*Drink it!*"

I didn't know whether to laugh or cry, so I slowly sipped the water after letting the mud settle to the bottom. At times, it felt as though we were on Candid Camera or a movie set and Hopalong Cassidy would come riding up on his steed at any moment. I pictured the director saying, "Cut, that's a wrap!" and then I would awaken.

It was unforgivably rude of me. They were proud, hard-working Greek farmers entertaining their wealthy American cousins. I don't recall if anyone else was struck in the same way, but that journey back in time shook me to my core, and I realized being in their presence had been a rare honor.

We had been blessed and spoiled, and I didn't take that lightly and was humbled by it.

As we peeked into the building at the dirt floors they slept on, we saw the wooden planks, which had been stuck into the manure wall as it hardened, leading to a second floor. A raised hearth fired with twigs sat below a makeshift wooden covering outside the building, where Maria was preparing a meal for us. The air, which was fragrant and moist from the sea, helped stimulate our appetites. If I close my eyes, I can still smell the aroma of fresh herbs and garlic.

They must raise their own chickens, I thought, because there wasn't a supermarket anywhere in sight, nor did they have refrigeration or electricity. They lived by oil lamps.

We were there for several hours, as Dad and Maria caught up on the many years they had been apart. After serving us a simple meal that was utterly delicious—accompanied by homemade hard-crusted bread and string beans Kapama with onions, garlic, lemon and tomatoes—she topped off the evening with a wedge of freshly baked, sticky-gooey baklava that Anna had helped her mother prepare.

On the uneventful drive back through the cornfield to the hotel, Dad chuckled to himself. I'm sure he wondered what we were thinking.

Finally, he said, "What did you think of the rabbit we had for dinner?"

He was kidding, right?

10

A MAY TO DECEMBER ROMANCE

MY EIGHTEENTH-BIRTHDAY GIFT from my parents was the snazziest teal-blue Chevy Super Sport convertible, making me the envy of my class.

The greatest surprise though, was mounted under the dash. They had installed a 45-rpm record player, just like the one we had seen in Kalamata. (This was long before CD players in cars had even been conceived.)

Pulling up to the curb with the top down, the wind streaking through my hair, I put a record of "Johnny Angel" by Shelley Fabares into the player. My classmates gathered around and couldn't believe their eyes. They hadn't seen anything like it before, so they all piled in and we took a spin around the block.

Yes, of course I was showing off.

Early one evening, while cruising around town, I saw my friend

Jesse Lo Bianco coming out of the corner store. He had been a chaperone at the Youth Recreation Center at the Roosevelt Commons where I spent most of my free time as a child. The town had provided a safe haven where kids could learn crafts and finger painting, or play kickball. We could even go for pony rides.

I yelled out, "Hey, Jesse, you wanna go for a ride?"

He jumped in and we drove up to the Palisades Parkway and stopped at one of the scenic overlooks. We walked along the pathway enjoying the spectacular view of Manhattan as the full moon began to rise over the skyline.

When we got back in the car, he spontaneously leaned over and gave me my first real kiss. Sparks flew!

"Oh, no, this can't be happening!" I exclaimed. "Jesse, you're married. We shouldn't be doing this!"

"I'm sorry," he said. "You're right. Let's go."

Although we had known each other for years, his kiss surprised me. We laughed about it, and feeling rather cocky I drove back to town.

I couldn't get the kiss out of my mind. In my dreams I thought, I'd really be lucky if I could find someone like him with whom to spend the rest of my life.

Upon finishing high school, Class of '62, I couldn't bear the thought of leaving my parents or Jesse behind. So for six years, I attended night school at the Teaneck campus of Fairleigh Dickinson University, earning a bachelor's in business administration. Often after class, I'd fill in for Dad to give him a break, closing the Inn at one or two o'clock in the morning.

The Inn was the local gathering place, and Jesse and many other townsfolk often stopped in with some friends. Occasionally, he came in alone. We often talked about our families and shared stories of our lives at great length. As we kidded with each other, a rich companionship had begun to develop. He'd stay until I closed the

Inn, and then he walked me to my car.

That one kiss we had exchanged was not something easily forgotten. I found him irresistible, and it wasn't long before a second kiss. This time I didn't pull away, although I struggled with a strong sense of guilt. His beautiful come-hither smile was drawing me in.

When we kissed again, I experienced something I had never felt before. My knees buckled, my thighs quivered, and I had a fluttering sensation in my heart. I'd never before known such joy. I wanted more, and although he was twenty-six years older than I, that seemed inconsequential.

While he expressed his love for his wife, Sandra, he also confessed his sense of loneliness and his need for intimacy. He explained that after three miscarriages, Sandra had nearly died during the birth of their son, Matthew. The doctors had advised her that she would never be able to carry another child to full term. From that day forward, her fear kept her from being intimate with Jesse ever again.

Though he remained committed to their marriage, given their Catholic faith, he was conflicted about what had been evolving between us. We were, however, connecting with each other on a very deep emotional level.

I, too, was lonely and had an unfulfilled desire and longing to be with someone, since my high school years had been so devastatingly isolating. Life was becoming confusing yet irresistibly arousing. It had my moral compass spinning out of control.

Jesse told me, "Please don't feel that you have broken up our marriage—that happened long before you came into my life."

We knew that our relationship was wrong, but it felt so right. It was not a life I would have chosen for myself, but I do believe that it was heaven-sent. Jesse gave me a love that so many others only wish they could have had, a love that I would not change for anything in the world.

We soon began finding time to sneak away. When we kissed there were fireworks. My eyes closed and I shuddered. He was a real turn-on.

What I was feeling seemed like the beach scene in *From Here to Eternity*, and there was no doubt that I was falling in love with him. He was a perfect specimen of masculinity, with shoulders broader than the statue of *David*. His stride was like that of a president, and his soft blue Sicilian eyes captured my heart. He also had a full head of gorgeous gray hair flecked with hints of silver.

It didn't take long to realize that we'd soon make love, but I wasn't sure exactly how, since he was the first man I'd ever been with.

One evening he said, "Will you come away with me for a little while?"

"Sure. Where are we going?"

"I know a cozy little bed and breakfast we can go for a few hours to be alone."

In the hushed calm of our room, he slowly undressed me with great finesse, admiring my figure. I could feel the ripple of his muscles under his shirt, and then I undressed him. I couldn't believe how beautiful his body was. We kissed passionately, but restrained our desire for each other. He was gentle and respected my lack of experience.

Then we dressed and drove back. We hugged for a long while before parting. He left for home, and I left with a grin on my face that lasted for days, as I dreamed of what had taken place and what was still to come. This was the beginning of a splendid love affair.

On the next highly anticipated rendezvous, feeling more relaxed with each other we quickly undressed. I knew this was going to be it. The intrigue was intoxicating.

He delicately tickled my skin; he kissed me and then asked if it was okay; I knew that I would never be the same.

When he collapsed into my arms with his full weight, breathing heavily, he asked, "Are you alright?"

Too weak to respond, I simply nodded. We chuckled and caressed each other as we tried to catch our breath.

Kissing my tears of joy as they trickled down my cheek, he whispered, "I love you, Jane."

"Oh, Jesse, I love you too."

"We need to be careful and patient," he said, "and I'll try to see you as often as I can."

Soon we dressed and slipped back into our normal daily routines.

He left me breathless. I could hardly wait to be alone with him again. The memory of his aftershave was making me nuts; the expectations drove me wild. My pulse quickened as I gasped in anticipation. There is no greater feeling in the world.

I had been a virgin; he proved to be a very skillful lover. We began meeting more often and my thoughts of him consumed every moment.

We were falling madly in love. He *was* the man of my dreams, and I loved him more than life itself.

Once we had accepted our destiny, our remarkable love affair lasted for twenty-five magnificent years.

We devoted our lives to each other and cherished every brief encounter that we shared. Not wanting to waste one single perfect second, we never once argued or raised our voices to each other. I am eternally grateful for these priceless memories.

THE FAMOUSLY VOLATILE RELATIONSHIP between Katharine Hepburn and Spencer Tracy and their off-screen love affair, brought about the most convincing chemistry in movie history.

I believe that Hepburn summed up this special kind of love

when director Clarence Brown once asked her, "Why the hell don't you find a guy you can marry and raise a family with? Otherwise, when you're older you'll be all alone."

She replied, "Yes, and I'll look back at all the fun I had." As if finding someone else when you're *already in love* is that simple.

In 1993, I watched Phil Donahue interview Hepburn. It was late in her life, yet she was still full of piss and vinegar. She spoke of the splendid life she had enjoyed with her family in Connecticut, where she learned to swim, dive, and ride horses. She had also been a debutante. She was tough, independent, strong-willed, and witty, yet feminine. With the exception of tough, I believe I share many of those qualities.

That evening, I sat down to write her a letter. I explained how our lives had run a parallel course, although we had chosen different career paths. I expressed how grateful I was to know that she, too, believed that the kind of love that we had shared was undeniably the most beautiful gift. Having heard that she also loved flowers, I painted a watercolor rose for her and enclosed a photo of myself from the Hope Cotillion. My profile was similar to one I had seen of her in a photo.

Hepburn was living in Manhattan at the time, so in my letter I asked if I could have the pleasure of meeting her. Remarkably, she wrote back. She kept the painting and returned my photo with a lovely note thanking me for bothering to write, adding, "Too many people—not enough time."

During her interview with Donahue, he had asked about her illicit twenty-five year affair with Tracy, to which she responded "We just simply loved each other. Nothing more to say."

Katharine Houghton Hepburn

II - 11 - 1993

Dear D. Jane Albanese -

What a charming letter - Thank you for bothering -

It's really not possible for me to meet all the lovely people who want to say hello - Too many people - Not enough time -

All the best of luck to you -

Katharine Hepburn

11

A Surprise Trip to the Cape

Jesse and I simply loved each other, too. As our affair became addictive, it also began to present a series of obvious challenges.

Not the least of which was when Jesse and his family vacationed, and I traveled with mine. It was difficult tearing ourselves away from each other as we snatched our precious moments together.

Nevertheless, we made the best of it. Since he and his family usually traveled locally, I found a way to show up on the spot, often saying, "Don't be surprised if I magically appear."

Each summer he and his family spent a few weeks down at the Jersey Shore. Jesse loved to fish. Being the independent person that I was, and a prankster in my own right, I'd drive down to the beach, disguise myself with a hooded parka and dark sunglasses, and walk along the water's edge right in front of Jesse, careful that his wife wouldn't notice. She would be in the cottage making lunch or searching for seashells farther down the beach.

As I passed him, I'd say, "Hi, Stootz" (a nickname that stuck). Startled, he freaked out, looked around for Sandra, and then tried to find a way to fish by the pier where we could steal a kiss. I know that, for me, that very brief encounter was exciting enough to last until their vacation ended and they returned to Tenafly.

The following year, Jesse and Matthew, his son, were fishing on one of the jetties in Cape May, New Jersey. I waited for him to come back to the beach, but it took too long, so I asked a young boy who appeared to be familiar with the rocks if he could take a note out to the end of the jetty and give it to the older man with the gray hair. The note simply read, "Turn around."

I was cracking up inside. When he got the note, he told Matthew that he had to pee and would be right back. I saw him returning to the boardwalk and as I jumped the rail, I landed just a few feet in front of him.

He said, "You're a crazy nut!"

"Yes, I'm crazy about you."

We snuck under the boardwalk and smooched for a few moments, and then he went back out onto the jetty. I drove home content as a clam in its shell.

On another occasion, Jesse and three fishing buddies took a trip to Cape Cod without their wives. I knew they were driving up there in Sammy's four-wheel-drive Jeep, but I didn't know where they were staying and had no idea how big the Cape was. It was going to be a bigger challenge than I expected. I told Jesse, "If you see red flags flying in the sunset, you'll know that I'm there."

I convinced my sister Linda to drive to Cape Cod with me for the weekend. She was one of our confidantes. We stopped in Boston first to visit our cousin Arthur. I explained that we were playing a prank on a friend, and asked him if we could switch cars for the weekend, so we wouldn't be spotted, and he agreed. Linda and I had bought some long-haired wigs and oversized circus-type sunglasses. We laughed ourselves silly, realizing that we were two nuts and thinking there was no way we'd be able to find them. The only clue we had to go on was that the Jeep was an Army fatigue green with Jersey plates.

With my sense of mischief, we began our search. Linda and I took a room at a cute motel at the lower end of the Cape. I didn't want to drive too far for fear of passing them. We had dinner and went to bed around ten that night, figuring we could get an early start in the morning looking for the green Jeep.

As we walked out onto the morning dew, we noticed a Jeep of that color parked in a motel lot just across the street from where we were staying, and it had Jersey plates. *That couldn't be them, could it?* Surely there were many Jersey fishermen up there.

We got into our costumes and turned the car around so we could see who owned the Jeep. Within moments two men emerged. I thought I recognized one of them, but wasn't sure about the other—and then Jesse came out with Sammy. What an amazing stroke of luck! They packed their gear and headed for the beach.

They drove about a mile and a half, then pulled onto the sand and disappeared behind a dune. I tried to see how far the Chevy could go without getting stuck, but quickly realized it was going to be impossible to follow them. So I parked the car and we crept around the dune. They were gone, leaving only their tracks in the sand.

We trekked for a while, hoping to catch a glimpse of them, but we couldn't see them at all. I said to Linda, "Let's get back in the car and drive to the other end of the beach."

As we did, I noticed a small airport with a big sign that read "Sightseeing Flights for $49."

"Come on," I said excitedly. "Let's go rent a plane."

All the while I had the red crepe-paper flags ready to display. Linda was beginning to think I was a little loony—she was probably scared, too—but she was a good sport. We got into the open cockpit of the yellow sightseeing plane, fastened our seat belts, and pulled on our goggles. I explained to the pilot that we had to find four fishermen and then drop the red flags out of the plane. He, too, probably thought I was crazy, but he went along with the prank.

We circled the end of the beach where we had seen them heading. Sure enough, there they were. We dropped the flags. Then the pilot looped around a few more times as we watched the men running toward the flags. They must have been thinking someone was sending them messages, but since nothing was on the flags, I'm sure they were puzzled and simply went back to fishing.

I couldn't imagine what Jesse was feeling, other than, *Oh, no she can't really be here,* can she?

Linda and I went sightseeing around the rest of the Cape and then waited for the men to return to their motel. As the sun was setting, we went for a walk wearing our long-haired wigs.

Suddenly I noticed Jesse and the man I hadn't recognized coming toward us on the other side of the street. Jesse told me later that he had recognized us and told his friend he was going to go over and talk with those girls. The friend went back the other way, and Linda, Jesse, and I met. We hugged and laughed, and then asked Linda if she'd mind going for a short walk so we could be alone for a little while. She agreed, and Jesse and I snuck in a very quick, wildly passionate moment as he kept shaking his head in disbelief.

12

Hope

Just after Christmas 1965, at the age of twenty-one, I was invited to make my debut into society at the Hope Cotillion Debutante Ball at the Waldorf Astoria. The cotillion was the annual gala, named in honor of the S.S. Hope navy hospital ship originally built and operated by Project HOPE.

Of the many highlights in my life, this remains at the top of the list. Eleven girls from prominent families in the area came out that year. We all wore white. It was like a dream I'd never dreamed come true.

Mom and I shopped for my ball gown. The one we chose had a delicate pearl-beaded neckline, and it flattered my twenty-one-inch waist and voluptuous bust. There was a large, floor-length satin bow like a bustle at the back, complemented by white gloves rising above the elbow. I'd never looked as pretty before, and

I certainly have never had a twenty-one-inch waistline since.

When I saw my reflection in the mirror, I felt like a ballerina perched on top of a music box.

Mrs. Stuart Alexander was the Grand Dame of the evening. We all met at her home in Park Ridge for four fun-packed, grueling days of rehearsals. With the help of a choreographer, we learned the art of the curtsey and three dance routines. Over and over again we practiced, until she felt we were ready for the performance of our lives.

For the dress rehearsal the night before the gala, our fathers, looking proud and dapper, joined us in their white ties and tails in the Grand Ballroom at the Waldorf. It was an honor to be included in the event—in fact, the whole week seemed as if we were preparing for a Broadway production.

My mother played hostess to our friends, many of whom had been on the Caterpillar that snowy winter's eve years earlier, and several of my best friends were there as well, including Leo.

The International Debutante Ball—a different, much larger event—was being televised the same evening. The young women participating there were the crème de la crème, the next generation of the international elite who presented themselves to the sons and families of ambassadors, world leaders, and captains of industry. The girls at that event were the well-heeled scions of the world's most elite families. Our group was from the New York metropolitan area only.

When Jesse got home that night, they were introducing Miss New York. Not realizing it was a separate event he was upset that he missed seeing me, thinking I must have been Miss New Jersey.

I could hardly wait to tell him all about it the next day, and he was relieved to learn that what he had seen was a different affair, and that our event had not been televised.

Mamie Eisenhower was the honorary chairperson of our Ball.

Also in attendance were the King and Queen of Norway, New York Mayor Robert F. Wagner, senators, and other dignitaries.

To me, Dad looked like the handsome prince that he was. With tears in his eyes, he said, "Honey, you look amazing."

Each of us, escorted by our fathers, was introduced as we walked to the center of the stage and curtsied. We then made our way down the steps and straight across the dance floor before returning our dads to their tables. The audience stood and applauded as we made our way back to the center of the ballroom, where we lined up for our performance.

The night was magical. Accompanied by a full orchestra, we were joined by our partners and went on to perform our dance routines to "Moon River," " Winter Wonderland," and "Singin' in the Rain"—umbrellas and all.

There were speeches and an elegant dinner, and then our fathers were reintroduced as pillars of the community. We had the opportunity of dancing with them as if at our own wedding receptions, a highly emotional moment for Dad and me. Soon, our escorts tapped our fathers on the shoulder and swept us up to dance the night away.

My escort, David, was a professional dancer who had taught me the high-stepping tango that we had rehearsed several times. As we took the floor, feeling confident and looking stellar, everyone moved aside, forming a huge circle to watch us dance to "Blue Tango" by Leroy Anderson. Like Ginger Rogers with Fred Astaire, we twirled around the dance floor and through the curved archways of the ballroom as he lifted me through the air. After a burst of applause, the others joined in.

Soon the alumnae from previous cotillions, with their dazzling red sashes, entered the room with their escorts, and together we pin-wheeled around the ballroom. We posed throughout the evening for formal pictures by the cotillion photographer. The New York society press from the *Times* and the *Daily News Magazine* were there; they covered the event on their front pages with the gorgeous platinum-blonde debutante, Segrid Oberg, on the cover. We all had our photos in the center spreads the following week.

We had made the headlines!

It was, after all, the "Hope" cotillion—the spirit of hope for the future of our lives. It seemed to offer endless possibilities of

prosperity, joy, and fulfillment. Linda had the same opportunity the following year, but she turned it down. Unlike me, she never liked being at the center of attention.

TRYING TO DECIDE THE COURSE of my future while working during the day, I decided to take a two-week travel agency course in New York City. Having traveled as extensively as we had, it was right up my alley. When I completed the course, my first job was with a local agency in New Jersey. I loved the details and felt it was something at which I could excel. Still elevated by the great poise of the cotillion, I knew that I could conquer whatever life presented. It gave me an exceptional advantage into my first venture in the real world.

I worked hard to learn the business and memorize airline fares to the most commonly traveled cities. I also took advantage of the numerous travel perks, and I knew that I had found my place in the business arena.

One of our steady customers was a young Englewood resident named John Travolta. He loved to fly and would come into the office every other week or so to buy a $49 ticket on Mohawk airlines. In the late 1960s, Mohawk ran this special rate: You could fly wherever they went, then get on the next flight, and the next—for the entire weekend. John had become a regular passenger with them, and I believe this is where his love of flying began. He later earned his commercial pilot's license and owns several planes.

A few years later I moved to a different agency, where my bosses recognized my potential and soon asked, "Would you consider becoming a partner in a branch office we're about to open?" I was flattered and felt that my attention to detail was paying off.

Only twenty-eight at the time, I brought my father in on the discussion, and he thought it was a great idea. Dad and I met with my bosses, Nick and John Faye of Presidential Travel in Fort Lee, to discuss the details. Dad put up some money and, voilà, I was a partner. Although my head was spinning with nerves, I was confident that I could do it.

Linda had been working at the Inn but seemed restless, so I asked, "Why don't you learn the travel agency business and join us?" To my surprise, she did—and she also became a partner. We worked hard to learn the ins and outs of the business, to be sure we could hold up our end of the bargain. I began learning the back end, helping to handle the accounting—including billing and accounts receivable, learning the published fare and commission structures, and how to make the weekly payments to (IATA), the International Air Transport Association. Things were going smoothly, and Linda was learning the industry quickly as well.

In the second year, we had a lengthy battle with our two partners when we discovered that Nick had been having private meetings with my father to ask for more money. I began to question why Linda and I hadn't been included in the conversations and suspected something underhanded was going on.

Sure enough, on closer examination we discovered that Dad's money had been passed through the branch office and into their original agency. We had been too proud, trusting, and naive to even consider such a possibility, but our trust had been betrayed. After a series of painstakingly long discussions that revealed the truth, Dad said, "Hon, instead of taking them to court, you and Linda take over the branch office, and I'll take care of the rest."

"Dad, I don't think I know enough."

"You'll be fine," he said, "because you're always good at what you do."

Although I felt far from ready, we did just that—knowing he would be there to help if we needed him. Like my father, I was always looking to be challenged and, although it was not exactly what I'd had in mind, a challenge had come knocking on my front door. And I knew I had to give it my all.

Two years later, we learned that we would be losing our lease in Fort Lee to a Jack LaLanne franchise, which forced us to relocate. Linda and I battled over where to go. We searched all of Bergen County but found nothing quite suitable that we could afford.

Then I had an idea.

"Dad, can we move the business into the lower level of the Clinton Inn and create an office there?" I asked. "The rent would be cheaper than anywhere else, and the space is large and empty."

He gave it a great deal of consideration, then finally said, "If you can convince Uncle John and Uncle Jim, you have my approval."

Shaking in my boots, I went to speak with Uncle Jim first. After I explained the situation, he replied, "It's fine with me." Then he added. "Now, good luck with Uncle John."

Everyone knew Uncle John would be a hard nut to crack, so I took a deep breath and drove to his house. He welcomed me in and listened to my impassioned plea. He had many questions: "How big will the office be? Who's going to pay for the construction? How many employees do you have?" I was really nervous, although I knew all the answers. When he realized that I was serious, and that we had found nowhere else to go, he reluctantly agreed.

A few handy friends, a carpenter, and I laid out the office plan. It was going to be lovely. We had selected an off-white, stucco-textured panel for the back wall where I had placed a large, free-form burl wood clock. The sidewalls were paneled in maple, so brochure racks could be hung there. We scheduled the start of construction three weeks before Christmas. I asked the contractors to get there at 7 a.m. to begin.

Much to my surprise, Uncle John arrived a few minutes later. He screamed at me, "You can't take up this much room!"

"But I showed you the plans," I said. "What's changed?"

I had explained we needed room for seven desks and some storage, but I guess he hadn't translated that into real space. The whole lower level of the Inn was empty, and we were only taking about a quarter. He stopped the men. I called Dad for help, and together they worked it out. We started again the following week, even earlier in the morning. By the time Uncle John arrived, the two back walls were already in place. He yelled some more, but we just kept working.

Our office was completed late on Christmas Eve. Linda had not at all been in favor of being at the Inn, so she stayed away during construction. She didn't want to be "too close" to home—and didn't want anyone to know her personal affairs. When she finally came to work, she made sure it was only for a few hours a day, which began to cause a rift between us.

The perks of owning a travel agency, however, offset the friction. While trying to keep the business afloat and build the corporate end, I also got to take advantage of the many travel discounts.

I retraced all the high points of our family's journeys, often staying at charming boutique hotels for just three dollars a night. Occasionally I'd splurge and stay a night or two at one of the luxury hotels that we had visited earlier. I also traversed less-traveled pathways to tiny picturesque villages. I skied the Swiss Alps, swam in the Aegean, and shopped at the Baccarat and Lalique showrooms in Paris, shipping home a few stunning crystal pieces to add to my treasures.

At the Vatican, I felt blessed when I touched the robe of Pope Paul VI, and relished the moment when Pope John Paul II came out on his fourth-floor balcony at Castel Gondolfo, to bless the huge crowd standing in the blazing afternoon sun.

Waiting for the clouds to clear over the Matterhorn in Zermatt, Switzerland, a few friends and I lay among the fragrant, lush grass on the perimeter of a cow pasture. We dined on a bottle of wine, a wedge of Swiss cheese, and a freshly baked baguette still warm from the oven, and we enjoyed the fresh air of the Alps.

With the exception of Wyoming and the Dakotas, I've also seen all the lower forty-eight states.

One of my favorite trips was when a group of agents and I ran the rapids on a rafting trip down the Salmon River in northern Idaho. We camped out along the shoreline for six nights during a drought that made the rapids more severe. Forty of us rode in two ginormous forty-foot rubber rafts.

Fresh eggs, whole chickens, steaks, and lobster tails were carried on the platforms between the pontoons of the rafts. The bottled drinking water, soda, and beer—lots of beer—stayed cold in big nets tied to the side of the raft. There is nothing like the crisp mountain air and frigid water to build your appetite. When we pulled over for the evening, our guides set up the grills. The food was hearty, delicious, and very satisfying.

It was a magnificent trip with forty new friends. We slept under a starlit sky. There were no port-o-potties, just large trees to hide behind. Careful not to pick poison ivy, we used maple leaves in place of toilet paper. We quickly, very quickly, bathed in the nude in the frosty water. Then, as we sat around the evening campfire, we roasted marshmallows and told tales of our lives back home.

Once back on the river, we sang, "You Picked a Fine Time to Leave Me, Lucille," over and over again, and then "A Hundred Bottles of Beer on the Wall." The more beer, the more choruses.

As our guides scouted the route ahead, the rushing water echoed through the canyons and birds soared high against the cirrus clouds above. There were many deeply spiritual moments, when we realized that we were but a tiny part of this massive world.

The third day out, our raft unexpectedly collapsed as we got caught up in an enormous hole. I was knocked unconscious when my head hit the front of the folded pontoon. Other people got cuts and bruises. Luckily for me, someone grabbed my life vest and hung on until we reached a calm stretch. I awoke feeling four inches shorter and wished that one of the other rafters was a chiropractor.

No such luck, so we continued on downstream 'til we reached the lower campground, at the end of seven invigorating days. We parted with tears after a week of belly laughs and fond memories.

EACH TIME WE PULLED OUT OF PORT on a Windjammer tall ship cruise, "Amazing Grace" was played over the loud speakers. We snorkeled in the water above the third largest barrier reef in the world off Grand Bahama Island. The clarity of the turquoise waters and the glow of the neon-colored coral formations that grow some six-stories tall, highlight an abundance of tropical fish species, turtles, and eels.

I've also had the pleasure of driving across this great land of ours three times. I've visited every point of interest along the way, from New York to Seattle's Space Needle, and from the Grand Canyon to South Carolina's famous South of the Border, as well as from San Diego to the rugged coastline of Maine.

I've even had the opportunity to pull the umbilical cord of a glider as we rose to 4,000 feet on the thermals of the clouds over my favorite airport back in Blairstown. For over an hour the pilot and I glided over the treetops, so close you could see robin eggs in their nests. Then we'd rise again by making lazy circles on the air currents that lifted us back up. As we rose, the temperature plummeted. Then, finally upon making our approach, we landed effortlessly—with barely even a bump. What a thrill!

Over the eighteen years of my travel agency experience, I spent time in Memphis and toured Graceland; stayed with friends in Hot Springs, Arkansas; dined on Chicago's Magnificent Mile; explored the great national parklands; and visited New Orleans, home of Dixieland Jazz.

I was living the high life and loving every minute of it. I had found my wings, and I was prepared to soar like an eagle.

13

YOU SOUND JUST LIKE MOM

THE MOST FUN I HAD EVER HAD with my sister, Linda, was on a trip to Munich, Germany. Did you ever find something so funny that you lost control, laughing so hard that you wet yourself? One Friday night, Linda and I were catching a 9 p.m. flight out of JFK to Munich. We checked in, everything was normal, and we left the runway on time. As we were flying over the tip of Long Island, I was looking out the window and said something lame that tickled Linda's funny bone, and she said, "You sound just like Mom."

We started to laugh, and the harder we tried to stop the sillier we got. Two hours into the flight, a petite older lady who was sitting in front of us got up on her knees and turned to us. We thought we were doomed, but she just wanted to tell us how delightful it was to hear us laugh, and that she was enjoying whatever was cracking us up.

The trip promised to be loads of fun, and I suppose we did catch a few winks before our arrival. I was a seasoned traveler, prepared for whatever contingency might occur. I had lightweight rain gear, an umbrella, a sweater, extra socks, and such. Though it was early summer, the Munich weather could be unpredictable. Linda, on the other hand, made sure she had her mascara and a curling iron. Umbrella? Why would she need one?

You guessed it—the skies opened and it poured like cats and dogs for the first two days. That got us laughing all over again as we tried to share my umbrella and rain jacket.

We finally found a department store and looked for an umbrella or parka or something for her. We went up to the third floor, where we found what we were looking for. It looked just like mine—but how do you open it? This wasn't brain surgery; there had to be a simple solution. Ah, we finally opened and closed the umbrella successfully a few times. Once I had the hang of it, like anything else, it was easy.

I gave Linda mine, and as we left the store I couldn't get the damn new umbrella to fully reopen to save my life. I just sat it, half open, on my head, so the rain would shed off my shoulders, not letting the dilemma spoil our day. We howled so hard we could barely walk a straight line, and we hardly cared what there was to see—we were having too much fun.

Taking pictures was futile in the rain, so we bought lots of postcards as we headed through the charming old city, and we booked a few bus tours. As we got on one bus—I can't remember where we were headed—we still had the giggles.

Shortly thereafter, a rather peculiar odor came from a seat or two in front of us, and we just lost it, cracking up again. When we stopped for lunch along a beautifully scenic roadway, one of the other passengers came over to us and said, "What on earth is making the two of you laugh?"

Her name was Elvie. I'll never forget it because Linda kept calling her Alfie. Elvie, short for Elvira, lived in the Swiss Alps, but she had spent many years in Elmira, New York. So Elvira from Elmira soon caught the bug, and we spent the next three days laughing our way through the picturesque German countryside with her. She was a bright and interesting woman, and we looked forward to seeing her each day.

We asked her what she missed most about living in the states, expecting her to say something profound like "American freedom" or "wide-open spaces," but she said she missed cranberry sauce. We couldn't believe it! For years thereafter, we sent her cases of cranberry sauce each year for Christmas. I cherish that memory of Elvie and Linda.

ON ANOTHER OCCASION, when I'd asked Linda to cancel an airline reservation for me, I had marked our reservation card with the word *cancel* across the front. I asked that when she completed the cancellation, she would add the *ed*, so that when anyone else looked at the form it would be clear that it had been *canceled*.

I was going about my own business but could hear Linda on the phone with the airline.

All of a sudden I heard her say, "Thank you, E.D." She quickly flipped around, hoping no one else had heard her. We had. Embarrassed, she started to laugh uncontrollably, hung up on E. D., and then we all burst into tears of laughter.

As soon as we could catch our breath, we called Dad to tell him the story. At first he said he couldn't tell whether we were laughing or crying, but then he began laughing with us and he could hear our whole office cracking up in the background.

THESE STORIES REMIND ME OF THE LAST TRIP I took to Europe

before moving to Florida a year later. I wanted to fly to Sorrento, Italy, to buy a cameo. I loved fine jewelry, and Sorrento is famous for its cameo industry. Travel agents are frequently offered discounted travel to tourist spots (called fam-trips), so they can gain firsthand knowledge of the area to better sell the location. On the Fourth of July weekend in 1980, our office was offered a fam-trip to Sorrento with a stopover in Rome. I jumped at the opportunity and discovered that I knew most of the other agents who were also going on the trip. We were headed for a good time.

Friday night, the traffic to JFK was heavier than usual. I had left the office in plenty of time, but the typically one-hour trip took close to two-and-a-half. Who could have prepared for that? And in the 1980s there were no cell phones to check on a flight's departure status. I knew I was cutting it close but kept on crawling in traffic to the airport. I dropped my bag at the curb—it was safe to do that back then—parked the car in short-term parking, and sprinted back to the terminal. (I was able to do that back then, too.) I ran up to the counter and discovered that, due to air traffic control, the flight was being delayed for four hours. Relieved, sweaty, and exhausted, I located my friends, and we adjourned to the lounge.

The four-hour delay meant that we couldn't take the first tour upon arrival in Rome. So they gave us three options: we could go right to sleep, or shop, or, without rest and a shower, go to Castel Gandolfo to see Pope John Paul II. No guesswork there for me—after seeing Pope John XXIII in 1961 and Pope Paul VI in the late 70s, I wasn't going to miss an opportunity to see John Paul II.

Half of us chose that option, so we hired a few taxis and took the hour-long trip to his summer residence. (It actually took well over an hour, because one of the taxis ran out of gas, which was exasperating. How the hell could you run out of gas when you're taking people to see the Pope?)

We were already so punch-drunk by then, all we could do was laugh. The taxis pulled up near a card shop, and we got out while one of the cabbies went for a can of gas. As quickly as possible when he returned, we jumped into the cabs and hurried off. Did we stop to count heads? No, of course not! One of our travel mates was still in the card shop and we hadn't noticed. Unfortunately, the poor guy missed the Pope, and had to find his way back to the hotel.

Castel Gandolfo is high on a hill, so the drivers let us off at the closest point. With cameras flying in the wind, we ran up the steep cobblestone path. It was above 90 degrees Fahrenheit, and we hadn't slept in what felt like a week.

We were fifty feet away when, at the stroke of noon, the clock struck twelve times. Stopping to catch my breath, I leaned against a large stone wall, and suddenly heard a loud roar *on the other side* of the building. We were at the *back* of the building; that was where the drivers had left us off. We asked a uniformed Pontifical Swiss Guardsman, "How do we get to the other side?" He indicated there was no room there, but added, "The Pope will also come to this side at 12:30." *What a relief!*

We had a few moments to rest, and sure enough Pope John Paul II did come to our side. He was four flights up, and his head, from that angle, was the size of a pea. Camera at the ready, every time he raised his arms to greet us, I'd look through the lens—and down came his arms. I have two full album pages of Pope John Paul II's head—he's barely recognizable. We did feel blessed by him nevertheless. Good thing we were young. It was all very funny and thrilling, and if we hadn't laughed we would have been crying.

We collapsed in our hotel rooms and missed dinner; at least I know I did. I slept like the dead, having been up since the morning before. The next day was one of leisure. Then we headed by bus to Sorrento, Capri, and the Blue Grotto.

We ran from the bus to a boat that would take us to a smaller boat, which took us to the rowboats that took us into the Grotto. I don't think I have ever seen anything so tranquil and breathtaking. It was cool and serene, and the crystal-clear, aqua-blue water appeared to be lit from below. It is an amazing phenomenon. I dropped a quarter into it and watched it twist and turn for what seemed like an eternity. I didn't want to leave and wished I could have jumped into the water to refresh myself.

We returned to the bus, had a sumptuous lunch at the top of Capri, and then moved on to Sorrento. It was a bright, hot, sunny Sunday afternoon. *Sunday!* The shops would be closed. I couldn't believe my luck. I had come all that way to buy a cameo, and the shops were closed.

What they hadn't told us, however, was that the shop owners would open on Sundays for the tour buses. I was very relieved and spent an hour or so shopping. I came home with the most gorgeous round, chocolate-brown-and-white cameo I'd ever seen. It was hand-carved and signed by the owner of the factory himself. On it, there is a couple in love sitting on a bench in the woods, a tiny bluebird on her shoulder. I love the memory of our trip to Sorrento and that beautiful piece of jewelry, and I will never part with it.

In later years, through difficult financial times, I sadly had to sell most of my good jewelry for the gold content, in order to survive. I even sold the gold watch that had been given to my father on his fiftieth birthday by our gang and then given to me upon his death. But I've kept the cameo.

We returned to Rome and prepared to leave for the airport the next day. As travel agents, we were flying on a standby basis. It was the Fourth of July weekend, which meant nothing to the Italians, so we figured we shouldn't have a problem getting on flights back to New York. But the whole world seemed to have the same idea. There was not a single economy flight available to anywhere in the world from Rome that day or the next, or the next.

I went from airline to airline until I finally found three first-class seats to London. From there we would still be on standby, but three of us did make it back to New York the next day. Some of our friends were stranded in Rome for another week. It was an expensive trip but worth every moment.

As I recounted this story at the office the next day, I had my legs elevated because my feet were swollen beyond recognition. After the heat, the long flights, and the Mimosas on the flights, my toes had completely disappeared; the toenails were just sitting on top of elephant-like stumps. How funny was that? In addition, the meeting I had returned for had been canceled. My feet eventually got back to normal and I went about my business, grateful for the fond memories.

Book Two

Turning Point

14

A Crack in the Armor

We were all still living at home on the east hill. Tommy was about to be married for the second time, and Linda and I were excited about going for the final fittings of our bridesmaid's gowns. Tommy's fiancée, Frances (or "Nifty," as she preferred to be called), was a lovely girl with gorgeous blond-streaked red hair, a bubbly personality, and a very pretty freckled face. We loved her and were eager to welcome her into our family, though I wondered what she saw in my big brother.

One evening, knowing Mom and Dad were out with the gang and Linda was on a date, I'd gone to bed early. Tommy had stayed up a while to watch a movie.

I was awakened from a deep sleep by ear-piercing screams coming from the other end of the house. I leapt to my feet, feeling disoriented, frantically thinking, *Oh, my God! Please let Daddy be okay.*

As I rushed to see what was wrong, the screams got louder. I thought he had died, and fear overcame me—thankfully, though, he was the first person I saw when I got to the den. Mom was still screaming, and she was pulling Linda's hair.

"What the hell's going on?" I screamed.

I was shaken to the core, and as I approached them Linda freed herself and ran to Dad. I seized my mother's shoulders, trying to calm her. "Mom. *Mom!* What's wrong?" I cried out, but she wouldn't stop—she was hysterical.

In the chaos of that moment, I hadn't noticed Tommy was right on my heels. He must have thought that I was hurting her. He grabbed me by the shoulder and punched me in the face as hard as he could. The blow nearly lifted me into the air. As I back-pedaled, I almost crashed through the sliding glass doors on the other side of the room.

When the marbles in my head stopped bouncing around long enough for me to get up, I ran into the kitchen and grabbed a butcher's knife. Everything was happening so fast it was like being in a bad Hitchcock movie.

Dad came running to me, yelling, "Honey! *No*! Put it down!"

I threw it back in the drawer.

Linda picked up the phone and, with trembling hands, called the police.

The incident was so completely foreign to us, I couldn't grasp what was happening and was hoping it had all been a horrible nightmare, but the pain in my jaw told me otherwise.

Our old friend Detective Jack Powell soon pulled into the driveway. I was still trying to wrap my mind around what was going on. Sure we had our little family spats, but never a knock-down, drag-out fight like this.

Powell separated us and took Tommy, still in his pajamas, out on the balcony. Before we knew it, my brother was driving away.

When Powell came back in and started talking with Dad, he asked me, "Are you alright?"

"Yeah, I guess so."

"You and Linda go back to bed, we'll take care of this."

It must have been two or three in the morning by then, and I wasn't going anywhere. Linda was crying, and Mom had stopped —but what the hell had happened?

Too much partying?

Upset and embarrassed, Dad briefly explained the situation to Detective Powell and asked him to keep the incident as quiet as he could. Powell said that he would, and then left.

My jaw was swollen, my eye felt glued shut, and the side of my face was turning black-and-blue. I grabbed a bag of frozen peas and held it to my cheek.

My father embraced Mom, and they cried together. Then he put her to bed.

Dad, Linda, and I stayed up till dawn, trying to sort things out. It seemed that she and my mother had gotten into an altercation and harsh words were exchanged, then things spun out of control.

There'd been nothing unusual about any of them being out late, so I couldn't tell what had triggered the hostility. Clearly, something had sparked my mother's aggressive behavior.

"What happened? Why was Mom pulling your hair?"

Linda explained, "When I got home, they must've just gotten in. I sat next to her on the couch, and she started yelling at me for being out so late. Then she grabbed my hair and was screaming curse words at me. She called me a whore. Dad tried to stop her...and I guess that's when you came in."

I asked, "Why was she so angry?"

"I don't know. I've never seen her like that before."

"Were you out drinking?"

"No, we were at a friend's house, but we weren't drinking."

"Do you think Mom might have had more to drink than she could handle? I hate what booze can do to some people."

Dad explained that they had been out to dinner with the D'Agostinos, celebrating their anniversary.

"Everything seemed fine," he said. "We had a few drinks with dinner, and then Jim popped a bottle of Champagne. I hadn't noticed anything unusual about Mom's behavior, but she doesn't do well mixing drinks. That, though, doesn't explain what happened."

I suppose Tommy had just reacted—thinking he was being protective—but he hadn't stopped to assess the situation as I had been trying to do. For me, the irrational punch he'd thrown at me put everything over the top—and I sensed that we might never be the same.

"There's no way I'm going to be in their wedding now," I said.

"Yeah, me either," said Linda. "That was really scary. I don't know why he had to hit you like that."

I said, "I really feel sorry for Nifty, but I'm not going back to try on the gown again."

Dad was deeply upset and concerned. We all hugged and then finally crawled into bed as the sun began to rise, hoping to make the incident go away.

I could hardly wait to tell Jesse the next day. He wanted to find Tommy and beat him to a pulp, but since my family was unaware of our relationship, I made him promise that he would let it lie.

Tommy and I are very different and never really got along well, which I can only assume began when he tried to overturn my baby carriage, or when he left that lump on my head in Venice. So, though cordial, we usually kept our distance.

As he entered adulthood, he seemed angry, resentful, and perhaps inadequate somehow. He always had an *I'll-get-even-with-you* kind of attitude. By the time he slugged me, he had been in and out of several colleges, the navy, and a brief marriage to a woman with a young daughter. Alcohol had also begun playing a significant role in his life, and I wanted nothing to do with it or with him. He began to distance himself from the family, which I considered a good thing.

Ours had, I thought, been a family built on solid ground—precious and high-spirited, the very essence of what a wonderfully loving and close-knit family should be.

That feeling was lost during those early morning hours.

Mom had a good night's rest and remembered none of what had happened the night before. We didn't talk about the incident again and acted as though it hadn't occurred. How strange! I think we were all in shock, and I believe to this day that Tommy has no idea what actually took place that evening. Neither he nor Nifty ever asked—and he never apologized. I've often wondered what he told her. I'd have thought that she'd want to know the truth about why we chose not to participate in their wedding. I suppose they were too busy embarking on their future together. They married two weeks later, as planned.

Over the years, as they began to raise a family of their own, we remained distant. Although we spent time together at holiday dinners, Tommy, having usually had a few nips before we arrived, was frequently nasty and rude. I often ate my Christmas dinner alone in the other room on that sacred day, not wanting to watch three or four football games at the end of the dinner table. He called me a freak, so I withdrew from any discourse with him.

PEOPLE SOMETIMES SAY MY EXPECTATIONS are too high. Maybe I am a dreamer, but the extraordinary bliss we had all enjoyed during our younger years had come to a screeching halt. We began to grow further apart, and it affected each of us, I'm sure, in unspoken ways, as it seemed to seep into every other aspect of our lives.

We had often seen our parents and their gang party and drink.

There was a season of Brandy Alexanders and old fashioneds, and then they went on to rusty nails, or J & B on the rocks, but I never once detected that any of them had gone too far. They were highly respected, successful, and dedicated businessmen and their wives, and there seemed to be no need to get drunk—they were already high on life and laughter. They danced and told jokes and thoroughly relished being with one another.

But over the years Tommy—and later his daughter Kristi were plagued by alcoholism and other addictions. Kristi also suffers from anorexia. Now that she's a mother herself, I hope she rises above her demons and raises a loving, healthy, and successful family of her own.

She was one of the prettiest babies I had ever seen. Her wisps of blond hair softly framed a perfectly shaped little head, and she was a sweet child. Her eyes melted your heart, and her smile lit up the room. As she matured, we were close.

When Kristi was fifteen or so, she and I went to the mall. I loved being with her; she was like my BFF. Before getting into my car, she asked, "Aunt Jane, what's it like?"

"What's what like?

"Sex."

"Sex?" I exclaimed. I was shocked but tried not to show it, as she pulled out a Playgirl magazine to show me pictures of naked Adonises.

"Where did you get that?"

"A friend at school gave it to me."

My mind raced as I tried to think of what to say. Wanting to be honest with her, I said, "Sex is the most wonderful experience of life. But it's very important to be with the right partner. Sex just for the sake of having it, isn't nearly as gratifying." I paused, then asked, "Have you tried it yet?"

"No, of course not."

I turned a stern eye on her, "*Really?*"

"Yeah."

"Do you have a boyfriend? Someone you'd like to have sex with? Is he pressuring you?"

"There's a boy in school that I really like, but I'm not sure he likes me."

"Have you kissed him?"

"Yes."

"How was that?"

"I liked it."

"Did he touch you?"

"Just a little, but I didn't know what to do."

"Have you asked your mother about sex?"

"No—I don't want to do that."

"Well, maybe you should. Sex is a very natural thing, and she was your age once. She'll understand."

We talked some more, and she wanted to know how you do it and what it felt like. I cautiously described my first encounter to her. Luckily for me, it had been with a man with whom I was deeply in love. He was gentle and caring, and although I was scared at first, I felt safe. I knew that he loved me, too. If I conveyed nothing else to her, I wanted her to understand how important it was to be careful and not get pregnant. I asked, "Do you know how to protect yourself? You do know that it only takes one unprotected sexual encounter to get pregnant, right?"

"Yes, I know."

When we got to the mall, I said, "Let's change the subject. Where do you want to go first?" And off we went.

I hadn't given the conversation much more thought until one day when Nifty called me and said. "How dare you talk to my daughter about sex!"

I was flabbergasted that Kristi had made me look like the bad guy. "I did what I thought was best given the circumstances," I said, knowing full well that she'd likely believe Kristi over me anyway.

Nifty had never tried to get to know me, nor I her, since the wedding. I'd always had great respect for her ability to tolerate her husband's lifestyle and behavior, and for the lovely way in which she had raised her children.

Her attitude though, brought into question whether or not she could view both sides of a story. Rather than pouncing on me for doing what I believed was right, she should have asked me what had happened and why the discussion with her daughter had occurred in the first place. At that moment Nifty showed me who she truly was, and as Maya Angelou once said, "When someone shows you who they are, believe them the *first time*."

15

NEW BEGINNINGS

THE TURMOIL OF THAT LIFE-ALTERING clash stayed with us, as the frayed edges of our family solidarity began to unravel. Linda and I had been trying our best to make a go of the travel business after taking over from our partners, but soon we too started to struggle.

To compound everything, it was not long after that episode that Jesse told me he was going to retire and move his family to Clearwater Beach, Florida. I was stunned. The fracturing of my family had left me feeling forlorn; other than my dad, Jesse had been my only safe haven and I couldn't bear losing him. Up to that point, we had secretly hidden our affair for thirteen spectacular years.

When he retired, he and Sandra flew back and forth to Florida, looking for a new home. We had many conversations about what would happen to our relationship. He explained, "Leaving you is one of the most difficult decisions of my life, but we can no longer afford to live in Bergen County. You mean the world to me, and, oh, how I wish you could come with me. I'm so sorry, honey. Please try to understand."

He attempted to assure me that I would find another wonderful man to love, but I knew that was only a pipe dream, and it would take a long time for my heart to mend. I'd cry myself to sleep and felt sure that my life was over, until one day a dear friend said, "Jane, you're in the travel business—you can fly down to see him whenever you'd like."

Grateful for her comment, I realized that she was right. This became a new challenge, and I began commuting to visit with Jesse every month for *six very long years*, barely able to see him for more than a few hours at a time. Our love was the most important thing in my life, and I needed his comfort and support.

One day, as we approached the seventh year of commuting, I could no longer stand leaving him. I fell to the floor and wrapped my arms around his legs so he couldn't go. Up to that time, I had departed each month with a lovesick, broken heart, realizing that I had no choice but to move near him. That defining moment changed the trajectory of my life. As I became more restless and torn, I recognized it was time for me to spread my wings. Eventually, Linda took over the agency.

BY THEN, I WAS A WOMAN OF THIRTY-SEVEN, and my mind was made up. I began preparing to move to Clearwater, excited yet frightened beyond words, having never before lived away from home. In my visits to Florida, I had fallen in love with the warmth and charm of the area, and although I knew I would miss my family terribly, I was looking forward to living there.

When I told my parents of my plans to move, the rumors they

had heard about Jesse and me having an affair were confirmed. Mom snooped through some of my personal things and had discovered a birthday card I was giving to Jesse, and she and Dad confronted me.

"What's this?" she demanded.

"Why were you going through my things?"

My father jumped in, "Never mind that. What's going on with you and Jesse?"

"Dad, I'm madly in love with him, and I can't stand being away from him for another moment. But I can't bear the thought of leaving you and Mom either. I have to move closer to him—please understand and give me your blessing.

"We can't do that," he said. "You're making a grave mistake. He's a married man."

I asked them to try to comprehend how upset I was and reminded them that I was old enough to make my own decisions. Mom later told me that she'd felt I was abandoning the family.

It was so hard to explain how lonely I had been all the years following my high school experience, where I didn't fit in.

When they realized that my move was inevitable, they decided to give me a going-away party on the night before I was to leave and invited all my aunts, uncles, and cousins, and the entire gang was also there. I guess they didn't realize how much harder that made it for me to go, or maybe that was their plan. At the end of the lovely evening, I cried as I hugged everyone and said, "See you soon."

I kissed Mom and Dad goodbye and left the party. They didn't even get up from the table and wouldn't walk me to the car. I felt completely rejected by them, which made me need Jesse all the more.

As I began the long drive the following morning and reached the point of no return, I called them. It felt as though there were icicles hanging on the phone line. My only salvation was that I knew that Jesse was less than eight hundred miles away, and that gave me the peace of mind that I needed.

Shortly after arriving in Florida, I had put a small deposit on an adorable home that was being built just two miles away from where Jesse and Sandra had moved.

One day after moving in, Dad called and said, "Mom and I would like to come down to see you."

"Oh," I exclaimed with great enthusiasm, "that would be great! When can you come? I miss you so much."

A few weeks later, I met them at the Tampa airport. We hugged and cried; I was so glad to see them, feeling that they hadn't deserted me after all.

They liked the neighborhood I'd chosen, and I think they were proud of me, although I understood that they were also upset by the thought of their eldest daughter leaving home without being married.

They only stayed a few days, but I think they felt a little better about my move when they saw that I would be safe. I was in my own home in a lovely neighborhood with great neighbors.

After settling in, I took a real estate course and, when I finished it, placed my license with a business broker. My boss was an older Irish gent named Patrick O'Neil. His gentle manner was endearing and he mentored me, teaching me the tricks of the trade. He was a heavyset man and had great character in his handsomely dimpled face. There was always a little curl at the end of his lips like the remnants of a leftover smile, and softness filled his light hazel eyes. His curly white hair was cropped short, and he was forever in long-sleeved button-down shirts with his plaid necktie slightly askew. I found him very attractive.

Several months later, on the Fourth of July weekend, as I was recuperating from an unexpected second partial hysterectomy (the first had been at age twenty-eight), Mom came back to stay with me in Florida; Dad would be joining us in a few days. When Jesse came to visit, he and I spent some private time in the den while Mom watch TV in the living room.

He had been there with me as I faced the surgery, and we had grown even closer now that he was just a bike ride away. Jesse was the first and only man I had ever been with, and we were madly in love. I couldn't breathe without him. I had never before experienced such an impassioned emotion.

ONE EVENING AS I WAS KISSING JESSE GOODNIGHT, Mom, hiding behind a column in the living room, said, "Make sure he doesn't come here while your father's here."

Why was she hiding—*what the hell was that all about?*

I said, "When are the two of you going to grow up and realize Jesse is the man I love?"

Immediately, I felt my comment had been disrespectful, and I was sorry for that. I was also frustrated that she was not accepting of Jesse after all that time. Being in love with him was the most precious gift of my life, and his love had given me my first true feelings of worthiness and an extraordinary sense of happiness and belonging. Though the immorality of our affair never left my conscience, my boundless joy with him overpowered those feelings.

Deep down, I certainly knew that there was no way my parents could fully accept Jesse. What we were doing had to be extremely difficult for them to swallow, given the level of dignity with which my parents had lived.

As Jesse rode away that evening, I went back inside to speak with Mom, but she had already withdrawn to her bedroom.

The following morning she gave me the silent treatment, and then she went next door to my neighbor, Marie, to ask if she'd drive her to the airport to pick up my father.

"Mom, don't bother Marie," I said. "I'll drive you to get him." But she wanted nothing to do with me.

Marie looked at me, shrugged her shoulders, and said, "It's okay, I'll take her."

I suspected that Mom would do just about anything to keep Dad from coming to see me after that retort. It seemed she was perpetuating what appeared to be a deep-seated dislike of the daughter with whom she always felt a need to compete. It was not a competition—I was merely a daddy's girl, she was the woman Dad had always adored.

Although I wasn't supposed to drive with the stitches still in me, I had to speak with my father personally. Once at the airport, I had them paged. I couldn't find them and returned home, hoping that they might have taken a cab there. Later I discovered that Dad never heard the page—although Mom did, and then she took him away.

I was very upset and didn't know what she had told him, but could only surmise that it had to be an exaggeration of the truth—because I knew that my father would have insisted on coming to see me virtually under any circumstance. Her explanation must have been something severe enough to change his mind.

Family dynamics may be complicated, but love conquers all—or so I thought. I didn't know where they had gone. I tried calling them at home and at their place in Boca Raton, but there was no answer.

A week or so later, when they returned to New Jersey, Dad wouldn't accept my phone calls. I pleaded with our staff at the Inn to get him on the phone for me, but he refused. What could she possibly have told him? I decided to write him a letter to explain what had taken place.

He finally called me and said, with sadness in his voice, "Honey, Mom threatened to divorce me if we went back to your house that day."

"Why'd she do that? It wasn't a big deal."

When he heard what had actually taken place, he was dismayed and said he wished that he had followed his instincts.

"I don't understand why her anger and need to lash out was so out of proportion with what you said to her."

I, too, was confused by her anger.

During her stay with me, Mom hadn't given me an inkling of her being upset with Jesse and me. Apparently, I hadn't understood the depth of her disapproval, and I guess I hadn't recognized how uncomfortable our visits might have been for her.

I loved how Dad and I were always able to talk things out, and I was so thankful for his support. Mom and I were different, never able to discuss anything without disagreeing. She would lash out and then walk away, allowing no further discussion. Dad, on the other hand, had a clear understanding of my need to express my individual characteristics and to be true to myself. Mom never did.

16

No Thanks, I Just Got a Haircut

Weeks later, on October 19, my thirty-eighth birthday, the phone rang at three in the afternoon. It was Linda calling to wish me a happy birthday—and then she put my cousin Arthur on the phone.

"Hi, Jane," he said. "Your father died this morning."

"Your father?"

"No, *your* father."

In disbelief, I turned to Jesse with tears choking at my throat. "My–my father died today," I said. "I've just lost my family."

Verbalizing that thought surprised me, though it was exactly what I had been feeling for some time. It was one of the most painful days of my life.

I was so thankful for that one last conversation with my father, knowing that we both had peace of mind and an understanding of what had actually happened between my mother and me.

He was my world and the sunshine of our lives.

He'd had a massive heart attack. In that moment, the unraveling of our family became all too real. I was devastated by the news. I wished that I could have been there with him and, of course, I worried about my mother.

Dad dying on my birthday was, in an absurd way, a sanctified gift to me. It was as if he were saying, *I'll always be here for you, honey.*

Instinctively, however, I knew the road ahead would be less than perfect for our family. We had not only lost him, but our way of life. His unconditional love was the glue that had kept us together, and we would now certainly grow further apart.

The arrangement Dad had with his brothers was that if one of them died, the others would buy out his family's share of the business.

The Clinton Inn was more than a second home to us; it was our pulse. And although I had left the area, the fact that it was no longer ours created unimaginable complications. It was as if my father had died twice. I know Mom was especially crushed by his loss, and was lost herself without him.

I couldn't get a flight until late that evening, arriving home at midnight. It was a difficult trip, and fear of the future raced through my head.

As I look back, I'm not sure if Mom ever fully recovered. It was as if she reverted to the insecure young woman she had been before they married. Dad had always kept her in balance, and though she had grown with him, she seemed to have lost her sea legs. She had often snarled at the people and things that bugged her over the years, a behavior which Dad had been able to keep in check. I'm sure the gang tried to understand her new fears and challenges, and they were kind, patient, and loving, but it took her a long time to find her way.

The love and respect our extended family and friends demonstrated enveloped us warmly as we made funeral arrangements.

As we were leaving the funeral mass, we saw people still trying to make their way *to* the Greek Orthodox Cathedral of Saint John the Theologian—a moving tribute to a great man. There were so many cars that the roads were blocked for miles in both directions from the church to the cemetery.

The entire cortège pulled under the porte-cochère of the Clinton Inn before proceeding to the burial. A hundred or so of our employees lined the sidewalk, sobbing in disbelief. Their eyes met with ours in pain, as their beloved Mr. Pete passed before them for the final time.

Each of the nearly four thousand sympathy cards that I read included a hand-written note. I was looking to save a few. Two in particular profoundly touched my heart, encapsulating the essence of the others.

> *Dear Emily,*
>
> *It is still incredible to us that he is gone. Our memories go back over 30 years, and we will forever treasure them. It is very rare that a human being like Pete passes among us, and we are all better for having known him.*
>
> *... Milton*
>
> *Dear Ms. Emily and family,*
>
> *Our grief and tears join yours for the loss of our beloved Mr. Pete. You will never fully know what he has done for me and for my family; we shall never forget him.*
>
> *... Irene*

Yet another said, "In all the years of being fortunate enough to know Pete, I found him to be a kind and gentle man of great wisdom, understanding, and humor. I was lucky that our paths crossed."

It was remarkable to note how many lives he had touched in extraordinary ways. They thanked him for making their mortgage payments, or paying for their child's surgery, or even buying a car for one of our dishwashers when his was totaled in an accident. Many notes thanked God for sending such a great man to live among us.

To this day I am astonished by how fondly my father is remembered by the people of Tenafly. He's still "Mr. Pete" to them, an ordinary man with an extraordinary talent for bringing love, laughter, and great food into our world.

AFTER THE FUNERAL, Mom admitted to me that she had threatened to divorce him if he went to see me that day back in Florida, and she apologized. She told me that Dad had been bringing me a fourteen-thousand dollar check as a housewarming gift, and she said she would give it to me a few days before I went back.

By then she had to have realized the enormity of what she did back at the airport. I tried my best to forgive her—she had lost her lifelong mate, and I felt sorry for her. There was no way she could have predicted that he would die before I got to see him again.

They had been blessed with a good marriage of more than forty-seven years, and I know that she understood "being in love." I think that might be why I couldn't completely comprehend why she couldn't accept the love that Jesse and I had for each other.

I'D LIKE TO SHARE A TASTE of how I remember my dad.

One evening at the Mt. Carmel Masquerade Ball, he was the cat's meow. Standing only about five-foot-six-inches and portly, he was dressed in a Little Lord Fauntleroy costume. His white tights held him tight under his purple velvet pantaloons. He wore a matching vest and a long, curly white wig with a highly plumed purple hat. The whole crowd at the church burst into laughter and applause, giving him a standing ovation when he walked in. He fit the part. They could hardly believe that the sophisticated gentleman and restaurateur would let his hair down like that, but they also knew that he was a man of great humor.

After the ball, all were invited back to the Inn for bacon and eggs. I wish I could find the photos of him dressed in that costume.

Another cute ditty also comes to mind. Every Sunday evening for many years, Mr. and Mrs. Bishop frequented the Inn for dinner. They were quietly elegant in appearance and very proper in their speech. Dad, keenly aware of remembering names by association, connected the Bishops with The Pope in this case. And, one evening, as they arrived, he said, "Good evening, Mr. Pope."

Without a moment's hesitation, Mr. Bishop replied, "Thanks for the promotion!" and they cracked up.

Two of Dad's favorite expressions were, "No thanks, I just got a haircut," and "Que será será"—*what will be, will be*.

If we asked him, "Do you want a cup of coffee or whatever?" He'd say, "No thanks, I just got a haircut."

He kept us laughing because he was laughing so hard himself that we couldn't contain ourselves. He'd slap his knee and tears would streak down his face from his half-cocked, lazy eye.

As I approach my golden years, I recognize the truth and wisdom of "Que será será," and try to live by it, although clumsily at times.

Peter Chagaris 1906 - 1982

17

WELCOME TO VERO BEACH

A FEW MONTHS AFTER DAD'S FUNERAL and my return to work in Florida, I took a new client to see a meat distribution business that was for sale. It seemed like a very interesting enterprise, and subliminally, I sensed my father saying, *If the client doesn't buy it, you should.*

The client didn't—and so I did!

The food business was in my blood, and my entrepreneurial spirit knew that selling real estate wasn't what I wanted to do for the rest of my life. Although I was astounded by my own decision, I felt confident that I was making the right move. When I met with Arthur Lidstone, the owner of Maple Ridge Gourmet Foods, for the second time, everything fell into place. As we negotiated the sale, I asked if he would consider swapping the business for a condo I owned in Boca. We went to see it, and he was willing. He also agreed to stay on for a few months to teach me the business. It couldn't have been easier.

My boss, Mr. O'Neil was surprised but pleased for me, and he helped facilitate the deal. The papers were drawn up, and the deed for the condo was transferred to Lidstone.

I ran Maple Ridge as he had instructed. Within a year, however, I thought there might be a better way, and I converted the meat-distribution operation into a gourmet-food mail-order business—it was not an easy task, to say the least. It gave me the opportunity, though, to combine my love of food with my love of the arts. Although it was uncharted territory, I'd always relished new experiences that tested my abilities.

Untrained in computer graphics at the time, I hired Les Davis, an art director; an expert food stylist named Nicé Minor; and David Ewart, who was a food photographer. With the help of my assistant, Susan Caryl, we created an award-winning sixteen-page full-color mail-order catalog. It was awe-inspiring to me, and comparable in quality to the one Omaha Steaks, our biggest competitors, sent out. We carried prime sirloins individually vacuum-sealed, jumbo shrimp stuffed with crabmeat and Asiago cheese, extra-fine loin lamb chops, and homemade four-pound cheesecakes, among many other delicacies. On the first go-round, the catalog won an Addy award at the American Advertising Federation Competition.

After months of preparation and negotiating with suppliers, Nicé had the delicate task of preparing and styling the food on the plates to make them look picture perfect, an art unto itself. As she created a place setting with a napkin, utensils, flowers, and a wine glass, she would use a hypodermic needle to create bubbles in the wine, giving it the illusion that it had been freshly poured. She lightly oiled the steaks and the chops so they looked like they had just come off the grill.

We spent ten days holed up in David's home, using his kitchen and living room as a studio while shooting the entire catalog. The first mock-up was soon ready to go to press, along with the film (Digital cameras had yet to be invented.) I had gotten several quotes for the printing and settled on a major print house in Chicago. I flew there for the production.

I'd never seen a printing press that large in my life. The process started off with a huge roll of paper three feet taller than I—and ended with the finished product at the other side of the building. That first year we printed 300,000 catalogs, purchased mailing lists, had the product ready to go, and we were on our way. Having the first new catalog in my hand was an inspired moment.

Back in Florida, we were ready to launch the newly converted business from our 10,000-square-foot warehouse. There were two enormous walk-in freezers, conveyor belts, forklifts, plenty of room for storage of the packing materials, and I had built myself a gorgeous, knock-em-dead office. I wished my father could have seen the process, and hoped he was proud of me.

Over the course of the next three years, we printed and mailed a total of 900,000 catalogs.

Susan and I ordered and received the products, answered the phones, and took the orders. We managed the mailing lists, made the bank deposits, and computerized everything. We felt like pioneers and worked well together, and we laughed all the time. We also updated the catalog each year with new photos.

With the help of a few part-time employees, we packed thousands of nearly coffin-sized Styrofoam coolers with literally tons of dry ice surrounding the frozen food, and shipped them off to places far and wide around the nation.

In our marketing scheme at the end of the first year, I had been in contact with SkyMall and TWA, and began to enter into negotiations with them to get our catalog into the seat pockets of their domestic flights. We began receiving repeat orders and believed we were onto something big. It was exhilarating.

Treat Yourself To The Very Best
MAPLE RIDGE
GOURMET FOODS
MAPLE RIDGE
GOURMET FOODS

IN THE AUTUMN OF THE FOLLOWING YEAR, while I was on my way to Chicago for the printing of the second catalog, I stopped off in New Jersey to visit my mother on Labor Day weekend. My heart still ached for her since our lives had changed so drastically upon my father's death.

Late one beautiful afternoon, she and I took a ride along the Hudson River. The leaves were bursting with crimson and gold. The deep cerulean blue of the sky made a breathtaking backdrop for the Manhattan skyline, and thousands of tiny windows across the river glistened in the sun. As we entered the town of North Bergen, I said, "Mom, do you know if Dom Albanese is still alive?"

"No, I haven't heard from him in years since he remarried."

We took a chance and stopped by his house. No one was home, so I left him a note that read, "Hey, bum, why don't you stay home once in a while?" I tucked it behind the doorbell, not remembering that he rarely used the front door. A few weeks later he called my mother to say, "I was sweeping the porch and just found the note today. How are you?"

"We're fine, thanks. How are you? Jane and I were out for a ride and we thought we'd stop by to say hello."

"It was good to hear from you," he told her, adding, "I buried Virginia two months ago. Please give Jane my regards. I'd love to see you both."

Later that evening, Mom called to tell me that Dom had called and that Virginia had passed away. She said, "Don't call him." That seemed odd, and I wondered why, but knew I had to give him a call to express my condolences. It was good to hear his voice.

Dom and I had always had a special kinship, and we'd spent many long hours together after his first wife, Angie, died years earlier. I never knew Virginia, and so we had drifted apart.

I called him again a few times over the next several days to comfort him. In one of our early conversations, he mentioned he was going to Orlando to visit his middle son, Ray, and his family, whose grandson was celebrating his first birthday.

"Do you think they would mind if I join you at the party?"

"Oh, I'm sure they'd love to see you again. Come on over."

When we met in Orlando, I could hardly believe my eyes. Dom hadn't changed a bit—it was wonderful seeing him. As soon as he saw me get out of the car, his beat-up old tweed hat went flying into the air as it had so many times before, and we embraced.

Dom was a man with whom I shared a very special bond.

It was also great seeing Ray and his family. After the party that evening, we headed back to my place in Clearwater but somehow missed the turnoff. Apparently, after passing all the Orlando hotels and resorts, I headed east, not west. In the dark, the highway looked the same to me. Up to then I had never been lost in my life. The next sign we noticed, however, read "Welcome to Vero Beach"—some two hundred miles away from my home, on the opposite side of the state. We laughed like crazy, then I realized I could cut across the state and take Route 60 westbound to get back home. What a relief! The road was narrow, dark, and kind of creepy, but we finally made it. Dom never let me live it down. Truthfully, we were talking a mile a minute, catching up on all the years we had been apart. He was filling me in on the details of his wife's illness and what his sons had been up to, and I was telling him about Jesse and my new life in Florida. So we got to my place at 2:30 a.m., slightly later than expected.

We visited each other for a few days before he returned to New Jersey, and then we kept in very close contact by phone; our bills running up to hundreds of dollars each month.

A month or so later, Dom came back to see me in Florida, and I introduced him to Jesse. Although I knew he was not in favor of our relationship, he was cordial, and I was experiencing euphoria unlike anything I'd known before. Though they were both a generation older than I, these two men, who had been very special friends to me for nearly my entire life, were together for the very first time. It was clear they liked each other, and had circumstances been different, I think they could have become good friends.

I called my neighbor Marie over to take some pictures of the three of us. As I looked at the photos, I had to laugh. They were two very different-looking men. Jesse was built like a football player, tall and broad, now with a beautiful full crown of pure white hair, his eyes a soft blue, and his engaging smile sparkled in the sun.

Dom, on the other hand, although taller, was nearly bald, slender, and had deep grooves carved into his face. He also had expressive blue eyes that would charm you when they gazed into yours. Both had large, broad Italian noses and boisterous laughs that were hard to forget. They were self-confident, loved life, and were extremely playful. They had both loved their mothers and had great respect for women, which I found an endearing quality. Their personalities were very closely aligned; I'm sure that's what had attracted me to them in the first place. It's hard to describe the great love I felt for each of them. They had both played a major role in my life in different ways—Jesse romantically, of course, and Dom, who was like a best friend, more casually. My love for them both, though, was undeniable.

Having Jesse part-time was far better than not having him at all, however flawed and imperfect the arrangement. The intrigue and excitement of stealing a few precious moments of each day were exhilarating, and we wanted to capture every moment of the great love that we felt for each other.

Jesse left after the first meeting with Dom and returned again the next day. We were having a good time together. One evening when I kissed Jesse good-bye, Dom retreated into the den. When I went to find him, he seemed pensive, so I asked, "What's going on with you?

"Jesse's a really nice guy, but he's married. He can't take care of you."

"I know that, Dom, but I'm crazy about him."

I didn't think any more of it. Then Dom returned to New Jersey after giving me a warm, loving kiss and bear hug at the airport. He had been the second man to kiss me, if you remember, on my sixteenth birthday, after Pat O'Brien.

Dom and I kept in touch by phone, but he seemed distant, and I wondered why. We had always been able to communicate our feelings to each other. That was in part why I loved Dom as I did. One day he called and said, "I'd like to come down to see you again."

"Great, when? I'll pick you up at the airport."

Soon his visits became more frequent, and we'd call my mother laughing like hell at the fun we were all having. Dom often expressed his disapproval of my relationship with Jesse. I found those comments upsetting, but also provocative.

Why was he so upset? What was he thinking? It was my life, and I was perfectly content with the tremendous love that Jesse and I shared. I wondered whether Dom was simply trying to protect me, or if maybe he was beginning to have romantic feelings for me himself. But I never put much credence into the thought.

One day when Dom was back in New Jersey, I asked him, "Why don't you give my mother a call and take her to dinner? I know she's still missing Dad, and I'm sure she'd love to see you."

He said, "That had never occurred to me. I'll do that." I believe they had dinner a few times, and I was happy for them.

My journey with my parents' gang and that older generation had put me on a path that might seem unsuitable or peculiar to others in some way, but I was an old soul and not your typical young woman. I saw it as quite normal—my normal. I had always been with older people, and I fit right in. It was certainly within my comfort zone.

Around the same time that Dom began visiting more often, I started to notice that Jesse's health was showing signs of deterioration. The look in his alluring eyes was becoming painfully distant. I didn't know what to make of it, but since I was not his wife, I couldn't go to the doctor with him to determine what was happening. I was very concerned.

Then, suddenly, he just wouldn't show up as regularly as he had so many times before.

I began to notice that when I asked Jesse's opinion about something, anything, he'd merely say, "I don't know." That wasn't like him at all either. It was devastating, and I was frightened—it seemed that he was failing quickly. He had always been my rock, but when Dom visited I began seeing less and less of Jesse. Dom, fortunately, was helping to fill the gap.

Aware of everyone's disapproval of my affair with Jesse, I had prayed that, when the time was right, another wonderful man would come along and sweep me off my feet. I couldn't have written the script any better; in truth, I had written that exact prayer many years earlier, and tucked it into my Bible.

Much to my amazement, Dom was *that* man. We actually started dating long-distance. We also often spoke and laughed with my mother on the phone. At age eighty, Dom was still working as an architect up north, and I was entrenched in my business. Soon he began commuting between New Jersey and Florida on a weekly basis. I had constructed an office for him on the second floor of Maple Ridge to ease that commute, with a drafting table and all of the tools of his trade, allowing us to spend more time together. We played golf, dined out, and laughed a lot, and before we even realized it, a true romance had begun to blossom.

One day I discovered through a mutual friend from Tenafly that Jesse was suffering from Alzheimer's. I was missing him terribly and was devastated by the news, and I couldn't imagine living without him. He and I had enjoyed an unforgettable ride of deep love and devotion to each other. Soon, though, I began to recognize that Dom had been placed into my life to help me pick up the pieces as Jesse's health worsened.

Then on one of Dom's visits—it was an ordinary Tuesday afternoon—I caught a glimpse of him out of the corner of my eye. He kneeled next to me by the photocopy machine. I thought it a bit strange, but he took my hand and said, "Jane, will you marry me?"

I thought he was kidding at first. I was stunned and started to laugh and said, "Would you do that again?" But he was serious. And he did it again.

I had never been married before, except to my business. Dom was so much older than I, but I knew he was also tons of fun to be with. It felt surreal. My emotions running wild, life quickly passed before me, and I realized that as I was losing Jesse, I couldn't imagine living without either of them. So, much to my surprise, I said, "Yes, I will absolutely marry you."

His quick wit and loving upbringing, I felt, were sure to lead to an idyllic marriage. Although Jesse had occupied my heart for the prime of my life, this transition was something that I knew had to take place. I felt secure in Dom's arms, and I had always longed to be married one day.

Thoughts of my parents came to mind, knowing how pleased they would be that their friend Dom would be taking care of their little girl.

Girl—I liked that; by then I was forty-two. Dom and I had always cared deeply for each other. He told me one day, shortly after proposing, that he had wanted to make me a "respectable" woman; for him, marriage was the next and necessary step to make that happen.

There was a lot of preparation to be done as we planned for our upcoming nuptials. First, we had to tell both of our families, most of whom were up north.

Dom left for home, and the next day he went to see my mother to tell her the wonderful news. Since we were in high season at Maple Ridge, I was too tied up to leave. We planned his conversation so that I would call moments after he told her.

I immediately detected something other than surprise in her voice but assumed we had merely caught her off-guard. He would tell his five sons the following day.

Then, as if on cue, Jesse rode his bike over to my house one final time. I hesitated at first, but then told him that Dom had asked me to marry him, and that I had accepted.

True to his character, Jesse replied, "I knew one day that someone would take you away from me, but I never thought that he would be older than me."

Holding me tightly to his chest, he went on to say, "Thank you for loving me. You've been the light of my life, and I will love you until I take my last breath."

The indescribable depth of passion we shared in those intimate moments as we clung to each other cherishing our sad and final embrace, lingers in my soul.

His weakened, fading eyes filled with tears when he rode away that day. The great love that Jesse and I shared can only be described as a once-in-a-lifetime fairy tale, in which butterflies dance in the sunlight and a splendid peace overtakes the world. I am so lucky to have loved and been loved by that delightfully funny, tender, and adorable man.

Dom was there for me with compassion and understanding of the love that Jesse and I had shared. I'm truly fortunate that his love and devotion to me had begun to take over the reins of my heart.

Long after Jesse's passing, the memory of our love still draws a tear to my eye. His bellowing three-tone laugh will forever echo in my soul.

BEFORE LONG, OUR THIRD CATALOG was ready to go on press, this time in Atlanta, where I had gotten a better price. Dom and I flew there to proof them and watch as they came off the colossal, city-block-long press. It was another proud moment and a great thrill for me when they handed me a stapled, trimmed, and completed catalog. I could feel Dom's pride.

In a celebratory mood, we dined at the Ritz Carlton, sipping Champagne cocktails and enjoying each other's company. I asked the waiter, "Do you serve prime beef here?"

"Yes, ma'am, that's all we carry."

"Great. I'd like to order prime rib, end cut, English cut, if that's possible."

Dom preferred a center cut.

As the dinner plates arrived, looking as though my father had prepared them, I could swear I felt *Dad* put his arm around me as he always had. I could even smell his cologne, but as I whipped around in my chair, nearly toppling over to see who had brushed past me, no one was there. Bursting into tears, I cried, "Dom, my father was just here!" We knew that he was giving us his stamp of approval, and we wept.

The waiter rushed over. "Is something wrong?"

"No," Dom said. "We just got engaged, and we're full of emotion." But we both knew better.

"Oh, congratulations!" he said, and he bought us another round of drinks.

Comforted by Dad's affirmation, I flew back to Clearwater to prepare for the onslaught from the holiday mailing, and Dom returned to New Jersey. That was Labor Day 1987.

18

A Love Triangle

With Christmas fast approaching, I flew up north to be with Dom. We were eager to share the holidays with our families and friends, and to see the lights of Broadway.

The night I arrived was bitterly cold. Dom and I went directly from the airport to my mother's house to pick up the winter coat that I had stored there for my visits.

My key wouldn't work in her front door. We tried repeatedly and walked around to the side door, then realized that the locks must have been changed. When we drove down to Linda's office to get the new key, she said, "Sorry, I can't give it to you." But she wouldn't tell us why.

"What? What the hell's going on? Why can't I get the new key? I want to get my coat."

"I can't tell you."

"Well, you go get the coat for me."

"I can't do that either," she said.

"What do you mean, you can't tell me, and why can't I get my coat? *What's going on?*"

I was about to lose it but struggled to maintain my composure —not wanting to spoil our Christmas plans.

Baffled by her behavior, Dom put his arm around me and said, "Come on, honey, let's go buy a new coat. The hell with this."

We drove to the mall before going into the city.

New York pulsates with excitement around the holidays. People are busy scurrying from one beautifully decorated store to another, carrying more packages than they can handle.

The enticing aroma of giant salted pretzels and roasted chestnuts blended with the smells of the bus and subway fumes as we strolled along the gum-encrusted streets. Christmas carols and police sirens, church bells and honking horns blanketed the city with mystical sounds of happy chaos.

Then, right before our eyes, we witnessed a chilling tragedy: A young woman's body fell from the sky. The streets were jammed with people as we walked toward Radio City Music Hall. Oddly, though, there was an open spot just off to my left, where the curb met the street. I ducked as I caught a flash of color out of the side of my eye, and I couldn't imagine what it was. People gasped, and someone screamed, "Oh, my *God!*"

It was dark, but as I looked over, the first thing I noticed were her patent-leather shoes—platform spikes with a bow across the front. Thankfully, I couldn't see her face, but from her shoes, I assumed she was probably in her early twenties. She was wearing black silk stockings and a red coat or robe.

A man in the crowd ran over to her, saying, "Stand back!"

Another called out, "I'm a doctor! Give me some room. Someone call 911!"

Rattled to the bone, I looked up but couldn't see anything; the city lights were glaring in my eyes. We didn't know whether she had jumped or been pushed from the high-rise apartment building. People started crying; most were speechless, in disbelief. One woman fainted and collapsed on the ground.

At that sobering moment, time froze. The city went silent in my mind. My feet felt like lead, and my voice, when I could finally tune back into it, seemed to have an exaggerated and elongated edge. Within moments we saw flashing red lights coming from all directions. They got brighter and brighter, then suddenly the sirens stopped as the ambulance came to a screeching halt right in front of us.

Having never experienced anything like it before in my life, everything for me seemed to move in slow motion. I wanted to run but I wanted to stay—to comfort her, although there was no way that she could have survived that fall.

Dom reached for my arm. "Honey, I don't feel so well," he said. "I have a pain in my chest."

We pushed through the crowd and returned to New Jersey by ferry. I was feeling sick to my stomach, too.

I couldn't get the young woman's fate out of my mind. What had gone so wrong for her?

When we disembarked, I drove directly to Mike's house. He and Sonny, Dom's youngest and oldest sons, had wanted to talk with us about our engagement. Although it was not a good time to do so, they had insisted.

Dom's pain had subsided, so we tried to explain that it had been a harrowing day—first the lockout and not being able to get my coat, then the girl dying in the city. With everyone's anger and bizarre actions, the issues we were already dealing with were now compounded, but none of it seemed to faze Mike or Sonny in the least.

I began to shiver like a frightened cat sitting on Mike's sofa in my new red woolen coat, as he began asking, "Why do you want to marry such an old man? What could the two of you possibly have in common, and who's going to take care of him should he get sick?"

I was forty-two and Dom was eighty, and although some people might find our age difference unconventional, we had everything in common and knew exactly what we were about to embark upon. We had been friends my entire life and we felt as though our souls were intertwined. Yes, he was thirty-eight years my senior, but psychologically, he was the youngest-thinking man I'd ever known. Dom was blessed with great energy and superior wisdom, and he had a happy-go-lucky, childlike disposition.

"We're in love with each other," I said, "and I'll take care of him should he get sick."

I thought we had quieted their fears, but Sonny went on to say, "If we come to your wedding, we're not going to enjoy ourselves."

An odd comment, I thought, so I chose to ignore it. That was their problem.

His sons and I had all grown up together—we even played basketball in their backyard—so I wasn't quite sure where their questioning was coming from. Over the years, had they paid attention at all, they might have noticed the affection Dom and I had for each other, but they were too busy living their own lives. Why couldn't we be allowed to live ours?

My parents had been good friends with Dom and Angie for over fifty years. After having five boys, he and Angie had treated me like the daughter they'd never had. Dom often enjoyed telling the story of bringing me home from the hospital with my parents when I was born. We clearly understood our history and the chemistry that we had shared, and we knew we were meant to be with each other.

After Dom lost Angie, which was right around the same time that Jesse moved to Florida, no one knew how much time Dom and I had spent consoling each other. We were like bosom buddies. I would cook for him either at his home or at mine, and we'd often take long walks holding hands and talking about the trials and tribulations of life.

The day after the incident in New York, Dom's chest pain returned, so I took him to Hackensack Medical Center. After completing a battery of tests, the doctors performed an angiogram. They came to me and said, "Two of his arteries are severely blocked, and we're going to try a balloon angioplasty right now, while we're in there."

It worked. The following day, I took him back to his home to rest.

It didn't leave much time for me to find out what was going on in my own family. Why had the locks been changed, and why wouldn't Linda let me in? I knew that my mother was spending Christmas in Arizona with Tommy and his family. They had moved out there to begin a new life, but I was still taken aback by Linda's offensive attitude.

When we returned to her office a few days later and asked about the locks, she repeated, "I can't tell you."

"What?...Wait a minute. Why can't you, *or won't you*, tell me what's going on? What the hell's wrong with this family?"

Through her pursed lips, and with a smirk, she refused to say. I thought maybe someone had tried to break in. There was no conversation or disagreement that would have led us to believe that we had been the cause of their hurtful conduct.

Confused and angry, I lost my cool, cursed at her repeatedly, slammed my fist on the desk, and stormed out of her office. I tried reaching my mother but couldn't get through. No one seemed to care about what Dom and I had been going through, including his sons. They hadn't come to the hospital and barely even inquired about him.

Dazed by all that had taken place, Dom and I spent a quiet Christmas at his home in North Bergen. We returned to Florida as soon as the doctors released him, feeling as though we were heading down a bumpy road. I had so many unanswered questions. What could we possibly have done to cause such discord? It should have been the happiest time of our lives.

When I finally reached my mother by phone, she was distant and cold. In the interim, I had called several of our family friends from the gang to see if they knew what lay at the root of her behavior. I finally discovered that my act of compassion for her several months earlier had backfired. They said, "You've stolen your mother's boyfriend, of course she's upset."

"*What?* How could she possibly think that?"

I had never given it a second thought when I asked Dom to take her to dinner. They had each been living alone in New Jersey, and I was right about her loneliness. But I never thought for a moment that she saw Dom as a possible suitor.

The fact that Dom and I had both misread my mother's feelings toward him and her desire to be with him, shook me to the core. My sense of remorse cannot be overstated.

Then, to complicate the situation even more, the same weekend that Dom asked me to marry him, we discovered that my mother had told some of her bridge-playing friends that she was dating an old friend—Dom Albanese. I was devastated to hear what she had told them, and I was heartsick. We thought she would be delighted by the news of our impending wedding; instead she was embarrassed and humiliated.

Trying to console her, I continued to reach out, but soon she stopped answering my calls. My relationship with my mother had been severely damaged by our engagement. The distance compounded everything, so I flew back home to explain, and I pleaded in vain for her understanding.

Her comments were bitter and cutting. She said, "What about Jesse? You have him."

"Jesse is sick," I said, "and we are no longer together. Why are you so angry with me? You knew Dom and I were seeing each other. We talked with you on the phone so many times when he and I were together, and we were all having so much fun."

She angrily walked away from me, uttered something under her breath, and then said, "Get out!"

"*Mom, please,* I beg you, please, don't do this. I'm so sorry."

"Get out, and don't come back!"

"What? *Are you disowning me?"*

A question I wish I had never asked, because she simply replied with, "Yes, I'm disowning you!" And she went on to say, "If I had known it was going to be you, I would have had an abortion."

I tried to let that stinging comment roll off my back, hoping that she didn't really mean it. It was as if she was trying to erase me from the family scrapbook. She wanted nothing further to do with me. She had been hurt to the quick, and she *did* mean it.

I had already lost my father; now I feared losing my mother, too. Mom had always said, "I've had the best, and no one could ever take Dad's place." In my naiveté I had believed her, and I'd assumed that her friendship with Dom was simply platonic, as it was for him.

Concerned for my mother's loneliness, I had unintentionally created a love triangle. Now her comment "Don't call him," began to make sense. Dom's proposal had been as much a surprise to me as to her. I then began to realize that our engagement must have been the reason the locks had been changed. But why wouldn't Linda or my mother just tell us that?

The pain of being estranged from my family overshadowed our engagement and, later, our marriage. On top of everything else, Dom had continuing health problems, the economy was slipping into the dumpster, and I was about to lose the business I cherished and had worked so hard to build.

I'd always thought I could handle anything that came my way, but my spirit was broken once again when my mother refused to come to our wedding. I've had great difficulty bouncing back from that blow. Having never been married before, I longed to share our love with our families.

At one point, I had to ask myself whether, somehow, Dom and I deserved this treatment. I suppose, with Dad gone, there was no telling the depth of the fear and anguish that lay beneath the surface of my mother's life. It seemed that the rhythm of our lives had been cracked open like an eggshell. The wonderful family life we used to have, had, for me, come to a devastating conclusion.

On learning of my family's deepening rejection, Dom's sons stuck to their conviction that our marriage was not a good thing, and they made our lives very difficult. I felt sure, though, as his sole caregiver, that I could prove my love and concern for their father and that I would eventually win them over. Much to my dismay, that would not be the case.

One day, Sonny said to me, "I hate you, and I don't know why."

I had no comeback for that!

Everyone's conduct and disapproval only drew Dom and me closer to each other, as we were deeply in love—making the best of a very disturbing and unpleasant situation.

Although our life together started off fractured, and no place felt safe or welcoming, we knew we'd be okay. We still had great hopes for the future; we had each other; we shared a tender and intimate love; and our strong faith in God gave us the encouragement we needed to carry on.

19

FROM BLACK MONDAY TO A SUN-STREAKED SKY

SEVERAL MONTHS AFTER OUR ENGAGEMENT, on one of Dom's visits to see me in Florida—July 5, 1987, to be precise—I showed him an exercise I was using to stretch my vertebrae.

We were in my garage when, before being properly hooked to a gravity glider (a contraption that enables you to hook your boots to a bar and then rotate upside-down), an unexpected sneeze crept upon me, and I was propelled backwards eight feet into the air. I landed on the top of my head. My thighs smacked the ground over my head—behind me—and my chin was tucked into my chest. I couldn't breathe. In the blink of an eye, the freak accident left me wedged between the wall and the car. It was an exceedingly painful and dangerously contorted position.

Frightened beyond words and thinking I might never walk

again, I begged Dom to help untangle me. He gingerly brought my legs back over my head. I screamed in pain—yet thought I would die right there if I remained in that knotted-up position.

Horrified but stubborn, I wouldn't let him call the ambulance right away. Once untangled, I tried with all my arm strength to pull myself up by the door handle of the car, but I had to give in. It felt as though my brain would explode out of the top of my skull. The pain worsened, and my breathing became more labored.

"Dom, you have to call them now."

In the emergency room they laid me on an ice-cold, stainless steel slab for X-rays. The technician told me to keep my eyes open so I wouldn't pass out and fall off the table. He was as cold as the slab itself as he barked his orders at me.

Incredibly, I had no broken bones, but all the muscles from the base of my skull to my coccyx were described to me as having been ripped right off the bone, as if preparing a chicken breast for the grill.

No surgery could repair my body, and I had no time for such a catastrophe. Susan and I had 300,000 catalogs ready to go out in the mail.

For several months thereafter, I worked lying in agony on a mattress on the floor of the warehouse taking orders, hardly able to move. With the upcoming holiday demands and the help of our temporary staff, plus Susan's unfailing assistance, we met all of our deadlines.

The memory of that savage pain is still fresh in my mind—and in my joints. I sought treatment with an orthopedist; he recommended a gifted, "magic-fingered" therapist and a massage therapist. I tried a pain specialist and several chiropractors before realizing that only time would heal my broken body.

My broken soul was a story of a different color. I needed and wanted my mother more than ever, but realized that she had never been supportive of me in the past. I assumed that her inability to be the nurturing mother that I had needed stemmed from her own upbringing, in which her stepmother, who was not a good role model, hadn't been there for her either.

October 19 of that year came and went, and other than the fact that it was my birthday and the sixth anniversary of my father's death, it appeared to be an ordinary day. We had a lot going on.

However, to the rest of the world it was Black Monday, the largest stock market crash since the Great Depression.

My catalog contained only luxury items. I was unsure what to expect, never having seen such a drop in the market before. It didn't take long, though, to recognize what it was doing to the business. After mailing the catalogs, we awaited the onslaught of new orders as we had for the previous two years. I was overwrought with angst when they didn't come.

Then, early one spring afternoon, as Dom returned from the restroom, I noticed that he had a large red spot of fresh blood on the back of his yellow trousers. I knew it wasn't good, but I was in so much pain I could hardly bear the thought of further complications. I feared losing him, as I had been unable to raise my arms to brush my teeth or comb my hair since the accident.

It drew us back to the hospital. We soon learned he had colon cancer. He had several more CT scans and biopsies, and while there he had more chest pain. When they did another angiogram they found that he had three new blocked arteries. The prognosis was bleak. On March 7, 1988, they operated on the cancer, followed *three weeks later* by a triple by-pass on March 21 to clear the blockages. He was brave in the face of it all.

As Dom lay in his hospital bed one morning while recovering, I tossed him his wedding ring and said, "Will you marry me on April 22? I'd like to keep our special anniversary date of 4-22-88." He loved the idea, and we were both delighted that we would soon be husband and wife after all.

Dom had taken the diamond from his pinky ring, which had been Angie's first engagement ring, and had it beautifully reset into mine. I loved it and I was honored.

We did marry on that gorgeous April day. In fact, we eloped. It was the most grown-up decision I had ever made, and it felt wonderful. We realized we didn't need anyone's permission, and since none was forthcoming, we resolved to run away and get married.

I had always pictured a candlelit church wedding, with my friend and counselor Reverend Harry E. Chase presiding, giving us his blessing. Unfortunately, that would have to wait. We knew we needed to postpone the church wedding we had planned in New Jersey.

So on a balmy Friday evening, we invited a few close friends, and we were married at a beautiful sunset ceremony in a park near Clearwater Beach. Justice of the Peace Quentin Richmond presided.

As a signature look, Dom had been accustomed to wearing bow ties, but I was impressed with his ability to also tie a perfect Windsor knot. He looked handsome in his dark blue suit, crisp white dress shirt, and smart, dark navy-and-gold paisley tie. I wore a very becoming off-white crepe dress with embroidered lace butterfly sleeves and a plunging neckline.

Dom was slightly hard of hearing and couldn't quite catch the marriage vows in Richmond's southern accent, so he ad-libbed and made up his own words. At age eighty, he knew he could get away with just about anything, and he was absolutely adorable. We all laughed with him. Then, with a cute little chuckle, Richmond said, "I now pronounce you husband and wife." A cheer went up, and goose pimples ran down my spine.

We'd done it—we were finally married! The rest of the evening was lovely. With a spectacular view of the Gulf of Mexico, you could almost hear the sizzle of the plump orange sun as it lay on the horizon and slowly melted into the sea. The cumulous clouds burst into shades of vivid watercolors, and just then a jet contrail streaked past as if to say "Well done!"

Though Dom was still weak from his surgeries, we enjoyed a quiet weekend honeymoon at a beach resort. It was good getting back to work on Monday, feeling stronger and more confident.

We spent the next few months in and out of Morton Plant Medical Center as our bodies began to knit themselves back together.

Although our recoveries were slow and painful, we both survived and in time were once again able to think more clearly. As soon as he was able, Dom returned to New Jersey and continued to work while trying to sell his home before moving to Florida to be with me.

I missed him and wanted to do something special to surprise him after all he had done for me. I knew he'd be coming down again the following week, so I borrowed a video camera and set it up in our living room. Dom's handsomely manicured hands looked naked without his ring, so I had a brilliant idea! On one of his visits to Florida I would surprise him with a new pinky ring. I designed it, had it made by a jeweler friend, and hid it in a box of Cracker

Jacks. When he arrived, he was very animated and excited to tell me about a new job he was working on. As we sat on the sofa he noticed the camera and said, "What's that?"

"It's a movie camera. Just ignore it."

"Is it on?"

"Yes. I want to capture these moments together."

That was the end of his curiosity, as he told me about the challenging new job.

I had opened the bottom on the Cracker Jacks box with a razor blade, replaced the toy inside with the new ring in a tiny baggy, attached a love note, and resealed the box.

I hadn't had Cracker Jacks in many years, so who'd have thought that he'd bring another box the same size with him from New Jersey, which he placed on the dining room table—he hadn't noticed the first one. I was cracking up at the coincidence, because now I didn't know which box contained the ring.

I grabbed one of them, hoping I had the right one, and we sat on the sofa kibitzing and sampling the Cracker Jacks. Being a gentleman, he offered me three pieces, and then put the box down and continued with his stories, interspersed with a few new jokes he had heard back home. Ten or fifteen minutes later, camera still rolling, he offered me a few more, took some for himself, and put the box down by his side again. Luckily it was a small box.

About forty-five minutes later, he finally came upon the "toy." He looked at it quizzically, then put it down next to him. I was dying of anxiety at that point. My whole surprise seemed to be ruined. A few minutes later he picked it up again and said, "This is heavy, isn't it?"

"I don't know—let me see."

When I handed it back to him, he opened the baggy and said, "Look! This looks real doesn't it?"

"Oh, it can't be," I said.

He still had no clue, but he held it in his hand weighing it, and said, "I think it's real!"

It took every ounce of my being to contain myself.

Suddenly, when he saw the card, he looked at me and said, "You! How did you get this ring into the Cracker Jacks box in New Jersey?"

When I pointed to the other box on the table, we burst into laughter, and then he cried and said, "I've never before been given such a beautiful gift."

Being the Italian lover that he was, he quietly took my hand and led me into the bedroom. The camera was still rolling. How funny was that!

DOM HAD BEEN RECUPERATING NICELY and my pain was subsiding, so we continued to plan our church wedding in New Jersey. We had new invitations printed and mailed them out to everyone again—but as we were preparing to leave for the airport, I noticed that he looked a little peculiar. The whites of his eyes, and his skin, were a pale yellow. We headed back to the hospital. They knew us there on a first-name basis by then. He had hepatitis and yellow jaundice, and was also afflicted with a bout of shingles on his face. So, once again, we postponed our church wedding and decided to wait and try again on our first anniversary.

By September of that year, the economy had plummeted, causing us enormous financial strain, which weighed heavily on my mind and my pocketbook. A piece of me died the day that I was forced to close the doors of Maple Ridge Gourmet Foods for the last time. I had invested everything there, including every ounce of my soul.

Dom and I were experiencing so much turmoil in our lives. Striving just to survive became our new lot in life. We couldn't seem to catch a break. Ongoing pain from my accident plagued me as we went from one medical emergency to another. By then, I was unemployed, and Dom's medical bills were mounting—his family stayed away, as did mine, and we had nowhere to turn.

Although we had each other, our world had become a very isolated place. It felt as though we were living in a vacuum. Our lives had been short-circuited.

I wanted to get in touch with Jesse for comfort and support, but I knew I couldn't do that to Dom, and by then, I no longer had a way of reaching him.

Like most women, I had longed to walk down the aisle, and a year later I hoped that I would still fit into my gorgeous sheath wedding gown. Its bodice and cap sleeves were embellished with dozens of pearl-beaded leaves wrapping around my now slightly larger waist. A sewn-in necklace of larger pearl teardrops graced the small of my neck. It had a long sweeping train, and it now just barely fit. I had a tulle veil that covered my face; fingerless satin gloves completed the look.

On April 21, 1989, Dom and I finally married (again) in the original old stone edifice of the Tenafly Presbyterian Church. It was a thrill to see Reverend Chase and Dom waiting for me to join them at the altar. My ninety-one-year-old uncle Peter Chagaris, Dad's namesake, and my dear friend George Spencer, who had been our family's interior decorator for the many renovations at the Inn, both walked me down the aisle. Dom was Catholic, so we also invited Father John Murray, a family friend on Dom's side, to assist. The church looked lovely. Each pew was decorated with a tall candlestick, handmade off-white floral arrangements and flowing satin bows. As we renewed our wedding vows, Dom promised to love me forever, even on Jewish holidays!

I felt pretty and sensed that the memories of Jesse, which had dimmed in the background of my life, were setting me free like a butterfly awakening from its cocoon.

But the absence of my mother left a huge hole in my heart. Surprisingly, though, Linda did come to the wedding, and we were delighted when she apologized to Dom for misjudging his intentions.

When we had to cancel the ceremony twice earlier in the year due to Dom's health, I had asked Linda if she would call some of our guests to tell them that the wedding had been postponed. She had refused, and as a result, my dear friends, the Wulsters from Blairstown, who had to drive over an hour to get there, arrived as scheduled, but there was no wedding. The following year, when I did finally walk down the aisle, they were unable to attend.

Dom's sons also came, and believe it or not, they enjoyed themselves. In fact, at the end of the evening they gathered around and serenaded me with their rendition of "Mamma, Solo Per Te la Mia Canzone Vola."

20

Broken Open

My family's estrangement lasted for our entire marriage. I felt certain that my formative years, when life was sweet and my father was alive, gave me the strength and the sanity to withstand such a barrage of misfortune. I had always been a person of great inner strength; my character remained intact, yet I knew that Dom and I couldn't handle much more stress.

The loss of my business forced me into personal bankruptcy. In sheer desperation one day, I reached out to my brother for help. Tommy represented the family and my father's estate. We hadn't spoken in years, but I had heard he was now sober, and I hoped he had matured.

Explaining the severity of our circumstances, I begged him to help prevent the bankruptcy from happening. His quick response to my plea was, in essence, "You've made your bed, now lie in it. We won't help you."

I pleaded in vain for compassion and understanding.

Then finally, after months of reaching out for someone to care about us, Tommy did say he would consider helping. But in order to do so, we would have to meet the following conditions:

• I needed to have a psychiatric evaluation.

• I needed to get a complete physical exam.

• We needed to give him our financial statements for the past two years, as if we were entering into a high-stakes business venture with him.

I couldn't grasp what had driven his hard-assed behavior.

Grateful, however, for the possible breakthrough, we tried to comply with his wishes. We were, by then, living on Dom's social security and the little bit of savings that he had left from the sale of his home. His medical bills were skyrocketing and there was very little remaining for anything else, never mind a psychiatric evaluation and a full medical exam. I didn't have medical insurance or two nickels to rub together after the loss of my business.

Fortunately, we had the presence of mind to speak with Reverend Phil of the Methodist Church we attended in Florida, and explained our situation. He arranged and paid for the exams, and for a month's mortgage. We were deeply indebted to him for his help and understanding.

It was comforting to hear that both the psychiatrist and doctor found me to be perfectly stable and in good mental and physical health, aside from the residual pain from my accident and the stress of our circumstances.

We sent all the documents to Tommy, and we waited for his response.

...And we waited.

I was beginning to feel completely hopeless.

Then, Dom noticed a lump at the end of his open-heart surgical scar, and when we checked it out, they discovered that the colon cancer had metastasized to his liver. We received confirmation, in a second opinion, that Dom's advanced liver cancer was likely terminal. He was put on chemotherapy three times a week, then off for a week. After nearly two years of this regimen, his options were running out. I was his sole caregiver, and since we were isolated from our families, there was no help on the way. His sons rarely kept in touch, and I still had no response from my brother. Our calls and pleas for help went unanswered.

Eventually, I did get through to Tommy by phone. That was when he told me with great pride in his voice, "The decision-making process is at my sole discretion, and I say, *No*."

He went on to say, "Your expenses are too high. Why can't Dom" (age eighty-six and dying of cancer) "mow the lawn to save that expense?"

Was Tommy trying to teach his forty-eight-year-old little sister a lesson? He also suggested that I get a job.

I said, "Who'll take care of Dom while I'm at work, even if I could find a job?"

Perhaps he was measuring my life by his own broken yardstick. This whole experience left us exhausted and overwhelmed, and I felt it was another personal assault on my self-worth.

After getting off the phone with Tommy, my stress level, fueled by an ongoing sense of abandonment, overtook me. And I also knew I would soon lose my husband—my only ally.

In fear and desperation, I grabbed hold of the toaster oven and slammed it to the floor. I thought I was losing my mind.

We had complied with my brother's demands, bankruptcy was looming and inevitable, and Dom's doctor's reports were grim. Life began to no longer matter.

Burdened with depression and an agonizing sense of doom,

I was too tired to try anymore.

The sleeping-pill prescription that I had renewed that day was sitting on the kitchen counter. I emptied the bottle into my mouth. Before I realized what I had done, Dom tackled me to the floor screaming, "Nooooo!"

When my head hit the ground, the pills went flying all over the room. I doubt if I swallowed even one.

Like an athlete, he sprang up from the floor, grabbed the phone, and dialed 911. This, apparently, caused more excitement than the local police department had seen in a long while. Fire engines and squad cars descended upon our home, as the first responders burst through the door.

Night was falling; the sirens and flashing lights drew the entire neighborhood out of their homes. What in the name of God was happening to us?

The police immediately separated me from Dom, and before we could explain anything, my hands were handcuffed behind my back. The pain was as excruciating as it had been the day of my accident. My shoulders felt broken. My heart was shattered, my soul crushed. I wished I had swallowed those pills—our lives were being completely traumatized, and I longed for mine to be over!

The police lifted me off the sofa by my arms and forced me in the back seat of a patrol car as I screamed in pain, trying to explain about how I had fallen, nearly breaking my neck and back, just months earlier. They didn't care, and they left me sitting there for what appeared to be an hour. I didn't know what to think. They rushed back and forth, and then stayed in the house for a long time.

Where was Dom? Why couldn't I be with him? Was he okay? I needed him. It felt as if my heart was about to burst. The pain was insufferable.

I begged God not to take Dom away from me; we had never

been separated for even a moment through our long ordeal. Why wouldn't the police let us be together? What was taking them so long? He was gravely ill, and I was extremely worried. What if he had died without me by his side?

The neighbors were gawking, not knowing what to do or say; they did nothing but stare, whisper, and point. Watching them watching me was dreadful, and the physical pain was beyond agonizing. Why didn't any of them try to find out what was happening? Why didn't they try to find Dom?

Soaked with sweat, I felt like a madwoman.

I wish I could say the next twenty-four hours were a blur, but I'd be lying. The torment of that experience is so vividly scorched into my memory that I will never forget the horror of that day.

I prayed for God to have mercy on us!

I recall a note from long ago in which Reverend Chase wrote:

> *As I have observed, suicide is not necessarily a sign of mental illness. It is an act of desperation. I am convinced that every intelligent person, and every artistically sensitive person (and Jane, you are both) has seriously thought about it at least once. I understand you're feeling desperate—without hope. You seem to be all alone, devoid of family or a network of support.*

FLORIDA HAS A LAW CALLED THE BAKER ACT: "An involuntary Baker Act is when a person is taken to a receiving facility for an examination when there is reason to believe that he or she is mentally ill and, because of his or her illness, the person has refused voluntary examination; the person is unable to determine for him or herself whether examination is necessary, and without care or treatment, the person is likely to suffer from neglect or refuse to care for him or herself..."

I hadn't been given the opportunity to refuse anything, and

I certainly was not about to hurt anyone else. I was overwhelmed by years of emotional and financial stress, of isolation and pain, and by others' lack of concern and indifference.

I pleaded with the officers for compassion, asking to be un-cuffed, trying to explain, but they wouldn't listen. I cried out for Dom. "Where's my husband? Please, help me. I need him."

I was taken to the emergency room of the local hospital and had to wait for a doctor to examine me. When one arrived, I was still crying and badly shaken up but thought for sure he would understand. All I remember about the doctor was that he was young and tall, and he wore a long white coat with a stethoscope flung around his neck. He took one look at me, and said, "Did you try to kill yourself?"

"Yes, but—"

"Get her the hell out of here!"

I was beginning to think that maybe I was evil and deserved to be treated like an animal. I still couldn't find out where Dom was and whether he was okay.

I spent that painful night handcuffed to a metal cot with just a sheet and army blanket at the local psychiatric facility. The place smelled disgusting. There was no air conditioning; the weather was humid and sticky, and it was dank and dark in there. This horrible place had a cold, eerie feeling about it. I thought there were no more tears to be shed, but I was wrong. In the black of the night, the other detainees kept yelling, "Shut up, cry baby," and "Shut up, I can't sleep."

I was so frightened and I wanted to scream. More importantly, I wanted to die to kill off the pain. I needed Dom to hold me, but I didn't even know where he was. I was incarcerated and helpless.

This can't be happening to me; I'm Peter Chagaris's daughter! How could life have taken me from the Grand Ballroom of the Waldorf to the pits of the earth? *Dad, please forgive me!* I'm so ashamed—this is unbearably humiliating.

When I needed to go to the bathroom during the night, I tried to pull myself together as I called for the guard. The three-toothed armed guard unshackled me from the metal cot, and then re-handcuffed me to his thick, hairy wrist. That giant of a man stood in the doorway of the bathroom with his gun drawn, watching me pee.

The light from the single bulb hanging from an electric cord gave me a good look at his face, and there was a strip of filthy flypaper coming down from the ceiling. He grinned, exposing his rotted teeth as I pleaded for privacy. He was ugly, with bushy eyebrows and inflamed zits on his face. His hair was messed up, and his uniform shirt was half-unbuttoned, showing the sweat running down his chest. Although ugly, he seemed gentle enough, just doing his job. But it felt as though he was enjoying the shame that I was feeling. I wished I could have escaped from my own skin and flushed my humanity down the toilet. Maybe then the nightmare would go away.

Like the results of a branding iron, the scars of that unbearable calamity are forever burned into my soul.

The following day, exhausted and overwhelmed, I was the last to be interviewed; it was about one in the afternoon. The psychiatrist, a slender man dressed in a short-sleeved striped shirt and a black tie, did listen. He looked at me, decked out in my diamond jewelry and sweaty clothes and asked, "What are you doing here?"

I composed myself long enough to explain what had led me to that point. We spoke for almost half an hour. I asked, "Do you know where my husband is? Is he okay?"

He said, "He was here earlier inquiring about you, and he appeared to be fine, although he was clearly concerned about you."

The doctor's eyes softened as if to say, "I'm sorry." He offered me the first sign of hope, understanding, and empathy. Then he touched my hand and said, "I'll get you out of here as quickly as I can."

A few hours later, I was released, after my second mental-health evaluation had also declared me perfectly lucid but clearly suffering from severe physical pain and duress.

It angers me when people, even degreed psychologists, say that anyone who attempts suicide is mentally ill. That may be what the textbooks say, but I know for sure that *I am not!* Life, all by itself, can drive you to an extreme point of hopelessness and despair. Most times, my outward appearance is one of poise and strength. But given the stress of our circumstances, I felt as brittle as a hand-blown glass ornament that had been shattered and rendered worthless.

I spent the next three weeks in bed, trying to sort out what had happened. My husband was never able to express the anguish he had been feeling knowing what his call to 911 had done to me. He sat by my side, praying unceasingly.

Then one day Dom quietly said, "What about me?"

I was grateful for that comment, it shook me back to reality, and I remembered that he needed me, too.

Although I was the butt of everyone's anger, I recognized that I was not the only one being affected. I eventually allowed Dom to hold me tight through the night. I could feel my body uncoil as I began to relax in his arms—I loved him so for that, but I knew he wouldn't be with me much longer.

The outlook was bleak. Time marched as slowly as wooden soldiers stuck in the swampy sludge of a minefield.

Then, five days *after* the bankruptcy was finalized, Tommy called and said that he was going to pay off the liens that had been placed against our home. We were thankful, but also repulsed by his deliberate timing. He could have easily prevented all the trauma, but chose instead to say, "Look what I'm doing for you now."

He made sure that the papers we needed to sign arrived on our wedding day, which caused Dom and me to leave our reception for over an hour to read and sign the papers, and it also sickened and angered me as it put his name at the forefront of our special day. Then, when we reached the Williamsburg Inn, where we spent a few nights on our honeymoon, more papers arrived. For us, Tommy's warped sense of humor was not funny. We were, however, relieved that our home would be spared.

His lack of empathy left us feeling raw and vulnerable. Dom and I clung to each other, knowing we had so little time left.

"Oh, for wings like a dove to fly away and rest"(Psalm 55:6).

21

Goodbye My Love

Late one September afternoon, while we were sitting in our Florida room, God's light broke through the storm clouds of our lives. Just as we were feeling trapped in what appeared to be a hopeless situation, we witnessed a miracle!

The sky blackened, the wind whipped the air with tremendous force, causing our orange tree to dust the grass as if it were a weeping willow, and the rain pelted our windows like buckshot.

Suddenly there was a deafening sound barreling toward us. As I looked out the window, I saw what appeared to be a mobile home *flying right over us*. I rubbed my eyes as all kinds of thoughts raced through my head. Was I dreaming? What was that thing?

This was shortly after Hurricane Andrew had decimated Homestead, Florida, in 1992, and had I been dreaming, the reverberating sounds of glass shattering and trees snapping would have shaken me right to my feet.

There was no time to explain.

"Get up! *Get up! Hurry!*" I screamed.

By the time I could pull Dom up off the couch and get him to the protective cover of our hall closet door, the tornado had passed.

Moments later, we ventured out the front door. The neighbors to our left were already beginning to gather in the street, counting heads. The sun was beaming brightly in the vivid blue sky, and steam rose from the pavement. As we looked to the right, nothing there was familiar. The homes had been leveled to their concrete slabs; the roadways were clogged and piled high with cinder blocks, demolished boats, fragments of trees, enormous sheets of twisted metal, and overturned cars.

What I thought was a flying mobile home was in fact just that. It had crashed into our neighbor's yard, its residents still inside, and they hadn't survived. Our yard was filled with crumpled aluminum siding, broken pieces of furniture, hubcaps, and electrical wires. Whatever trees still remained had sheets of metal and all sorts of debris hanging like tinsel from their branches. The huge old pine at the center of our yard had a two-by-four threaded through its trunk, like yarn through the eye of a needle.

Soon ambulances and fire trucks swarmed the area, looking for survivors, and news helicopters hovered above.

Remarkably, our home was spared, with only minimal roof, window, and water damage. My gorgeous Tiffany-style lamp lay smashed on the floor.

AFTER MY ENCOUNTER with the Baker Act, Dom and I rarely ventured out. We were lonely, deeply saddened, still completely separated from both our families, and you'd have been hard-pressed to find two people who loved their families more than we had.

For some time, we had wanted to move to Daytona Beach, where a few of my lifelong friends from our old Tenafly gang could surround us. No matter what we tried, though, we couldn't scrape enough money together to move out of the area where we now had so many unpleasant memories. The urgency of our move was accelerated by Dom's failing health, but our finances were caught up in the muck and mire of our splintered lives.

Without warning, God had sent a ferocious act of nature that proved to be a mystically paradoxical storm. Perhaps He was testing the faith of our neighbors who had lost their loved ones and their homes, as Dom's declining health was testing ours. This tornado was ranked an F5 (the strongest on the Fujita scale) with winds in excess of 260 miles an hour.

As we assessed the damage and cleaned up the shards of glass and wreckage from inside our home, we met with our insurance claims agent. We learned that our generous reimbursement was going to be more than enough to make the necessary repairs—and we would have a surplus sufficient to help pay for our move to Daytona.

In the following days, we received three phone calls from people sixty to seventy-five miles away, saying they had found some of the mail from our mailbox in their swimming pools or their yard. Now, there's *express mail* for you!

We needed to heal and feel safe once again, and we felt the move to Daytona would be the answer. On a visit to see Jinny and Bob Tanzola, and Eileen and Garry Felter, we used the insurance rebate to put a deposit on a vacant lot facing a lovely winding lagoon near them.

They had known Dom through his association with my parents, and were all great fun to be with. We looked forward to reconnecting with them in the hope of creating many new memories. Eileen played the piano as she had at our bon voyage party, and Dom still played the drums, so we hoped we had found the beginnings of a new life. Maybe we could return to some sense of normalcy.

Dom had designed the plans for our new home, and as part of the Pelican Bay development, it was finally built. After selling our home on Florida's west coast, we moved in on October 12, 1993.

Then, within weeks of each other, Bob had a massive heart attack and died, and on Christmas day Eileen died suddenly from pneumonia. I felt fortunate to be there for Jinny and Garry during their time of grieving.

Bob was a gentle, sweet, good-looking, and playful Italian, and he was a big-game hunter in season. And Eileen, at age ninety-one, was one of the prettiest women I have ever known. Her high rosy cheekbones were like a ripe peach. Her eyes were made up like a vaudevillians', and she wore a feathered bonnet or ladies' fedora even while in her bikini. Her full head of platinum hair was coiffed neatly around the hat, and her heart was golden.

So our hopes for a happy life with them were dashed, and we knew Dom's time was also quickly approaching.

The only loved ones I had ever lost up to that point were my grandfather when I was very young, my dear friend Emil Wulster, and, of course, my dad.

As difficult as that was, the thought of losing Dom was like losing my breath. After long days of helping him cope with his illness, we settled into our bed clinging to each other as if holding onto life.

On several occasions, the phone would ring at two or three in the morning. I nearly jumped out of my skin to answer it, and the operator would say, "I have a collect call from Kristi Chagaris. Will you accept the call?"

"Yes, of course," I said, as fear raced through my head. *Why would Kristi (my niece) be calling at this late hour?*

She was drunk as a skunk and just wanted to yell at me for

upsetting her father.

"Upsetting your father? Do you have any idea about what Dom and I are going through?" I said. "My husband, lying here next to me, is dying, and you're concerned about your father being upset? *How dare you!*" That didn't stop her from calling several more times, until I no longer answered the phone.

By the end of that summer, Dom's health had deteriorated and he was confined to a hospital bed in our brand new living room. I never tired of his lighthearted spirit. He was the easiest patient to care for, and he even tapped out some of his favorite tunes on the hospital table, before fading and lapsing into a coma the last week of August. On September 6, 1994, just eleven months after settling into our new home, Dom lost his battle with liver cancer. It was Labor Day, exactly eight years after we had been reunited.

Concerned about our neighbor's children, I had been praying that when he died it would be early in the morning, so they wouldn't have to see him leave.

I also hoped that Cathy, the kindest and most caring hospice nurse, would be on duty when it was his time to go. She wasn't scheduled to work that morning but had changed her plans for some reason. The night before he died he had a seizure that was terrifying; I had to crawl on top of him to keep him from falling out of the hospital bed.

I had asked the hospice nurses if the was anything unusual that I should expect before he died.

They said, "No, he will most likely just stop breathing." They never told me that a seizure was even a possibility. I was shocked and horrified. Is that what death looks like?

I told Cathy, "I have to go lie down—I'm completely exhausted."

Fortunately, sleep came quickly—I had been so very tired.

Cathy stayed by Dom's side as I finally collapsed into my own bed around 3 a.m., for the first time in more than three months, because I never wanted to leave his side.

She shook me a little after 6 a.m. For a second, I didn't know where I was, or who she was, but she said, "Hurry, it's almost time."

As we rushed to Dom's bedside he took his last sweet breath—with it, I felt as though he also took what was left of mine.

Within moments, Cathy and I received a *blessed* miracle.

"Did you see *that?*" She said with a gasp!

There was a six-foot-two steam-like vapor—a gentle, cloud-like substance that hovered over Dom for a long moment before going right up through the cathedral ceiling.

We were witnessing Dom's soul rising from his body.

GATHERING OUR THOUGHTS, Cathy and I began to clean up the living room before the coroner arrived. As we filled one of the large black plastic bags with all of his medical paraphernalia and then tried to lift it, we had a moment of levity when all the contents fell out the bottom and all over the floor. It was as if Dom was trying to make us laugh one final time.

It then became Jinny and Garry's turn to comfort me for a month or so, and neighbors brought their casseroles.

Two weeks later, I arranged a memorial service for Dom at the First United Methodist Church in Ormond Beach.

The bass drum his mother had bought for him so many years earlier was placed on the altar, draped in a stunning floral arrangement of calla lilies, lilacs, and gardenia. It was perfect. But my Dom was gone. One of the choir members sang "Ave Maria" and I asked the church to play a recording of Perry Como singing "The Wind Beneath My Wings."

After Reverend Phil said a few words and recited prayers, we concluded the ceremony with a flair as a tape of Dom, accompanied by his longtime musical cronies, played some Dixieland jazz. He would have loved it.

Fortuitously, as Dom had observed my family's treatment of me, he had the presence of mind to have a private conversation with each of his boys to be sure they were financially okay and able to provide for their families. He also expressed his gratitude to me for caring for him through his illnesses. Subsequently he changed his will just months before he passed away, removing his sons.

I said, "Hon, please be sure to send a copy to Sonny."

"No, I don't want to do that," he insisted. "I've already told them that I am going to take care of my wife as I expect them to take care of theirs."

He was very ill, and I didn't want to challenge him, yet I knew that he was leaving that burden to me.

Shortly after Dom's memorial service, which most of his sons did not attend, Sonny called to say, "I'd like to come down to Florida to discuss my father's will."

That was when I had to tell him, "I have the most recent version of his last will and testament, and I will send you a copy."

When they discovered that they had been removed, I was informed by another family member that his five sons had made a pact to never speak with me again. It became their *badge of honor.*

I was consumed with grief, and it would have been comforting for me to know that they were there for me, as Dom would have wanted. But that was not to be the case.

EVERYONE ELSE SOON MOVED ON WITH LIFE.

Jinny would call occasionally, and Garry would stop by on his bike to say hello, but they too were still grieving, and eventually they got back to their own routines, which didn't include me. The phone had stopped ringing. I longed for my family. And I felt sure that my heart was going to stop on its own and prayed that time would come quickly.

Terrified by my previous incident with sleeping pills, I was paralyzed with fear. I stared blankly at the walls as they closed-in on me. I couldn't eat and don't remember consuming any fluids. Where were the tears coming from?

It had been months since I had spoken with anyone other than Jinny and Garry during our brief visits. At times I couldn't tell whether my voice was audible, or if I was merely *thinking*. My soul was crushed, and I longed for Dom's laughing eyes and tall spirit.

It has been well documented that human beings cannot survive without love and an intimate connection with others, and I was no exception.

22

Music of Angels

Dom and I often spoke of his childhood memories. He loved playing the drums in his father's shoemaker shop, banging out tunes with two screwdrivers on the brass rivets of leather-seated kitchen chairs. Amid the smells of tanned leather, shoe polish, and the shavings from the foot-pedal-driven grinding stone, he'd play along to his father's Italian arias.

His eyes glistened as he described how his mother had secretly hidden twenty-five cents a week until she had enough money to buy him a bass drum, afraid to tell her husband what she was doing—not because she feared him but because she wouldn't accept a "no" from him. "Better safe than sorry," she'd say.

His mom, a petite little lady with a gentle, weathered-looking old-world face, was stone deaf, but she was the light and true love of his life. She gave him love unconditionally, and although I barely remembered her, I too loved her.

He expressed his excitement when he heard his mother was about to get hearing aids, and he could hardly wait for her to hear his voice for the first time. He raced home from school and said, "Mom, how are they, can you hear me?"

"No," she said, "I gave them back to the man. They disturbed my serenity."

Dom cried, deeply disappointed, but he respected his mother's decision and tried to understand.

I also recall him telling me how he became a Catholic.

"Growing up in Hudson County, my best friend Izzy and I, after playing stickball, would sit on the curb in front of a big old church until it got dark before heading home for dinner. The music of angels bellowed out of the large stone building. We sat there several evenings a week until, one day, my curiosity got the best of me. I told Izzy, I'm going to knock on that big wooden door and ask where the angelic music was coming from."

Dom and his gangly, sad-eyed friend Izzy often mused about what they would become when they grew up. Dom knew he wanted to be a musician, but he also knew he would need to find a real job—one that would allow him to support his family if times got tough. He decided to become an architect and design houses, because, as he said, "I know people will always need a place to live."

When he finally got up the nerve, he knocked on the heavy, wooden church door, and it squeaked open. A tall, gentle-looking man in a black gown filled the doorway and asked, "How can I help you, young man?"

In his herringbone woolen knickers and high-buttoned black shoes, Dom removed his tweed cap and asked, "Where does the music of angels come from?"

The man chuckled, saying, "Are you Catholic?"

Dom shrugged. "I don't know."

The priest asked if he had been baptized, but again Dom shrugged.

"Come in," he said. "What's your name?"

"Dominick Thomas Albanese."

"Well, Dominick Thomas Albanese, I'm Father Sebastian, and the music comes from our church choir. They rehearse here in the evening."

Dom looked around curiously and said, "What's a Catholic?"

"It's a Christian religion about God. Would you like to become a Catholic?"

Dom nodded.

"We must find out if you've been baptized. Can you go home and ask your parents?"

Head hung low, Dom answered, "I don't know. My mother is deaf, and my father is mad at God for some reason, so I'm afraid to ask him."

The priest said, "We must find out. Then I can teach you about the Catholic Church myself. Would you like that?"

Again Dom nodded, and he left for home to try and find out if he had been baptized. He made his way slowly, zig-zagging along the cobblestone streets kicking a bottle cap from one side to the other, wondering how he could find out.

His father was a loving but stern man, and Dom never understood why he was mad at God. When he reached the kitchen door, he felt lucky that he found his mother asleep at the table. He woke her gently and whispered, "Mom, have I been baptized?"

The lace from her garment was softly pressed into her cheek, and the light from over the stove caressed her face. Reading his lips she shook her head, indicating that he had not been baptized.

She had baked an apple pie for him, but without noticing or stopping to explain, Dom ran out the steps and all the way back to that big old wooden door.

Father Sebastian greeted him. "Well, what have you learned?"

"My mother was sleeping, but when I woke her and asked if I was baptized, she shook her head."

"Good, I will teach you, and then I will baptize you and give you a new Catholic name. But we will have to tell your father, because we'll need to have two witnesses."

Dom told me his knees rattled and he shook in his boots, but he couldn't wait to tell Izzy that he was going to become a Catholic. He thought maybe his dream of becoming a musician would also come true there with the church choir.

For several months, Dom met with Father Sebastian after school. He studied his homework and his schoolwork, and then, just before Easter, Dom told his mother what he had been up to. She cried and said, "Come, we must tell your father. He'll be proud."

They went off to find him.

In his heavy Italian accent, Dom's father said, "You mean to tell me you did this without me? I could not show you the way, yet you have found your way. Son, I am proud of you. Come, let's go talk to the priest. I want my people to be il tuo padrini (your godparents)."

Overcome with relief, Dom introduced Izzy and his parents to Father Sebastian. The priest's deep-set eyes, thick eyebrows, and wavy black hair matched his robe, and Dom had taken a liking to him. Dom said, "Father, I'd like my Catholic name to be Howard."

The priest chuckled a little and said, "Howard it is. Dominick Thomas Howard Albanese."

Dom's parents were delighted, and his father's best man had become Dom's godfather.

AFTER COMPLETING GRADE SCHOOL and without funds for college, Dom read every architectural textbook he could get his hands on.

He hung around with his friends, some of whom were studying to become engineers or architects. With their assistance, he tested his knowledge and solved difficult structural engineering problems. At the age of twenty-one, he went on to become a self-taught architect, successfully passing all of the exams. He always believed that he passed because of one specific test answer. The question went something like this: Who was Alexander Lipshitz? Where was he educated and what was he best known for? To which Dom replied, "I don't know, and I don't give a damn!" And then he laughed like hell!

His father said, "Only in America could the son of an immigrant shoemaker become an *architecto*."

Dom – center
1921

In his early career, Dom worked in New York on the design team that drew up the plans for the Bank of Manhattan Trust Building at 40 Wall Street. During that time, the Chrysler Building was also being erected. There was a great rivalry going on in the news papers, well before TV was invented, over which would be the tallest building in the world. Forty Wall Street was completed in 1930 and very briefly held the title of world's tallest building. Then, secretly, the Chrysler people raised a 185-foot Belgian-steel spire from within the structure as its crowning jewel, making it the tallest in the world the same year.

Dom also had the pleasure of designing another impressive structure, the Pittsburgh Post Office and Courthouse. He'd never had the opportunity to visit it until we were married some fifty years after its completion. We stopped there on our way to New Jersey for our church wedding. The security guards were not letting anyone into the building due to a highly sensitive case that was being tried there. Dom, carrying a set of the original plans for the building under his arm, showed them to the guard and said, "Do you recognize these stairs?"

The guard looked at him thoughtfully and demanded, "Where did you get those plans?"

"I designed them myself in 1931, *in ink on canvas*, and there's my signature to prove it. I'm here with my wife, and I'd like to see how the courtroom turned out."

We were escorted to the post office and then to the courthouse with its magnificently detailed plaster ceiling and intricately carved judge's bench. We tiptoed in quietly with the guard, since court was in session. What a great privilege and thrill for Dom and for me! I relished the pride he was feeling, as his eyes grew moist and he seemed to stand a little taller. I was glad for the opportunity to share that special moment with him.

Dom was a delight to be with. If he didn't have a drafting pencil in his hand or set of plans under his arm, he had drumsticks. He'd play on the dashboard of the car when we stopped at a red light or tap out a tune at the register in the supermarket. Crossing the

Howard Franklin Bridge, which connects St. Petersburg, Florida, with Tampa, we'd open the car windows and, at the top of our lungs, sing along with our favorite songs as I drove and he drummed.

He'd laugh at his own jokes and tease waitresses everywhere we went. He cried just as easily when he heard the song "Mamma" or "The Star-Spangled Banner."

His tweed hat went flying in the air whenever he was excited to see you and, with his eight-foot wingspan, he'd envelop you. His bold Italian laugh would either draw you to him or scare the wits out of you at first, until you got to know him. At six-foot-two, he was nicely built, though slender.

After shaving the few wisps of hair remaining on his balding and rather ordinary-looking head, I continued to cut his hair for him on a regular basis. Looking dapper, the warmth of his smile and those tender, soft, Sicilian-blue eyes captured my heart. The masculine crevices on his face, and his substantial Italian nose, lent great character to his overall appeal. Dom was a man's man, and all of my life I adored him. He was sensitive, hilariously funny, playful and charismatic.

I clearly remember many years ago, when as a young child, I'd go into my father's office and say, "Dad, call Dom."

He'd say, "Why? I don't need to speak with him."

"Aw, come on, Dad, please."

He'd pick up the phone and dial Dom's number, then hang up after the first ring.

I'd say, "Why did ya hang up?"

He'd laugh and explain, "If Dom doesn't answer on the first ring, he's not there."

"Well, maybe he's in the bathroom," I said.

So my father would dial again, the second time Dom answered on the first ring. I just wanted to hear how they greeted each other:

Dad would say, "Hi, you miserable guinea bastard."

And Dom replied, "Hey, you Greek son of a bitch."

Then they'd laugh like hell and hang up. I loved that repartee and how much they enjoyed each other, and I was happy as a lark for the rest of the day.

23

A LOT TO LOSE

ONE DAY OUT OF THE CLEAR BLUE, eight months after Dom's death, I got a call from my sister, "Hi, Jane, it's Linda. Mom wants to talk with you. Are you willing to speak with her?"

I was enormously thankful for their call. We talked for a while, or I should say, she talked. Flooded with emotion, I listened through my sobs. She wanted to try to rebuild our relationship.

Finally, I felt as though God had indeed heard my pleas and was watching over me. I believed His will would prevail after all.

On the one-year anniversary of Dom's death, my mother and I were reunited at the Clinton Inn. It was awkward not being able to go home, so I had taken a room there. That, too, felt surreal. We had owned it, but I had never stayed there before. I remember being apprehensive about seeing her after all that had taken place, but we hugged, cried, and apologized.

"Mom, we never meant to hurt you. We could have had a wonderful life together, all three of us."

She said, "I'm sorry too."

"Dom was so sick. Why didn't you ever call me? I needed you."

"I couldn't, I was so angry with him."

We were sitting on the satiny comforter on the edge of the bed, afraid to get too close. It had been eight years since we'd seen each other. She seemed happy that we were taking these steps to heal our relationship, and she was affectionate and motherly. Her hazel eyes were full of life, and I was happy to see that she looked surprisingly well. I felt haggard and worn, my eyes were gray and sunk deep into my head. The years of turmoil had taken their toll on me.

She wiped my tears and said, "What would you like to do now?"

"I came up to bury Dom's ashes at his mother's and father's graves in Woodbridge. Would you consider going with me?"

"Okay," she said. "When do you want to go?"

"I was going to go today. Could you come?"

"Yes, let's go whenever you're ready."

That in itself was an extraordinary gift.

We went to Dom's mother's grave first; she had been buried with her second husband. As tears filled my eyes, I opened one of the burial vases, sprinkled his ashes, and prayed for them to be reunited. A few miles away at his father's grave, I'd arranged to bury some more of his remains. What I hadn't expected was that there would be two chairs sitting on top of the artificial turf that the cemetery had placed around the two-foot hole they had dug to accept his ashes.

How had they known that there would be two of us? I was startled and assumed that, since most people have someone accompany them at a funeral, the two chairs were probably routine.

It was midday and the sun was bright and warm. We could smell the freshly mown grass. As birds chirped in the trees, Mom and I took our places. What a sight we must have been. I think we sat there for an hour, enjoying each other as we rekindled our love. We began to laugh as I told her some of Dom's favorite jokes. I could feel his spirit join us. My heart melted, and I was extremely thankful.

I'd often remember Jon Shepard, the man whose son I helped locate, and the love he and his family had for one another. I had longed for that and hoped that maybe we would have that loving family reunion after all.

A week or so later, I returned to Daytona. Mom and I started speaking with each other often. It was a whole new experience for me, and I loved it because I loved her.

Having to reinvent myself once more, I returned to college in Daytona, where I studied graphic arts.

My mother came to visit me and see our new home. It was stunning, but without Dom, it felt so empty. She and I visited each other every couple of months, either up north or down south. Life seemed to be returning to normal. Jinny and Garry would come over and they enjoyed reminiscing with her. Laughter once again filled the rooms. Jinny introduced Mom to the bridge group, and when she was in Florida, she felt right at home playing cards with the other ladies.

When I completed my two-year college course, I was ready to begin working in Daytona, but it didn't take long to discover that there were no job opportunities in graphics available there.

On one of her visits, Mom and I talked about that. I asked, "Do you think I could move back home with you to look for work up north?"

I loved being with her and I felt safe once again. My father had died fourteen years earlier, so I think she also relished the idea. She suggested I take Linda's old room and the middle room and fix them to my liking, so we shopped for new curtains and a new bedspread. She bought me a TV and a reclining chair. I felt a joy that had been gone for far too long.

I kept my home in Florida, so she and I could vacation there in the winter months. Mom helped me refinance the house, since my credit had been destroyed in the bankruptcy. The refinance also incorporated the second mortgage, which Dom had taken out to cover his medical bills. Thankfully the sweetness of life was coming back into view, so I began the rebuild one more time, trying not to dwell on the pain of the past. Although my family had missed our marriage in its entirety, I knew it was time to forgive them and move onward.

BACK THEN, PEOPLE STILL ADVERTISED JOB OPENINGS in the local newspapers. So when I found a package design company looking for a graphic artist, I called for an interview and went to meet the owner. To my great surprise, I was hired.

During that pivotal moment my life teetered, delicately balanced between whole and fractured. Mom and I were on the road to recovery, and our reunion brought back memories of the life we had once known. It took a while, however, for me to feel secure, and often I feared that if I actually smiled my face would crack.

Linda and I were also starting to gingerly rebuild our relationship.

I loved being home. Home, for me, is always where my heart is, and, grateful for a second chance with my family, I looked forward to going to bed at night. I hugged and thanked my mother for all she was doing to help us heal.

Yes, *God is good*. I could once again feel Him near. Though I often felt like Humpty Dumpty, I knew that, with modern technology and large doses of love, I could be glued back together again.

Being reunited with our circle of old friends was wonderful, too. They had aged gracefully and were delighted to see us back together again. Mom looked lovely for her age. She was then in her late eighties and still had a full head of beautiful white hair and the cutest little nose that we had often teased her about. With the exception of a few laugh lines, her skin glowed.

Life had been good to her, although she had been in a very serious car accident not long after my father passed away. I think a scotch a day fortified her resolve. I was delighted by her stamina, because I needed my mother to help me pick up the pieces of my broken life—and this time, *she was there for me*.

FEELING SAFE, I BEGAN TO UNWIND. Finally, I could take care of the itchy rash on my left breast. I'd had it for quite a long time, even while Dom was alive, but neglected my own health; there was no time to pamper myself. He needed all of my attention as he faced the many cancers and heart disease.

Luckily, he'd been able to put me on his health insurance policy just before he passed away, since I no longer had medical insurance of my own.

I went to see Dr. Joanne Blayne a gynecologist at the new Women's Clinic at Englewood Hospital. She seemed quite concerned about the rash. She took some needle biopsies, but everything appeared clear.

Upon further examination, she said, "I'm convinced that the bumpy reddish outbreak on your skin is an advanced form of breast cancer called *peau d'orange*. I'd like to do a few surgical biopsies as soon as possible to be sure."

"Breast cancer? I've had the rash for a long time. Are you sure?"

"I'll know more once we get the pathology reports back."

She performed more needle biopsies and three surgical biopsies and oddly enough, they all came back negative. The doctor and I were both puzzled. She said, "I recommend you see Ben Goldfarb for a second opinion. He's a colleague of mine."

I made an appointment, and Dr. Goldfarb, who was a much older man, very serious-looking and thorough, said, "If it were cancer, and you've had the rash for as long as you say, you would have been much worse by now. I'd like to do a few biopsies myself."

Immediately, I called Dom's insurance company to check and be sure they would cover the cost of all the procedures, since they were Florida-based and I was now living in New Jersey.

I explained, "My doctor thinks I may have stage-four breast cancer. I'm going for a second opinion. Can you tell me if the biopsies, and whatever other procedures they might need to do, will definitely be covered?"

After giving her all of the policy information, she said, "Yes, we will pay for at least seventy percent of the hospital procedures, since your doctor is in New Jersey."

Dr. Goldfarb then did several more biopsies, but they, too, returned negative. The doctors conferred, unable to come up with a definitive diagnosis.

I was even more confused, and I hoped that Goldfarb's findings had been right.

I knew for sure that I had to get at least one more opinion. A friend who had been a nurse recommended Frank Lichtenstein at Holy Name Hospital in Teaneck. Hoping for a positive report, I was shaking as I sat in his waiting room until they called my name. The rash on my breast was beginning to look like a jigsaw puzzle, and I needed to get to the cause of the problem.

Dr. Lichtenstein was not affiliated with the other two doctors. After examining me and studying the previous biopsy reports he took a few more biopsies himself.

"I concur with Dr. Blayne's diagnosis," he said. With a deep crease of concern in his forehead, he added, "I'm sorry, but I believe this *is* cancer and should be removed immediately."

Being built exactly as my mother was, I had a lot to lose. As she had always said, "We were first in line when large breasts were being handed out." Mom, Linda, and I were all well-endowed.

I told them both, "The doctors think I have breast cancer."

My mother's response was "Oh, you'll get over it."

Linda didn't comment at all. How dysfunctional was that?

I had gone to my doctor's visits alone, so I guess I shouldn't have been surprised by their unusually harsh reactions.

Once again, I felt cast aside. My mother and sister offered no support for this new trauma.

Scared out of my wits, I was trying to take in the whole picture and decide what to do. My *life* appeared to be at risk. What should I do? It would have been a much easier decision had the three doctors been in agreement.

Many years earlier, I recalled that my mother hadn't gone to the doctor with me when I went in for exploratory surgery due to endometriosis. I had just assumed that her behavior was normal. After the first partial hysterectomy, I woke up without a uterus.

Mom had driven me to the hospital and dropped me off at the door. Later, when she and my father visited, he was stunned when I said, "Thank God I'll never have my period again."

Dad said, "Yes, you will."

"No, Dad, I won't. They've removed my uterus,"

His eyes filled with tears. I could only imagine that he was thinking about my not having children. My dreams of having four, so that there would not be a middle child, had been dashed way back then.

Again, I wondered if my mother's upbringing could have skewed her ability to be the nurturing mom that I needed.

Once I made the decision to move ahead with the surgery, I opted for a *double* mastectomy, to be sure they got all of the cancer—plus I wanted to keep my physical body in balance.

I reconfirmed my insurance coverage and was assured that the surgery would also be covered. They agreed to pay seventy percent of whatever procedures needed to be done. The papers were signed, and I scheduled a date for the operation.

Mom dropped me off at the hospital entrance. As I was prepped for surgery, Dr. Blayne greeted me. Her eyes were tender, and she tried to comfort me as she gave me a sedative to calm me before being put under. That's the last thing I remember.

Upon returning to my hospital room, I was informed that the pathology report was in—and that *I did not have breast cancer after all, but rather a skin rash*, which could have and should have been treated with a topical ointment. I also discovered that two-and-a-half pounds of *each* breast had been removed.

Dr. Blayne said, "I'm thrilled that it wasn't cancer, but very sorry that you were put through such a traumatic experience."

My emotions escalated. I was devastated, and I felt unnecessarily violated and maimed, although, I, too, was extremely thankful that it was not cancer.

On top of that, I got the disturbing news that the insurance company would no longer pay for the surgery. Since it was not cancer, they considered it cosmetic surgery, which was not covered under Dom's plan. I called the woman from Blue Cross Blue Shield again.

"You told me everything would be covered!" I screamed. "I can't pay for the surgery or for the second and third opinions, biopsies, anesthesia, and the many other hospital-related expenses. I've recently lost my husband and have moved back to New Jersey to be with my family, and I'm unemployed."

"Sorry," she said. "Obviously, you must have chosen to have a breast reduction."

"What? *Obviously?* I loved my breasts. You must be kidding me. How can you assume that?"

"Well," she said, "the insurance will not cover the medical bills, since it wasn't cancer, so you'll have to go to court to prove that it was not elective cosmetic surgery."

I was exasperated. What else could happen?

My first impulse was to sue the doctors for a misdiagnosis.

My mind said, *Fight this*. My gentle soul said *I want my breasts back*. I made several phone calls to malpractice attorneys, but was advised that it would be an enormously difficult case to prove. No one would even meet with me when I mentioned I couldn't afford to pay the doctors' bills.

Once again, my mother stepped in. We negotiated the fees, she paid a portion of what was due to each doctor, and it was finally resolved.

This entire experience has left me breastless and restless. Eventually the physical scars healed nicely, but the emotional upset had warn me out.

24

THE FINAL BLOW

WORK WAS MY REFUGE, so when I received a call to return to my previous job, back I went, grateful for the opportunity. Designing and directing photo shoots for product packaging was soothing and distracting, and I loved the job.

Right around that time, my dear friend, Jeanne, was confronted with the unbearable task of removing her mother from life support. The doctors offered her mom no hope of recovery, and she lingered for months as the family was torn apart by the devastating decision. My heart broke for all of them, especially for her dad, and I prayed that my family would never be faced with that same set of circumstances.

It made me wonder if my mother had a living will. When I asked, she didn't know, so we checked with her attorney and discovered that she did not. The attorney was retiring, so, gathering her papers, we made an appointment with another lawyer who had been recommended by a close family friend.

As Mom and I reviewed the documents, we discovered that my name had been expunged from her last will and testament.

"Why am I not even mentioned in your will?" I asked.

"Yes, you are."

"No, my name has been removed. Don't I count at all?"

"Oh, don't be silly, your name is there."

We searched the documents again, and sure enough my name was not mentioned anywhere. She seemed surprised by that, too.

We then met with the new attorney, and in her conversation with him, she said, "Why isn't my daughter's name listed there?"

With a quizzical look on his face, he said, "You must have removed her sometime earlier."

My mother was quite sharp, and I wondered how that had happened. Why wouldn't she have remembered doing it?

"Well," she said, "I want everything divided equally between my three children, so add her back in."

I reminded her of the money Dom and I had borrowed, and she said, "I don't care about that. Dad and I had wanted everything divided equally upon our death. You've each gotten a lot of money over the years."

The attorney turned to me and said, "Would you mind leaving the room so I can have a private conversation with your mother?"

"No, of course not."

He called upon several witnesses, and they talked with her for well over an hour. I was not at all privy to their questioning and felt reassured that my mother's wishes would be clearly defined and carried out this time, without input or guidance from me or from anyone else.

That June, my mother and Linda had gone to Arizona for my

brother's surprise sixtieth birthday party. I thought it a little odd that I wasn't invited but figured that, having been estranged for eight years, Tommy's family was not yet comfortable with my moving back home. I hadn't yet reconnected with him—there were still unsettled feelings between us.

I felt like the prodigal daughter, although I hadn't squandered my wealth on wild living, but rather on trying to make a living as I cared for my ailing husband. I was confident that God knew my heart, so I was okay with not being invited. But I had hoped that I would have, at least, been welcomed home.

While my mother and Linda were away, I took another self-help seminar at the World Trade Center as I sought solace and guidance. I was grateful for this forum; it gave clarity to my circumstances and helped strengthen my character and my fortitude.

The sessions were long and grueling, sometimes sad or funny, but they were also instructional and intuitive. I like that kind of atmosphere; it works for me. I enjoy growing in knowledge of myself, as I believe we are all works in progress.

There was a spirit of gentleness and concern in that room as the coach explained, "You should expect a breakthrough by the end of the weekend, the depth of which depends on your position in life and your willingness to chart a new course." By then it was a familiar concept to me.

Difficult times had consumed our marriage—I had a wounded spirit, had lost my breasts, and had to leave my home in Florida. I was wrestling with it all, trying to sort things out.

The seminar gave me the tools I needed to separate the pain from the hope—hope of the future, allowing me to embrace my forward progress.

While rekindling my relationship with my mother, I felt a tentative yet extraordinary sense of gratitude. I was a changed woman—more fragile, more compassionate and sensitive, than

I had ever been. I had hoped one day to be able to truly relax and laugh wholeheartedly again as we rebuilt our family one step at a time.

My relationship with Linda, however, still seemed somewhat labored, so I called her from the seminar and asked if we could talk for a while.

When my feet are firmly planted, I am confident and sure-footed. I felt it would be a good time to work things out with her. We talked for a few moments, but she seemed nervous. Since my call was unexpected, I assumed that explained her behavior.

"I've missed you all so much," I said, "and I feel dead inside since I've lost Dom."

She snapped back, "You're not dead. You get up in the morning, and you're breathing."

"What?"

The remainder of the call was brief. Her unwillingness to open her heart in a trusting, loving conversation was obvious, so before hanging up I simply said, "Thanks, Linda. Maybe we can talk when you get home. I love you."

At the end of the summer in 2001, business at work had dropped off, so once again I was laid off. Mom and Linda returned from their trip to Arizona, and I was looking forward to spending more quality time with them. Something was different, though, when they got back. I couldn't put my finger on it, but I assumed we were all still readjusting to my return.

New curtains were hung in Linda's old bedroom and the TV, recliner, and a few new lamps went into the spare middle room. It was like having my own little apartment. I was delighted. Mom and I traveled to the shore a couple of times, visiting old friends, as we had so many times before, and we were having fun again. We even took a trip to California, retracing old memories.

Feeling confident, I went out looking for a new job and had several interviews. Nothing turned up right away, but that was fine, because I felt safe at home with my mother.

As I came in the front door on Tuesday, August 21, 2001, I called for my mom. I looked around downstairs, and then I heard her come to the balcony off to the one side of the vaulted ceiling overlooking the large living/dining room area.

"Hi, I was looking for you," I said.

She said, "Pack your shit and get the fuck out!"

"*What?* What did you say?"

That was not her kind of language. I had never heard her use the word fuck before.

I needed her to repeat it. She had to. She had to explain why, *this time*.

"What's going on?" I said. But instead of answering, she ran and locked herself in her bedroom. I had never in my life seen her run before either!

I double-stepped it up the stairs, "Mom! *Mom*, what's going on? Please tell me."

She didn't reply.

I couldn't believe it. An unbearable fear swept over me.

I flew down the steps and out the front door, jumped into my car, and drove around aimlessly, pulling over every few minutes because I couldn't see through the tears that appeared to be coming from the depths of my soul.

The gut feelings that I had upon their return from Arizona had been on target, and the target was on me. They had been to see my brother. I wondered what they had schemed, and why.

Now what do I do? I came upon a Catholic church. The doors were open, so I went in and sat there, weeping convulsively. Luckily, no one else came in. How do you pray at a time like that? I think I just kept saying, *please*, dear God! Please don't let this be happening.

When I went back to the house a couple of hours later, I wanted to ask my mother what I had done. Couldn't we talk this over?

I had thought everything was going so well—*but she was gone.* She had moved in with Linda. There was a note on the steps of the red carpet that led from the foyer to the living room.

It read: "Pack your shit and get out. You've got to be out of my home by the end of August."

I drove to Linda's house—my mother's car was there, but there was no answer at the door. I called Linda's number over and over again—but no one answered.

Was I dreaming? Was this another dreadful nightmare, or was it truly the Hell Hole that spun so fast your mind would scramble, and then the floor would drop out from under you? Their actions were irrational and deliberate—I was gasping for air. My world had fallen out from under me again.

What signs had I missed this time? Things were finally coming together for me. I couldn't wrap my mind around it. I had been treading lightly, not wanting to upset anyone.

Throughout my adult life I have sought counseling, and I face life's trials head on, without turning to drugs, cigarettes, drinking, or any other vice or medication. I'm not trying to pin a rose on myself (one of my mother's favorite expressions, "Mother, mother, mother pin a rose on me,") I'm merely trying to explain.

Again, I sought counseling with a priest who had come highly recommended. My thoughts were scrambled as I tried to paint as accurate a picture as I could, but after six sessions, he said, "Until now, I have not believed a word you've said."

I was stunned—shocked that he would admit such a thing, and the comment made me feel totally invalidated—abandoned once more. I don't know what finally convinced him that I was, indeed, telling the truth. After another visit, I stopped seeing him and wondered whether he, in fact, was the one who needed the counseling. I couldn't fathom why he chose not to believe me. Clearly my journey is difficult to visualize, but I had been seeking support and guidance, and couldn't understand why he would think I had fabricated the story. What would be the point?

I was traumatized and overcome, and I needed help. My family was throwing me away again like a worthless *sack of trash*.

Sitting on the foyer steps, my mind a jumble of conflicting thoughts, the phone rang. I ran to answer it, hoping it was my mother.

It wasn't her. It was an officer from the bank.

"Mrs. Albanese?"

"Yes."

"Your one-hundred dollar check bounced."

"That's not possible," I said, "there's more than forty-two-hundred in that account."

"No, ma'am, your account is empty."

I knew there had to be a mistake. Trying to compose myself, I told the banker I would stop by the next day.

I frantically kept trying to reach Linda, and I drove back and forth to her house, but they wouldn't answer the phone or the door.

First thing the next morning, I went to the bank. What I learned was for me the final blow.

My mother had emptied out my checking account. "You must have made an error and emptied the wrong account," I said. "My mother also banks here."

The young banker had the face of a cherub, and empathy was written all over it. "I'm sorry, ma'am, there's no mistake."

I had left Mom's name on my account from when she helped with the refinance of the mortgage, never considering a need to remove it.

I repeated, there must be a mistake.

"I'm sorry," he said as he nervously adjusted his tie.

I soon realized that they were trying to snuff out my life in a very calculated way—*but why?*

I made it back to the house, ran to my room, and grabbed hold of my childhood crucifix. "God, help me," I screamed as I clung to it. *"Oh, Lord, what do I do now?"*

I had just mailed all of my monthly bills—and I had to get to the post office and retrieve them before they went out.

It was drizzling as I jogged up the steps of the post office, and I nearly slipped. The postmaster was having a bad day and didn't want to be bothered with me. His black-framed half-rimmed-glasses were tilted over the tip of his nose, and he ignored me.

"Excuse me, excuse me," I said.

He never even looked up or acknowledged that I was panting, frantically trying to catch my breath and get his attention. His scruffy beard was well past a five o'clock shadow, and his uniform shirt showed signs of the heat of the day. It was hot, and he looked mean. His curly chest hair was showing over the top of his T-shirt, but he kept his head down.

"Excuse me, sir," I repeated. "I've got to get the envelopes back that I mailed a little while ago. Please help me—my mother just emptied my checking account!"

He finally looked at me. "What do you want?"

"I've got to get my mail back. My checks are going to bounce. My mother's stolen all of my money! Please help me!"

"I can't give them back to you," he said.

"I have to get them back. Please, let me go through the mail and retrieve my envelopes. They should all be together with my return address on them."

He reluctantly reached for the bin and said, "Here, look through these—if they're there, I guess you can have them. Otherwise, I can't help you. I'm not supposed to do this," he said.

I flipped through all of the mail, and luckily I found them.

"Thank you," I said, and ran back out to the car, careful not to slip again.

One of my weaknesses, of which I am keenly aware, is the

propensity to choose to die—not intentionally wanting to kill myself, but the pain. Those frightening thoughts were returning.

I was terrified.

When I called Marianne, my mother's neighbor, I was sure my voice was inaudible as I begged her to come over. Then I reached out to my Aunt Sophie. "My mother has emptied my checking account," I said. "Can you send Tom (my cousin) over?"

"*What?* What do you mean, she's emptied your account? Why would she do that?"

"I don't know! She *won't talk* to me. Please send Tom. I'm at my mother's now."

Tom's a gentle soul and the closest to me in age, and we've always gotten along well. Then I called four or five other friends. Natalie and I had been friends and golfing buddies since the late seventies, but we hadn't seen each other for several years because I had been living in Florida, consumed with Dom's health. She told me later that she couldn't understand what I was saying on the phone, and that it frightened her, so she came quickly. I'm sure I wasn't making sense to anyone.

Eileen Coughlin was the next call. I was grabbing at straws, trying to get as much support as I could, or I was sure I would collapse. Eileen's dad had been my father's doctor, and she and I had always been close. As I tried to explain that my mother had stolen my money, she said, "I don't understand."

"Can you come to my mother's house? Hurry!"

"I'll be right there."

When I called Sandy Seigel and tried to explain, she said, "Let me call Bill." He was her ex. "He lives in Tenafly. I'm down the shore and can't get there. Call me back, and let me know what's going on."

"I will, I will, thanks."

I had begged each of them to come to help me sort things out.

What was I going to do? How would I live?

They all showed up within the hour and witnessed me shaking uncontrollably. They surrounded me as we sat on the steps, then helped me up, and we moved into the living room. I couldn't catch my breath, and I was hysterical. They tried to comfort me. Natalie said, "Don't worry, it's only money. I can loan you some."

But it *wasn't* only money—for me it was like having my guts ripped out without anesthesia. I needed my family, I loved them, and I wanted them back. Nothing, no one, could *ever* take their place.

Tom said, "It will be alright. We're here for you."

I said, "Where can I go? I can't even get back to Florida now."

Bill Seigel said, "You can come and live with me for a while. I'm in my parents' home in Tenafly, and I have plenty of room."

"Okay, thanks, Bill."

They stayed until I could relax my shoulders and breathe. Then, Eileen, Marianne, and Bill left, while Natalie, Tom, and I further examined what had happened and tried to figure out why.

All of a sudden the front door flew open. It startled us. It was Linda. I had forgotten that she had left a message saying she wanted to talk with me.

When she saw Tom sitting straight ahead of her, she went ballistic. She charged into the living room, and then she saw Natalie sitting on the sofa next to me. She went right up to Tom's face with her index finger two inches from his eyes, saying, "I don't fucking appreciate you being here. This is none of your business."

Natalie spoke up and said, "If you want to talk with Jane, we'll leave. We're here to support her."

"I *don't* want to talk with her," she said as she swiveled around and darted back out the front door, slamming it behind her with great force.

I have often wondered what she had wanted to talk about.

Tom said, "You're not safe here. Did you see the rage in her eyes? Let me call my mother. You can stay with her tonight."

Aunt Sophie had had a few run-ins with my mother over the years and understood how explosive things could be.

Natalie helped me gather some things and then left for home. I followed Tom to his mother's house. He stayed for a while, explaining what had transpired. Aunt Sophie said, "You'll be safe here until we can get to the root of the problem with your mother."

When she called Mom at Linda's house the following day, my mother hung up on her. I was still shaking in disbelief, but felt a little safer with Aunt Sophie. We had long talks trying to figure out what had happened and she gave me a couple hundred dollars to hold me over, but said, "You can't stay here—I don't want to be in the middle of this."

I wondered why God would allow *me* to be the one abandoned? *Family was everything to me*, and the pain of losing them again was unbearable.

When I returned to my mother's house to gather my things, I was trembling and confused. I rested in my bed, praying as I stayed in a fetal position, begging God to take me.

Then suddenly, I heard the garage door go up. It was my mother and Linda. Maybe we could talk this out, I told myself.

When I came down the stairs, I said, "Mom, why are you doing this? *Please*, can't we talk this over?"

"You've got to be out of my house by the end of August."

Linda said, "We just came to get Mom's mail."

"Mom, I beg you, please don't do this. Can't we at least go to family counseling or have an intervention with a lawyer or doctor? Let's get someone to help us."

"We don't need counseling," Linda said. "You're the one who's crazy."

My mother had been helping me get back on my feet of her own free will. What gave them the right to steal my money? How did they justify that? Couldn't we have had a civilized conversation about whatever their concerns might have been?

The two things that I know for sure are: Had my dad still been alive, this tragedy never would have take place; and like him, I am a lover and a peacemaker, and I would have done almost anything to bring our family back together again. But I truly struggled with their deep-seated hatred of me.

GARY ZUKAV, THE AMERICAN SPIRITUAL TEACHER and the author of four consecutive New York Times best-sellers, including *The Seat of the Soul*, offers these great words of wisdom, which are often quoted: "If you are the one who has excluded your sister or daughter from your life, you are the one who needs help."

So who's crazy here?

YEARS LATER NATALIE COMMENTED, "I will never forget that night. I've never witnessed anything so cruel."

25

DAZED IN SILENCE

"THROUGH THE VALLEY OF THE SHADOW of death, I will fear no evil." Hadn't I already been through that valley? How was I going to get through *this one?* I couldn't begin to imagine.

I moved out of my mother's home by the end of August, as she had demanded. My cousin Tom rented a small truck to help me move my waterbed, the computer, and the desk my mother had bought for me, along with the TV, the recliner, and my personal effects. We moved everything into storage, which he also paid for.

On the first of September, I moved in with Bill. I am obliged to all of those who were there to help, but it felt as if my soul had been damaged beyond repair. For the next couple of weeks, I could feel the blood gushing from my heart. My head ached, my eyes were dead, and the emotional pain was intolerable.

Scared out of my mind as everything was caving in on me, I went to see Angie Bracconeri and asked her to call a priest for me. She was understandably upset and nervous. I needed help—I thought I was going to implode. I wished I could *just be done with it*.

Within minutes Father Tony arrived and asked, "How can I help?"

I told him what had happened and said, "I want my family back."

He sighed and said. "You can't have them back!"

"Why? Why can't I? I want them back!"

He repeated, "You can't have them back."

How could he say that, I thought—*how cruel?*

I didn't know where his comments were coming from, but he was right! I *couldn't* have them back. They didn't want me and had left me stranded—and, to this day, I have never received an explanation as to why it happened.

It was very cruel. But I had to accept it.

Although my thoughts were foggy, I continued to cling to my crucifix—*betrayed*—with a better understanding of how our Lord might have felt.

THEN CAME THE HORROR OF SEPTEMBER 11, 2001.

I was numb, consumed by my own pain, when my friend Muriel called and said, "Let's drive up the hill to the Palisades to see what's going on for ourselves."

For me there could be nothing more devastating than being discarded by my own family, especially the family that we'd had.

Why God? Why now?

I already felt as if a bomb had ripped my world apart, and I longed to be with Dom. The pain felt like a branding iron on the inside of my loins. In a profound way, though, it drew me closer to the Bible, which I held onto for dear life.

Not understanding the evil acts of September 11, we stood, dazed in silence, as many people gathered, each in tears and with unanswered questions. We were mesmerized, unable to believe our eyes, as the World Trade Center towers came down in thick clouds of mushrooming dust. It felt like we were watching a sci-fi movie, and they were fake buildings crashing onto the streets below. I don't think I was able to grasp the gravity of the situation and the loss of so many lives. Where does that kind of hatred come from?

Where did it come from in my own family?

Momentarily, everything had grown crystal clear. The world was indeed coming to an end. Mine already had—nothing could change that.

Strangers hugged, tears met tears. Some said, "God bless you," others intently stared into our eyes as words escaped them.

We drove back to Tenafly to plant ourselves in front of the television. Soon we heard of the crash at the Pentagon, and of the other plane crash in Pennsylvania where the passengers were calling their wives or husbands and parents from cell phones, to express their love, knowing they were about to die—the most remarkable display of heroism and deep love that I have ever witnessed!

It raised in me a sense of anger that is hard to describe. Many of them got to express their love as they crossed the threshold into eternity. To me, love is all that matters, and I know we cannot live without it. Though they died, they were loved, and those left behind knew of their love.

In stark contrast, my family made it very clear that they did not love me—by their deliberate demonstration of malevolence. It was unconscionable. What could I possibly have done to warrant such treatment? My heart continues to bleed, since I have never been able to find the answer to that question.

I had lost no one that fateful day, but had lost everything in the weeks that led up to it. Through these extreme circumstances I have come to recognize that life has a way of bringing you to your knees. And having faith, for me, is the only way that you can rise again.

It is my belief that, by God's grace, time passes and wounds heal, and that if you reach for Him, He will uphold you. I felt my faith was my only life preserver.

Are we the same today as we were before that horrible September day? I hope not. I hope we are far more faith-filled, loving, and compassionate.

Knowing God as I have come to know Him, I fully understand that life is a long, winding, sometimes painful road bringing us home to Him and to His eternal peace.

Half-heartedly, I began looking for work once again and a place to live while trying to sort things out one more time.

Unwittingly, I wore my broken heart on my sleeve. My eyes were bloodshot and swollen. For the next three months I lived with Bill. When I could pull myself together and unscramble my mind, I tried going on interviews.

Surely, I scared off all prospects by not being able to explain what I had been through. I knew I couldn't live with Bill forever, but I had no money and I also knew that I couldn't pay for the first and last month's rent and a security deposit for an apartment. I felt completely hopeless, worthless, and empty.

Then I received a call in November from the man with the package-design company, calling me back to work.

Two weeks later a one-bedroom apartment became available, but I couldn't commit to it, knowing I needed *$2,800* to move in. I couldn't imagine how I would pull that amount of money together.

I still couldn't believe what had happened to my family and to me. Time and again I called, but they wouldn't speak with me or answer the door. But I refused to give up trying to reach out to them.

As I write this, it's been a total of more than thirty-two years, with the five-year break in between, that we've been apart. I am sure that no amount of time will completely heal that wound. It reopens when I see a happy couple walking hand-in-hand or hear the hustle and bustle when friends plan holiday dinners with their families. I have spent far too many Christmases alone, wishing that someone would call who remembered that I might be by myself.

I often wonder if my family members ever think of me, as they plan *their* festive holiday meals.

I'm sure most people who experience great trauma and loss can attest to the fact that it is nearly impossible to begin the healing process without closure. I was robbed of that, too.

After September 11, with the world reeling from anxiety and fear, there were many church services and most of the chapels remained open late into the day.

Three men from Our Lady of Mt. Carmel Church, across the street from the Clinton Inn, perished that day. Another man escaped from the fifty-sixth floor of the South Tower. He frantically tried reaching his wife, knowing of her fear, since he had also been in the previous bombing of the Twin Towers, and they had lost their son in a car accident earlier that year.

The daily masses were packed and filled with sorrow, yet I returned each afternoon to sit in the presence of God, weeping mournful tears, not only for my loss, but for the sense of loss that every American felt. The sun streaking through the stained-glass windows created eerie images reminiscent of the splintered shards of steel that remained standing at the end of our magnificent city.

Candles were lit, and a few people were scattered through the pews, some softly crying, kneeling with their heads buried in their hands. Others said the rosary, or quietly whispered to those around them, but I sat alone, engrossed in an overwhelming state of despair. People who shuffled in and out were transformed into zombies in my eyes by the numbness I was feeling. A lingering, leftover scent of incense from an earlier mass hung low in the air. You could hear a faint church bell off in the distance; it too, seemed to be wailing in pain.

As I sat in church on the third day, a woman I didn't know sat next to me. She said nothing, just sat there. I hadn't noticed the time or the fact that I was the only one left in the church, and that day had turned into night. The following day she appeared once more, and she quietly said, "I'm Sister Mary. Can I help?"

As I shook uncontrollably, I couldn't respond. She rested her hand on my knee to comfort me.

It was the end of the week before I could speak with her. She was warm and loving, and I felt relieved that someone had cared about me. My friends did. They had been there for me that awful day when I needed them the most. But they had their own lives to tend to, and they were also struggling with the atrocities of that September memory. My grief was all consuming, and I was very frightened. My spirit had been fully extinguished. I felt lost, and I asked Sister Mary if I could meet with her for guidance once in a while. She agreed. When I explained what had happened, she said, "How can I help? Can I call your family for you?"

"I've tried reaching them every day," I said, "but they won't take my calls."

People all around the civilized world were reaching out to find their loved ones and to hold them tight. Mine hadn't even tried to find me. They showed no remorse or regard at all for my well-being. I still struggle with how to put those gut-wrenching, demoralizing feelings into words

A year later, on September 11, 2002, after a long, empty, and shattered year, Sister Mary looked for me at mass and said, "Jane, you were the first one I thought of this morning when I awoke." She was tender and compassionate, and offered me a sense of being worthy of love.

Sadly, she passed away a few years later, but not before helping me through the process of becoming a Catholic. I had found my church home during that heartbreak. Angie Bracconeri was my sponsor, and I felt closer to God at that beautiful Easter Vigil Mass than I ever had before.

To this day, I welcome the body and blood of Christ into my soul every time I'm at mass—it helps me get through another day and another week.

26

Lord, You've Got My Attention, Now!

Hi, I'm Jane Albanese, and I'm estranged from my family is how I introduced myself for many years after our second family breakup. There was no explaining it, that's just who I was. Couldn't everyone see the word *REJECT* tattooed across my forehead?

I had become a fraction of the confident woman that I had known myself to be.

Fortunately, through years of counseling and self-help seminars, I have come to recognize that it is not *who I am*, it is what has happened to me. I have since vowed to rise above it, by learning to draw upon my own dignity of self, to overcome the mental charade of being *"estranged from my family,"* and simply become Jane Albanese. I have found that that is enough, and it's freeing. It has allowed me to become a better version of myself.

That transition didn't happen overnight, but it might never have happened at all had I not made a conscious decision to love myself. This was not an easy task since my entire family—with the exception of Aunt Sophie and Tom—and all twenty-two members of Dom's family seemed to be telling me that I was unworthy of being loved or cared about. *No one has ever asked me for my account of the story.*

Sure, the experience of great loss still hurts, but it no longer defines me. I discovered that I'm bigger than whatever my "pain mantra" is.

When I was called back to work again, I was flat-lined. The boss knew something had changed, but I couldn't explain what had happened since the spring of that year when he laid me off. The next few weeks I worked as many hours as I could get, trying my damnedest to concentrate. I appreciated the work, and I did my best to live up to his expectations.

Two weeks later when he handed me my paycheck, I was stunned—and I stood there and stared at it for a long while. It came to *$2,805*.

Okay, Lord, you've got my attention *now!*

To me, that amount was a miracle. I could get the apartment with the $2,800 and have five dollars left over for an ice cream cone. Things were looking up once again.

Human as I am, though, that thought quickly left me when I questioned how I could survive without my family. How would I maintain two homes and all the expenses for both? Though I now had enough money to move into the apartment, clearly a blessed gift, how was I going to pay for food, gas, next month's rent, and next month's mortgage?

While I was living with Bill, he would cook and leave a plate of food out for me, and I'd never had far to travel. I began my road to recovery by paying the mortgage in Florida on my credit cards, and

I worked every waking moment when I could find someone willing to pay me. As time progressed I created my own freelance graphics business, called *Graphic Design by The Drummer's Wife*, in honor of Dom, and I took on several new clients.

Like a robot, I'd go from one job to the next, and to the next. Then I'd work from home evenings and weekends, seventy-five to eighty hours a week, six-and-a-half days a week, for *ten years*. It left little time to eat or sleep or rebuild my life, just work—work as hard as I could in order to survive.

I remember speaking with my doctor about how tired I was, and when I explained why, he said, "Do you realize that you may be solely responsible for unemployment in this country?" His comment made me crack a smile for the first time in months.

Recognizing that God was supplying the work, I would have daily conversations with Him about my future. My steadfast focus was on honing my craft and paying the bills. However, in more recent years, as the economy slowed and the business dynamic changed, work again became more difficult to find.

Like a duck, I've tried remaining calm on the surface, while paddling like hell to find the next move. My credit card debt was rising, and I was often out of work due to the seasonal nature of the graphics industry. But by attempting to bask in God's golden light, my faith has remained strong.

A girlfriend once said to me, "You're so lucky. I'd give anything to have a few days to myself on a regular basis." She went on to say,

"Last week, when the entire family was away, I got to paint and to read, which I love. Then they came home, and we went right back to the chaos."

"That's great, and I'm happy for you," I said, "but I don't think you'd want to change places with me. No one ever comes home to me—I'd give anything for a little family chaos." I could only sum up the comparison by saying, "No one shares the bills, no one takes out the garbage, or shops, or even cares about how I'm feeling."

I didn't mean to be mean, but I felt I had to explain.

She looked shocked but finally understood, and I was grateful for her validation.

I remember thinking, *No more fun, no more laughing, no more parties, no more love, no more joy,* just keep your nose to the grindstone. Survive and *God will provide.* I have no complaints in that department, just wishes and dreams of one day finding an intimate relationship with another human being and love in any of its many wonderful forms. I know that I still have much love to give.

I have never again been invited to a family get-together, not even to my mother's 100th birthday party at the Clinton Inn, which made the local papers when the entire family, including her great-grandkids, flew in from Arizona.

Unless you have walked a mile in my shoes, I doubt that you can grasp the depth of the pain caused by this American family tragedy.

I have lived a life of extremes—going from years of joy, laughter, and a wonderfully loving family, to decades of emotionally painful solitude, brokenness, and financial strife. When people notice the rejection I feel, and we speak of it, their first question usually is "What did *you* do to cause the rift?"

My journey has been unique and difficult to comprehend; but I find *that question* painful and exceptionally insensitive. Why would someone make such an unkind assessment right to my face without knowing the facts?

I don't know what I did or didn't do to warrant such radical behavior. I can't imagine what I could have done differently to avoid such treatment. They have permanently altered my life. Although my grieving has eased, I believe I'll go to my grave praying for them and for myself, never knowing how things might have been.

I miss the home Dom and I shared, and hope that one day I will be able to spend more time there. By working myself to a frazzle, I have been able to maintain the house, and I get to visit occasionally while I try to get some rental income during the high season in Daytona Beach.

As I continue to come to terms with what has happened, I can't help but recall when one of our longtime family friends said to me, "Why don't you leave them alone and go away?" Another said, "Why won't you just get the hell out of the way?"

Leave them alone—get out of the way, as if I were some sort of leper or monster. It was *my family* we were talking about. What version of our saga had they heard? Why wouldn't they have, at least, inquired about what I had to say? To have their vitriolic comments pour salt on the open wounds was more than I could or should have to bear.

No one should have to face the trials of life completely isolated and alone, without a moral support system.

In the first pages of this book, I shared lots of happy and nostalgic memories. They are, however, in no way meant to trivialize the unfathomable events that have stripped me of my family's love, or to minimize the shame I feel about who they have become.

Life without love is no life at all.

Book Three

The Rising

27

THE BIRTH OF A GIANT

A SERENDIPITOUS MOMENT CAME TO ME on November 27, 2006, while I was out of work again one day and turned on "The Oprah Winfrey Show." It was such a joy-filled and moving episode. You could almost feel the enthusiasm bubbling right through the tube—Oprah's favorite "Holiday Giveaway, Results Show." Results of what, I wasn't sure, but the audience was electrified, so I stayed tuned, needing a positive charge myself that day.

I learned that, the week before, Oprah had given a thousand dollars to every member of her audience. Her gift to them carried this caveat: They were not to use the funds for themselves or any member of their family, but had to pay-it-forward and do something kind to help someone else.

That day's show was the evidence of what everyone had done

with Oprah's gift. Each story was more riveting than the last. The audience was laughing and applauding, crying, even screaming with joy as countless audience members from the prior show proudly told their stories of what they had done with her gift.

The first woman showed a video of herself standing on the street corner in her hometown, giving one-hundred dollar bills to utterly unbelieving passers-by.

Another video showed two sisters from South Carolina who wanted to use their money to honor the woman who had helped raise them for more than twenty years.

"She gave us love, she gave us affection, and she gave us discipline," they said. "So on behalf of Oprah Winfrey and our friend's entire family, we presented a donation to her church to purchase a stained-glass window honoring her name.

"Our memory is bittersweet," one sister went on, "for as soon as we say her name, tears just get in our eyes. We miss her so."

Sadly, their guardian angel had passed away five years earlier, but they remembered her gift of love.

One of Oprah's recipients took her thousand dollars, went to her local supermarket, and waited to find shoppers who had carts filled to overflowing. She simply stepped up to the register and paid for their groceries. Can you imagine how both the recipient, *and the giver*, must have felt that day?

Astonishingly, a couple of friends in the audience took their two-thousand and, by gathering their family, friends, co-workers, and community leaders together, raised nearly seventy-thousand dollars. They completely paid off the medical bills of a local man who had been stricken with a debilitating neuromuscular brain disease and could no longer work. There was even some money left over to help fund his children's college tuition.

The *pièce de résistance* that day for me, however, was when two sisters from Atlanta got up to tell their story. They had taken that week off from work and decided to adopt a local woman's shelter. With two-thousand dollars and Oprah's name behind them, they contacted local radio stations and newspapers to broadcast their idea. Spending hours on the phone eliciting the help of everyone they knew, they got in touch with all the large chain stores, explaining their challenge. Before they knew it, semis and tractor trailers were being loaded with everything from diapers to bedding, dishes to dishwashers, refrigerators to toiletries, and everything in between that a woman's shelter could possibly need to be fully refurbished. Oprah's blessing reached far beyond these two sisters' wildest imaginations. In just one week's time they had compounded their two-thousand dollars into nearly *two-hundred-thousand* in donations and in-kind gifts.

On my side of the screen, I could hardly see through the cloudburst of tears that welled up from deep within my core, pulling heavily on my heartstrings as I witnessed the love they were all sharing.

Yes, I was crying for myself and for all I had lost. In spite of everything, though, I began to see a glimmer of hope through the excitement of Oprah's show.

I remember thinking that, if those two women could raise that kind of money in a week's time, maybe I'd be able to do the same thing in a year's time, although I didn't know how I was going to make that happen.

The unthinkable experience of losing my family for the second time had become my reality. My world was empty and broken, but through that TV show I was beginning to experience a warm, overwhelming feeling, like the lifting of a veil.

My memory flashed back to the jubilation I had savored when I helped reunite Jon Shepard with his son, and the joy that reunion had brought into my life.

At that very moment I recognized the gift that I had been given, the gift of being able to do miraculous things to help other people.

On that unusually dreary day in November, the wind was fierce, winter was approaching, and the trees were barren. A great chill came over me. Then suddenly, out of nowhere, I felt a flame reignite in me that I thought had been darkened forever.

I felt an urgent and enormous need to recapture that powerful sense of purpose and accomplishment. I could feel my mainsail changing course and hoped that it would heal my wounds and lead me to higher ground.

I knew that I needed to recapture a sense of joy that had been gone for far too long. The experience was emotionally thrilling for me; I began to believe that it was lifting me up to a new life. I had to find a way to bring compassionate, loving, and grateful people into my world.

Even the smallest acts of kindness can change the direction of a person's life, and I realized that there is no greater reward than helping someone in need.

Clearly, this is a premise that my family has never been able to grasp.

The pay-it-forward challenge came from the movie of the same name, based on the novel by Catherine Ryan Hyde, starring Helen Hunt, Kevin Spacey, and Haley Joel Osment.

Pay-it-forward is best described on the movie's website in this way: "At school, a young boy's class was given an unusual assignment—to think up a practical way to make the world a better place, and put it into action. The boy stumbled upon a simple way to change the world in this drama, coming up with the concept of paying it forward—do something kind for three people without being asked, and then request that they do the same for three others."

Inspired, I sat glued to the TV, watching Oprah's show; the weather began to lighten on that late-autumn day, as there were so many other stirring stories of amazing grace and generosity, followed by the reverent gratitude of their recipients.

Like Oprah, I wanted to start a movement to help others.

I remember saying to myself, "If Oprah can do it why can't I?"

Well, how many answers to that question do you need?

Although I've always thought big and have an entrepreneurial spirit, I didn't know what I was about to embark upon, yet I knew I could figure it out as I go. Or at least I *thought* I could.

Throughout my lifetime, I have been told that I have a highly tuned sense of native intelligence, defined as a metaphysical understanding of that which connects the mind, body, and soul.

My challenge, though, unlike Oprah's, was in many ways far greater. Not only did I have to create a charitable organization from scratch, I had to find a way to raise money in order to give it away.

How do you convince people to donate to a stranger, so their donation can then be given to help others who are in despair? And more importantly, how do you do it on two nickels and a credit card?

I was broke. What I really needed was a "godfather," or at least someone else who had walked a similar path and had a vision of helping others—hopefully, someone with money.

I had none of these. All I had was a God-given desire to pull myself up by my proverbial bootstraps before sinking further into the black abyss of desperation and shame.

That same afternoon I said to myself, "Okay, what's the first thing I need to do? Pick a name. How about Contagious Giving? That's what Catherine Ryan Hyde's novel and Oprah's holiday giveaway show were all about.

I was having dinner with Carol Caneriato and Sue DeMartini, two new church friends, and couldn't wait to tell them about my plans. They were part of the Cornerstone Retreat Core team at the Church of the Presentation in Upper Saddle River. I had attended a spiritual retreat there the year before. The following twelve months had been spent with our team as we got to know each other on a very intimate and personal level through the sharing of our life's stories.

My Cornerstone sisters had shown compassion beyond anything I had ever experienced. Their tender and loving words of encouragement had allowed me to release my pain. I'd felt safe among them in that holy and sacred space.

It was just a few nights after watching Oprah's astonishing results show that the three of us had dinner. As a graphic designer, I had already laid out a great-looking corporate logo for Contagious Giving and was looking forward to sharing my new concept with them.

They were amazed that I would even consider starting such an organization, when all they had witnessed during our biweekly meetings over the past year had been the broken me. I explained my need to rise above my pain by doing something kind to help others who were experiencing their own life-altering situations. My big plans monopolized the conversation, but my friends believed in my plan and encouraged me to move forward.

Carol, I later learned, was the treasurer of a foundation for people with celiac disease and knew some of the pitfalls and difficulties of running a non-profit organization. Recognizing my drive and passion, as well as my need to help myself in order to move on, she said, *"You go, girl."*

The next day I Googled "Contagious Giving" and, to my dismay, discovered it was already taken by a young man with AIDS. It shook me up. I was disappointed, but it forced me to quickly come up with a new name for my organization.

Seeking wisdom as I often do, I re-read some old letters from my dear friend, Reverend Harry E. Chase. Among one of them, I found the expression, "The giant doesn't know she's a giant."

I loved the word *giant*, but it had always seemed more appropriate when thinking about my father. He had been a giant of generosity.

"That's it!" I exclaimed. *"That's it!"*

I called Carol, told her that Contagious Giving had already been taken, and asked how she liked the name Giants of Generosity. We both loved it, so I Googled "Giants of Generosity" and, to my delight, all three domain names .org, .net, and .com—were available.

Seeing that as a very positive sign, I proceeded. I began looking up how to register a domain name, and I charged the fee for all three on my credit card, then I Googled how to incorporate a non-profit organization. Within two weeks, the paperwork had been filed and Giants of Generosity (Giants) was incorporated. Next, I decided to call local attorneys, inquiring about becoming a tax-exempt organization.

Having been in business all my life gave me a slight advantage, although I had never before considered starting a charity.

Already well into my third career, I was looking to start a fourth at age sixty-two. Just prior to the Oprah show, I had been working long hours until being laid off again. Not quite sure what I was getting myself into, I had another *"What are ya, nuts"* moment, but at the same time I knew for sure that I wanted to make it happen—and for my own survival, I *needed* to make it happen.

As I began researching everything I could find on how to run a non-profit, I was overwhelmed by the many details of the federal regulations and guidelines.

I called more lawyers and a few accountants, all of whom told me it would cost anywhere from seven to ten-thousand dollars to file the required IRS form to become a tax-exempt organization. There was no way I could afford that kind of money.

Feeling shot down once more, I asked one of the attorney's assistants, "Why is it so expensive to apply for the exemption?"

She said, "There's a twenty-eight-page report called form 1023 that you can view online. It needs to be filled out, by-laws would have to be drawn up, and a mission statement has to be developed." I felt discouragement creeping in, until I found the twenty-eight-page report the young woman had referenced online. At the risk of sounding cocky, I already knew the answer to the first few questions, since they were written in English:

Full name of the organization? "Got that."

Mailing address? "Got that."

Are you represented by an authorized representative, such as an attorney or accountant? Check box "No."

Organization's website? "In progress."

The IRS also requires at least three individuals to serve on the board of directors. This part would be the hardest, since my circle of friends was so limited due to the solitude and confusion that arose from my family situation.

I decided to print out the form, and I started writing, leaving the more difficult questions to the end.

Around that time, I was called back to work. In the meantime, I had also found a few new freelance graphics clients needing my services. So, all of a sudden, I was very busy again, leaving little time to get the application done. I stayed up late and squeezed in every possible hour to complete as much as I could.

If only someone would give me a few hours of his or her time to review the details and guide me through the by-laws, I thought, *I could work on the mission statement.* Then it would only be a matter of paying the $299 fee, not the exorbitant legal fee I had been warned about, and I'd be on my way.

At mass one Sunday, I saw a friend who was an accountant and asked him if he had ever done an application for a 501(c)3. He said that he had. I was beyond elated and went on to explain what I had hoped to do.

He said, "Come over this afternoon, and I'll take a look at what you have."

What a gift he was! We met for an hour or so. He perused the application and made some suggestions, then he helped me put the by-laws together. I had asked Susan, my assistant at Maple Ridge, and two of my new Cornerstone sisters if they would consider becoming board members; luckily, they all agreed. I still had some work to do, but on February 12, 2007, not quite eight weeks after being incorporated, I mailed the completed application to Uncle Sam with my check for $299—and kept my fingers crossed.

And then I waited.

28

THANK GOD FOR BEING PUT ON HOLD

HOW LONG WOULD THE GOVERNMENT'S APPROVAL TAKE? Would I be approved? Could I do this? It almost seemed too simple.

As I contemplated what to do next, I called a few friends, and some journalists, to ask them to come to a meeting, where I would explain my plan of action for paying it forward, and talk about my dream and vision for Giants of Generosity.

I arranged for a meeting room at the Clinton Inn, my old haunt. I felt safe within its walls.

On a very cold winter's night, with a foot of newly fallen snow and then freezing rain, the frozen parking lot was glazed over with shiny sheets of ice. The Inn's new management was in the middle of a major renovation of the lobby—everything was upside-down, covered in tarps, and thick with a layer of grayish brown dust.

I worried that no one else beside me would show up under those conditions. If even only one other person came, I would be pleased. I could talk about my plans for starting a charity to help people right here in our own backyards—people like me who were experiencing difficult times. Up to that point, with the exception of Carol and Sue, I had only been talking to myself. That, by itself, was a pretty scary thought.

At 7:30 p.m.—through ice, snow, dust, and all—twenty-one people were there, listening to what I had to say. I couldn't believe it. Why had they decided to come? To this day, I'm not sure, but I suspect forces greater than myself had something to do with it.

A few of my Cornerstone sisters were there. They knew all about my journey—in fact, at one of our bimonthly meetings I mentioned my plans even before completing the tax-exempt application. They each reached into their wallets to hand me twenty dollar bills. I've just recently framed my first one-hundred dollar bank deposit receipt.

A reporter from *PrimeTime News* was there, as were a few of my church friends, insurance agents, and even my hairdresser with her daughter and niece. As long as they were alive and breathing, I didn't care who they were or where they were from. I was excited. In preparing my speech, I had borrowed a top hat and cane from my good friend John Barrett, and was about to quote Winston Churchill. Not being a public speaker, I nervously stood at the podium, my eyes afloat with tears. Then I donned the hat and began.

"Welcome, thank you for coming. As Winston Churchill once said, "We make a living by what we get, we make a life by what we give."

I went on to explain that I had been going through a very difficult time in my own life, and that, after watching the Oprah giveaway show I was on a quest to help other people. I hoped to be able to help those going through all types of devastation—here in our own communities, not in some far off land. They were riveted by the Jon Shepard story and wanted to hear more about how I planned to help others. Not quite sure if I had captured them with my sketchy plans of raising money in order to help those who may have fallen through the cracks, I asked for their patience. Much to my amazement, three audience members came up to the mic to say they believed in what I was trying to accomplish, and they believed in me. I felt as though I had given a command performance.

As we parted that night I couldn't quite comprehend what had happened. I was beginning to feel like "an Oprah." As you can tell, my vivid imagination was running away with me. But people had listened, and they *had* responded.

That weekend I took a break, escaping to my favorite hideaway at my friend's home in Blairstown. I told Elli about the astonishing turnout and how excited I was for the first time in a very long while. We stopped to see her son's brand new office, and I couldn't help myself, so I told Derrick about my recent experience and about paying it forward.

His immediate reply was, "I've been waiting for you!"

"...What do you mean?

He reached in his wallet and he handed me an envelope with a red star on it and a five dollar bill inside. I looked at him quizzically. He went on to say, "A month ago, our pastor gave each member of the congregation an envelope with varying amounts of cash in it, asking us to find someone in need and *pay-it-forward*."

He had been waiting to find the right person. We said no more...then we embraced and felt God's hand working in His divinely mysterious way.

Clearly the pay-it-forward movement was spreading like wildfire. There I was, miles away from home, still connecting the dots.

My mind was running wild with ideas. I'd need a website, some advertising, brochures, flyers, press releases—and I'd need people to help.

Fortunately, I had the presence of mind to call or visit a few other local charities and ask for their guidance. Their generosity in sharing information was inspiring. They were able to show me how to design a press release and get an event published in the local papers.

Okay, I was getting the picture. Everyone I spoke with was intrigued with the idea of helping others here in our own communities. Though I live in an affluent area, there are still people who are in need. Sometimes, however, we choose not to recognize the reality of another's pain. I believe each of us as we walk this walk have our own trials, and many prefer not to make them public. I respect that.

ON MAY 1, 2007, A VERY OFFICIAL-LOOKING, large manila envelope appeared in my mailbox addressed to "Giants of Generosity, Inc." I stood, frozen, staring at it. *Was this a rejection letter?* I thought. I opened it gingerly and couldn't believe my eyes. The first word I saw was *Congratulations!*

I stood a little taller, no longer weeping.

Giants of Generosity, Inc. was officially a 501(c)3 tax-exempt charitable organization. That twenty-eight-page application, which I had filled out on my own back in February, had been approved.

Pleased beyond words, yet anxious, I couldn't find anyone to share my exuberance with, which seemed a familiar thread running throughout my life.

The shame of abandonment, if you're emotionally built as I am, haunts your soul, I suppose for the rest of your life. I've wanted so badly to bring love, joy, and hope back into my own life. That reason alone was the impetus for stepping out in faith, creating the charity in the first place, trusting God to guide me.

With the opening of that official envelope, my personal mantra changed once again, this time to "Hi, I'm Jane Albanese, and I am the founder of Giants of Generosity, an organization designed to help others who are experiencing desperate times."

Upon mulling over many phrases while trying to encapsulate what I wanted to accomplish in a singular mission statement, I felt compelled to express the breadth and scope of whom we'd help, leaving the door open to a variety of needs. By slightly modifying the pay-it-forward theme, our premise is simple: Do something kind for someone else without expecting to be repaid.

Trusting that the law of gratitude will follow its own path, I know those helped will share their blessings in their own way, in their own time—when they are able.

Many times in my own life, the walls have crumbled around me and I needed assistance on different issues and didn't know where to turn, often feeling destitute, scared out of my wits, even suicidal. I vividly recalled the time when I reached out to a suicide hotline and *was put on hold*. I'm grateful for that now, because I got so angry with them it made me snap out of wanting to die.

From my firsthand experience when Dom and I reached out to Reverend Phil for the help we needed to accommodate my brother's demands, I knew reaching out to strangers could be disconcerting. Intuitively, I understood that each case needed to be handled with care.

My goal was to touch the faces of those who were hurting and lift their chins to the light, offering them a renewed sense of confidence that *all will be well*.

As a designer, I couldn't wait to design a full-color brochure, which I had begun even before being approved. Not such an easy thing to do for yourself, especially when you also have to write the copy—thoughts from deep within your soul. I wanted to include every scenario that I could think of about how we could possibly help. When I look back on that first brochure, I'm embarrassed; it's crammed with small type and tiny images. Every thought in my head was there; how confusing it must have been to those seeing it for the first time.

Since I was also working full-time, months passed before I could complete the brochure. I had the new logo and the mission statement but still needed to clearly convey the vision of how I was going to carry out the mission.

Finally one day, with the newly printed brochures in hand, I started to walk the streets in and around my hometown, speaking with storeowners to see if they would allow me to leave some on their counters. For the most part, they said I could. The second day I headed out again, not quite sure if I'd honed my elevator pitch to perfection, but was ready to move on.

The pharmacist in a local apothecary listened to my plans for helping people in need, and she asked, "What kind of help do you mean?"

I told her that we wanted to help people going through desperate times, here, locally.

She said, "Can you wait for a moment?" as she tended to a customer.

"Yes, of course."

When she came back over to me, she said, "Would you consider helping one of my former employees?"

I was astonished that I might have stumbled upon our first case.

"What kind of help does she need?"

"Her name's Joanne. She's forty-two years old, and the mother of two young children. While she was doing laundry a month ago, she collapsed. Her young daughter found her curled up on the floor and called 911. She had suffered a massive heart attack and was rushed to the hospital. She is being treated with the best of care, but she has remained unconscious and has been put on life support."

Denise, the pharmacist, gave me Joanne's parents' phone number and asked if I would call them to see how we might help. Although Lucy and John had five other children, they were understandably vigilant about being at Joanne's side every moment. I called them and asked what we could do. Joanne, they said, had insurance, so money really wasn't an issue. That was a relief, because we didn't have any money to give at that point. I listened intently as Lucy told me about her daughter.

Then, in an almost embarrassed tone, she said, "Do you think you could have someone give Joanne a massage? I want her to be touched when we are not able to be with her. I sing to her when the hospital is quiet, late at night, and I know she hears me," she said. "I don't want her to feel alone when we leave her."

"I'll do my best to find massage therapists who will donate their services," I said, "and I'll get back to you."

I knew I also needed the doctor's permission to bring someone in from the outside. Once that had been arranged, I began calling everyone in the phone book to ask if any of their therapists would consider donating a massage once a week or so. I even called massage-therapy schools. Delighted by their response and compassion, I found three different therapists, and made the arrangements with the hospital staff.

Lucy was pleased, as well as surprised that someone whom she had never met would care enough to help her daughter. "It's comforting just to know that someone is thinking about us," she said.

I had been thinking about them more than she knew. Once

again I felt the hand of God on my shoulder and was blessed to be of comfort to someone who was hurting. For me, this was the beginning of my own healing: seeing my shaky notion of starting a charity to help others come to fruition.

Lucy wrote me this lovely note:

> *Dear Jane,*
>
> *Thank you. These words are inadequate to express our appreciation to you and Giants of Generosity for your work on behalf of our daughter, Joanne. We pray that one day Joanne will also be able to thank you personally.*
>
> *This note is brief, however our thanks are enormous and from the bottom of our hearts.*
>
> *Again, thank you.*
>
> *Sincerely,*
> *Lucy and Jim*

Sadly, after holding on for over a year, Joanne never regained consciousness, and passed away.

"God does not command that we do great things, only little things with great love." ... *Mother Teresa*

29

A Marshmallow Explosion

At Mass the following Sunday morning, before I could kneel in humble gratitude, my friend Rosemarie came over to me to say good morning. Her husband, John, was the accountant friend who helped me with the application.

"Jane, I was mugged in Bergenfield yesterday by two young men trying to steal my handbag in broad daylight," she said. "They got away with just fifty bucks and my credit cards, but tragically, a man who rushed out of his home to help me was pushed to the ground by the two thugs. He hit his head on a parked car, and he broke his neck!"

"What? In *Bergenfield?* Are you alright?"

"I'm a little bruised," she said, "but I'm so overwhelmed by his injury that I can't cope with the sadness I feel for him. It's entirely my fault that he got hurt. His name is Angel."

"Are you kidding me? His name is *Angel?* My God—will he be all right? Are you sure you're okay?"

"They're saying he's paralyzed from his eyes down."

"God help the poor soul!"

I was very happy to hear Rosemarie was unharmed, although a bit shaken up, and I was shocked by her story. That type of crime doesn't often happen in our sleepy little Bergen County towns.

Right after mass, I picked up the local newspaper. The headline read, "Good Samaritan Is Badly Injured in Bergenfield Mugging."

I felt a powerful connection with our creator that Sunday morning, less than seventy-two hours after handing out my first brochure. Although I was feeling nervous and inadequate, I was also excited at the prospect of doing what I had set out to do.

How could I help Angel? Such an unfortunate incident was exactly what I had in mind for Giants of Generosity, but I feared it was too soon and too big for me to handle.

I wondered what to do.

Looking at the article in the paper again, I noticed the reporter's name and called him.

"I'm the founder of a brand new charity here in Bergen County," I said. "I saw your article in the *Record* and hoped you'd be doing a follow-up story on how the Good Samaritan is faring?"

"This is a huge story for me," he said, "and we'll be doing another article tomorrow, because the suspects have already been arrested in the case."

"Would you be kind enough to indicate that Giants of Generosity will accept donations on behalf of the injured man?"

He agreed, and the front-page headline the following day read, "Fund to Aid Injured Samaritan."

That fund was the organization that *I had created*, and when I saw it in print I could hardly believe my eyes. Speaking of launching in a big way, we had made the headlines on a very important story! *Our first!* I hoped that someone would respond, and that we could bring in some money to help Angel Deida and his family. All the local churches and schools were also accepting donations on his behalf. It was spine-tingling, in spite of the fact that we were responding to a very tragic event.

I awaited the arrival of the first donation, while still working at my graphics job. Due to the severity of the case, we needed to come together as a community to help, so I felt confident that someone would respond, even though Giants of Generosity was a totally new and unknown charity.

As I approached my apartment two days later, I couldn't believe what I saw. My mailbox was overflowing with a whole bunch of white stuff that resembled an explosion of marshmallow fluff. As I got closer, I realized it was the mail—my box was overflowing with hundreds of envelopes addressed to Giants of Generosity. I marveled at how quickly people had answered the plea. Giants was only a few weeks old when I heard of the incident, and now the kindness of strangers filled not only my mailbox, but my heart as well.

I ran up the stairs, and then, hands shaking, opened the first one. When I saw its contents, my heart almost stopped. There was a lone five dollar bill, reminding me of the parable of the widow who had given her last two coins. In God's eyes she'd given more than all the rest, for perhaps she gave everything she had.

There was no note, just the five dollar bill. I was so curious about who this person was and what his or her story might be. I looked again for an enclosed note, but there wasn't one, nor was there a return address on the envelope. I couldn't even thank them.

Drying my eyes, I opened the next envelope. It had a hundred dollar check with a card saying, "God bless you for all you are doing." The next one I opened had a ten dollar check and the clipping from the newspaper. I found it intriguing how people responded to the one little italicized sentence in the paper at the very end of the article that read, "*Giants of Generosity is accepting donations on behalf of the family*," and listed our address.

I kept opening the envelopes wishing I had someone I could share that moment with. Anxiety crept in when I realized I hadn't even opened a bank account because I'd been waiting for the acceptance letter that I had just received.

There was fourteen-hundred and ninety-five dollars in those envelopes. Bursting at the seams, I had to find someone to tell, so I rang the bell of Bea Ginsburg, my wonderfully pessimistic neighbor, a lovely, white-haired ninety-two-year-old Jewish grandmother.

"Bea, you're not going to believe this," I said, as I explained what had happened.

"I really didn't have faith in what you were trying to do," she said, "because it's too big a job. I couldn't imagine how you would get people to send you money, so it could be given away to strangers. Wow, that's incredible!" And she started to laugh.

I was quietly astounded by the phenomenon myself. Here was a case where a local family was in need, and a new charity, acting as a vehicle to help, could practically command people to part with their money in good faith to help someone else. The power of the human spirit is a beautiful thing. I was glad Bea was home, or I think I would have burst with joy.

I had to find time to go to the bank with the legal papers and open a checking account. When could I do that? *Maybe on my lunch hour,* I thought. In the meanwhile I proudly endorsed each check with "Giants of Generosity, for deposit only for Angel Deida."

I didn't get to the bank the next day but wished I had, because when I returned from work, there was an even bigger stack of envelopes, all shapes and sizes. I wondered what the mailman was thinking! I thought, *Maybe there'll be another fifteen-hundred dollars.* By then my blood was boiling over with excitement. I slit open a dozen at a time—ten dollars, thirty-five dollars, a hundred and fifty dollars—most of them with notes asking if I could pass along blessings to the family.

Then came a five-hundred dollar check with a prayer for Angel's speedy recovery. Another check with a blessing for what Giants was doing. Another five dollar bill came without a note.

As I write these words today, tears still come easily at the memory of those generous and loving people, most of whom I will never meet. I sent each a thank-you note expressing my gratitude. I typed a hundred or so in the following few days after work, realizing that it might be an impossible task to respond to every one. Then I decided to send letters just to those who had sent a hundred dollars or more—that would be more manageable (and was required by law.) These donors had never heard of Giants of Generosity before this. We were brand new. But I wanted them to learn of my vision and of my passion for what I'd hoped to do.

Guess whose doorbell I rang again? Good thing Bea had a marvelous sense of humor. I was so overwhelmed I don't even remember the total for the second day. I had to find time to get to the bank, though. The next day, I made a substantial deposit as I opened the new account. I had put aside the hundred dollars that I had received from my Cornerstone sisters a few months earlier, and made sure that I made out a separate deposit slip for that money.

The third day the mailman not only filled my mailbox, but also left a tattered, old, three-foot-tall, fifty-pound gray mailbag next to the door, filled to the brim. I couldn't lift it, and made several trips up the stairs carrying as many as I could. *What had I gotten myself into?*

By the end of that week, we had received a total of nineteen-thousand-four-hundred and fifty dollars—not a dime of which was retained by the organization to defray expenses.

Bea Ginsburg was beside herself. "I guess I was wrong about the possibilities of starting a local charity by yourself. You're amazing!" she said, shaking her head in disbelief.

She wasn't the only one who was stunned. I quickly reached out to my Cornerstone sisters, told them about the remarkable experience, and thanked each of them for believing in me. Together, our faith in the project had made it happen. I also called upon them to help me make out the deposit slips and enter the names and addresses into the computer, so we could start building a mailing list. A few of my friends had good computer skills, but no one had time to spare, so I stayed up late at night and worked right through the weekends to get everything entered and deposited, along with mailing out the letters of thanks.

I rounded the check up to twenty-thousand dollars out of my own pocket and, with a sense of great pride, mailed it to the attorney who was working on behalf of the Deida family—grateful for everyone's generosity.

I wished my mother could have shared in the joy of these experiences, but that was not meant to be.

OVER THE COURSE OF THE NEXT FEW MONTHS, doctors performed a miracle for Angel. During a very delicate procedure, the broken bones in his neck were replaced with a titanium hinge and bones from a cadaver. After many months in rehab, Angel regained his ability to walk and to speak. I believe he was given a second chance at life due to his extraordinary display of heroism.

In my quest to keep the momentum going, I reached out to local churches, making them aware of our newly formed organization designed to help people like Angel.

I never imagined that, two weeks later, I would get a call from

Monsignor Arnholz of St. John's Catholic Church in Bergenfield, to tell me about a Filipino family in his parish.

"Mrs. Albanese," he said, "Bong Manansala is a forty-eight-year-old man who fell while playing basketball with his friends. He fractured his skull. Doctors are offering his family no hope for his recovery and recommended they pull the plug on his life support, allowing him to die with dignity."

His wife, Edwina, felt she couldn't do that. "Bong and I never discussed what to do in an unthinkable situation like this," she told me, "but since he survived the surgery that removed half of his skull bone, I must give him every chance to survive. We were childhood sweethearts and I can't bear the thought of living without him."

At first she didn't know what kind of help she needed, but soon afterwards, when she was unexpectedly fired from her job, she needed financial assistance. Although their circumstances were dire, the firing afforded her time to spend with her husband as he remained in a comatose state for the next *eighteen months*.

A month following that call, on a bright sunny afternoon, a few volunteers and I set up a booth at the Tenafly Street Fair. There we raised a few dollars to help this family and to make more people aware of Giants. I asked Edwina if she could come to the fair, so I could present her with a check for one-thousand dollars. There were balloons and kiddy rides. Live music filled the air, and there were also food and jewelry vendors and lots of excitement. When I met her there for the first time, she was fragile and stressed. We hugged, and she said, "I'm so grateful for your assistance—you don't even know me."

"Yes, but we do know of your husband's accident, and I'm so sorry for your pain."

Considering the severity of their circumstances, I felt the thousand dollars was so insignificant. Over time, I had the good fortune of spending many hours with this extraordinary woman as we got to know each other.

I didn't know what else to do to help, but the case was not going away anytime soon. I began reaching out to the Filipino community through their cultural newspapers, TV, and radio stations, telling the tragic story and asking if they could do a feature article requesting donations for the family.

They said that they would and, much to my amazement, within weeks they had pulled a fundraiser together to help them. They handed me checks totaling twelve-thousand-two-hundred-eighty-five dollars, to be given to the Manansala family. We continued to do what we could to help Bong and Edwina through that difficult and emotional time.

After the initial eighteen months, at Edwina's insistence, Bong's skull bone was finally replaced, although many doctors believed there was still no hope for his recovery. Within three months, however, her prayers were answered—*Bong awoke from his coma calling his wife's name.*

He had spent three long, painful years in the hospital. After fourteen brain surgeries, it was determined that *he was now also blind.* Miraculously, the doctors performed yet another surgery that restored his sight.

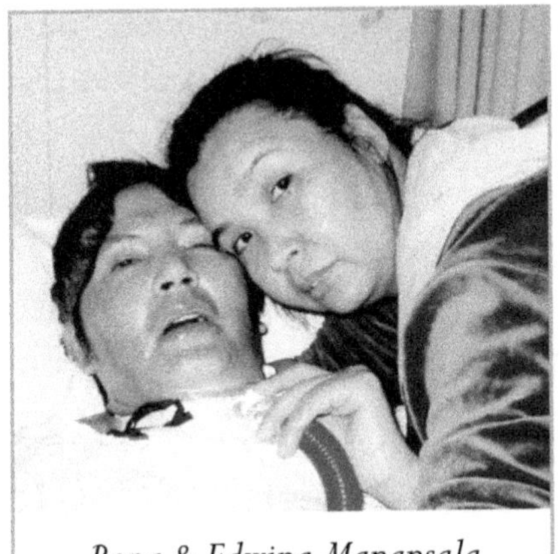

Bong & Edwina Manansala

Finally he was able to go home, still in very serious condition. Edwina, as his sole caregiver, not only struggled to care for him, but also had to take care of the medical and household bills, as well as their two children who were fifteen and twenty at the time. They were overwhelmed by what had happened to their father, and they had great difficulty coping.

During the course of trying to be there for Edwina whenever she needed someone to reach out to, she wondered why I cared about them; we had been strangers ‘til we met. Having spent a great deal of time together, I had the opportunity to share my life story with her. I think I may have needed her even more than she needed me. We cried often and broke bread together on many evenings, as Edwina coped with the tragedy.

I had purchased a special mattress for Edwina so she could lie in the hospital bed with Bong to comfort him. I walked alongside this family for eight long years, trying to help in any way I could.

We were in the process of trying to help refinance their mortgage to reduce their monthly payments—astonishingly, even under those circumstances, Edwina still had excellent credit—when a major storm was about to hit our area late in February 2010. The skies looked fierce, the power went out, and hundreds of sturdy-looking, elegant old trees were toppled, causing extensive damage throughout the county. You could smell burning rubber permeating the air from the transformer explosions.

Edwina had to get the February payment to the mortgage company by the end of the month. Not remembering that February is a short month, she thought she had until that Monday, but, February 28 fell on a Sunday that year, making her final option to get the payment in on time Friday, the 26th.

The weather was bitterly cold, and Bong, in his fragile state, had contracted pneumonia and was rushed to the hospital again. That same afternoon, Edwina’s brother George, after a long battle with sinus cancer, collapsed on her living room floor and died. In the extraordinary pain of her loss, she lost track of time and didn’t get to the bank that Friday, but she went early on Monday, before George’s wake.

She was too late, though, and her refinance was denied. I prayed with every ounce of my being, and tried with everything I had, but I could not convince the mortgage company to revisit this case. Much to our dismay, we both recognized that the refinance was not part of God's plan.

Edwina then decided to take Bong back to the Philippines, where she knew he could get more physical therapy at a much cheaper rate, since their insurance for therapy had run out here. Once that decision was made, I helped arrange to have their flight status upgraded, so Bong would be able to lie completely flat in business class for the very long flight back to Manila. Now and again I hear from Edwina, and although Bong's health has regressed, she is still happy that he's alive and able to be with her. I had hoped that Bong would one day walk again and return to the States, and become a guest of honor at one of our fundraisers.

Today, Edwina and I share a bond of sisterhood that cannot be broken. The emotional pull of walking alongside this family, who has suffered such a debilitating trauma, is the reason I exist.

"What I know for sure is that what you give comes back to you."
...Oprah Winfrey

30

THE AGONY OF DEFEAT

IT WAS BECOMING CLEAR TO ME that Giants of Generosity was not my new project, but *God's* project at work through me.

I knew I was onto something as these devastating cases kept presenting themselves. Immediately, I went back to the drawing board to figure out a way to bring in some money.

I called the Clinton Inn to see if they would consider donating part of their ballroom for a Giants of Generosity fundraiser, and they graciously agreed. In my research I came across an article suggesting that, when you want to introduce your new organization, do it with a bang—make a big splash! So I called the local newspaper to see how much a full-page ad would cost, and almost swallowed my teeth when I heard nine-hundred dollars. At that very difficult stage of my life nine-hundred was more than a splash, it was a tsunami. Thank God for plastic money.

Okay, so I had the Inn confirmed, and I could do a swan dive into the sea of the unknown. The Inn being my home turf, I felt confident, but what was the fundraiser going to be about? And who could I get to help me? My creative juices were flowing, and I was excited when I came across a psychic who was willing to donate an evening to do an audience reading. I had never been to a psychic before but was intrigued by the concept, knowing full well that it might not pique everyone's curiosity as it had mine.

With the entertainment in place, I thought about the graphics and put a flyer together. I picked a price for the event, called everyone I knew, especially those who had attended the first meeting I had on that very blustery winter's eve, to invite them to come to our first fundraiser.

It was June 3, 2007, when I officially launched Giants of Generosity with what I thought was a *big splash*. I designed the full-page color ad for the newspaper (putting the nine-hundred bucks on my credit card), and we were on our way. It was exhilarating.

I would make a speech thanking everyone for coming and discuss my plans to help people in distress here in our own hometowns. Beth, the psychic, had a few friends donate their musical talent, and I invited Joanne Chasmar's uncle as our special guest speaker. I thought his witness would help validate our mission and our vision. We had refreshments and were very organized; however, the night didn't go quite as planned.

As I arrived, all dressed up and feeling good, the singer, a Frank Sinatra impersonator, met me at the door and said, "Did you hear that Beth's son had an emergency appendectomy this morning?"

"No, I hadn't! Now what do I do?"

I envisioned greeting the guests at the door and giving them their money back. What a disappointing way to launch my new organization! I was heartsick. Then a phone call came—it was Beth, and she assured me that she would be there and the show would go on. I was relieved but still shaken.

Beth's daughter, who is a life coach, was also going to give a short presentation, and fortunately she also showed up.

As the evening progressed, however, things only got worse. My spirits were further shattered when my guest of honor, Joanne's uncle, didn't arrive until the event was almost over. I guess he didn't realize he was going to be the star of the show. He had a long way to drive and had been stuck in traffic.

The music and entertainment were good, but then, just before Beth was to go on to do her psychic audience readings, I introduced her daughter. She got up and started off with some interesting information about coping with life's difficulties…before she dropped a bomb!

I'm still hoping she didn't realize what she was saying when she said, "Well, I think we can all agree that all men *suck!*"

What the hell was she thinking? I looked for a crack in the floor to crawl into. I had hoped she didn't mean it and was only caught up in the moment, but she certainly knocked out whatever wind I had left in my sails. Of the forty-five or fifty people there, at least *half* were men, including her own husband.

I had lost my sense of balance and could hardly remember what I was going to say as I approached the podium. Joanne's uncle was still not there. I felt like a failure and wanted to abandon this whole charity thing.

I approached the mic again to introduce Beth. I have a vague recollection of her walking through the audience performing her psychic readings for the many who were there, but honestly, I barely remember what happened next. I was crushed! Could she read *my* mind?

Then, as we awarded the tricky tray items to the winners,

Joanne's uncle finally arrived. I thought, better late than never, but I wasn't even sure of that; for me, everything was out of sync. I asked him to say a few words about what had happened to Joanne and how she was doing, as well as what Giants had been able to do for her.

As I thanked everyone for coming, the affair concluded.

All the volunteers got up, saying, "Thanks Jane, we had a great time," and just left—leaving me alone to clean up and collect all the brochures, the cash boxes, the credit card slips, and the rest of the paraphernalia from the tricky tray raffle. With my feet aching and my heart broken, I went home and wept. It had been disastrous, even with all of the preparation—so much for a *big splash!*

I was new to fundraising, so I tried to think positive, but I was afraid to count the proceeds for fear of more disappointment. In the coming days, as I regained my composure and had the time to review the evening, I discovered, much to my amazement, that even with a few foibles and *the bomb*, which hopefully our guests hadn't been too offended by, we had raised close to three-thousand-five-hundred dollars that night.

That's when I knew for sure that God is able to rebuke the wind and the waves, and there was a great calm that came over me. We now had a small financial base from which to draw upon, and we could move forward.

We were just getting started, and there was so much still to be done.

31

CELEBRATING OUR FIRST ANNIVERSARY

THE TIMING OF OUR FIRST ANNIVERSARY as a local charity coincided with the debut of Oprah Winfrey's "Big Give" reality TV show. She called on everyone in the country to gather friends and family around the TV to raise funds to help others. Since she had been the inspiration for Giants of Generosity, it seemed appropriate for us to celebrate our anniversary with a cocktail party at the Clinton Inn, where there were two giant TV screens, so we could watch Oprah's debut show.

I had a lot to do to coordinate the venue with the timing of the TV broadcast; design the invitations, print and mail them; order an anniversary cake, see if the bakery would donate it; order the colored tablecloths, pick up the "Congratulations" balloons; set up a microphone; and so on. Was I missing anything? I knew I had to get people excited about coming to the event. Most of the men there probably hadn't even heard of Oprah's plea, but their wives dragged them out anyway.

I envisioned gathering around the giant screens, getting rowdy, and motivating our guests to *Give Big*.

And in spite of our being new at this, they did!

Caught up in the moment, as I spoke of the people we had already helped, there was a young woman in the audience who asked, "Could you use an old car to give to someone? I just got a new SUV a few months ago, and my old clunker is just sitting in the driveway collecting dust. It has about sixty-seven thousand miles on it and the seats are a little worn, but it does run well. I was thinking of donating it to someone, but hadn't gotten around to it yet. It probably needs tires," she said.

Astonished by her gesture, I said, "Sure, we'd be happy to take it off your hands. And you'll get a tax credit for the donation. Thanks so much!"

Of course, I did not know how to do that, but as I said early on, I was sure I could figure it out.

Our evening with Oprah was lots of fun. I believe everyone enjoyed themselves, even the men. It was only our second event in our inaugural year, and it was a wonderful experience and a great success. We had some more cash to help people in need. I remember feeling a sense of pride as I closed my eyes in sleep that night.

A few months earlier as I was reaching out to all of our local churches, there was one in particular, the Community Baptist Church of Englewood, that stuck out in my mind. On speaking with one of their deacons to describe my plans for raising money to help people here locally, they had responded with a five-hundred dollar check.

Before calling the deacon again about the car, I spoke with a man from the Lions Club in town, to see if anyone there knew what needed to be done to accept the donated car, and what the protocol was. He knew exactly what I needed to do with the title transfer and how we would determine the value of the car, as well as how much the tax credit would be for the donor. I find that when you reach out for help, people are generous with their time and information, and I was very appreciative.

As long as the Community Baptist Church had been so kind to Giants in their giving, that would be the first place I would start to look for someone in need of a car—beat-up old clunker that it was. I found a local service station that checked it out, replaced the battery, and donated four slightly used tires—and we were in business. *Just get the title and find a recipient* was all I could think about, and *oh, yeah*, let's see if we could get a local newspaper to cover the giving of the car. How exciting would that be?

When I got the deacon on the phone, I said, "Deacon Stannard, you've been so kind to us, I was wondering if you had anyone in your congregation who was in need of a donated car?"

"A donated car?" he said. *"You've got to be kidding!"*

I told him about our Oprah event, and how a young woman had donated her old car. "We've checked it out and, although it squeaks a bit—well, actually more than a bit—it runs quite well."

He didn't hesitate: There was a single mom in his church with three teenagers who had been commuting to work and to school by bus. In fact, the mother had to take three buses to get to her job.

The prospect was thrilling.

After speaking with her, the deacon gave me Estelle Butts' phone number. Not sure what her response would be, considering she knew nothing about Giants of Generosity or me, I treaded lightly, inquiring if she would be interested in taking a look at the car.

Her response was, "Why would you do something like that?

Why would you give us a car? We can't afford one."

I assured her that there were no strings attached, and the gift was coming from the heart of all who had been in attendance at our fundraiser. In fact, Michelle, the former owner of the car, wanted to be there as we transferred the title to Estelle and her family.

That was an exciting day. We had a huge red bow donated, and we taped it to the roof as I drove the squeaky old clunker to Estelle's apartment. A caravan of volunteers and spectators was in tow, and the camera crew from the local paper met us there.

All my life I had watched the *Reader's Digest* Prize Patrol. They would surprise unsuspecting winners on TV each year as they snuck up to someone's door and rang the bell to say, "Surprise! You've just won a million dollars!" I never really believed that was true but secretly wished I could find a job like that. And there I was—it was like a million dollars to the Butts family.

For me, it was a dream come true. I nodded, recognizing that Giants of Generosity *had arrived!*

These days, on television, we have home makeover shows, charity apprentice and cooking shows, and all kinds of ordinary people doing extraordinary things to raise money or donate their talents to help others. *It is contagious!*

Recently numerous natural disasters have devastated whole sectors of the globe, and as a caring people we have jumped in to help those in dire need. We do it because it is our obligation. We do it because it feels so good. Celebrities and billionaires who have been greatly blessed, do it in big ways (often for tax write-offs), but each of us, like whoever it was who sent us that first five dollar bill with no note for Angel, does it in equal measure out of the kindness of his or her heart.

Seeking to fill my own heart with goodness after my personal trials, that big red bow had more significance than you can imagine.

Why does the world fight? Seems to me, we're missing out on the beauty, joy, and true meaning of love and life. Can you imagine a world where each culture and nationality looked to be kind to others, a world devoid of jealousy and hatred? Yes, I've always been a dreamer, and maybe even a bit Pollyannaish, but think about it: Shouldn't kindness be the force that drives us?

At first I couldn't find Estelle's apartment, but then there it was. We were all trying to be quiet as I rang the bell; I rang it twice, then I finally heard footsteps. The door creaked open just enough for me to say, "Hi, Estelle? I'm Jane Albanese."

She knew we were coming, but she didn't know that "we" meant thirty of us. She was very shy and, I'm sure, a little embarrassed. She called her kids, and they all came out of the house one by one, looking perplexed. With the paparazzi snapping shots, Michelle, former owner of the clunker, handed Estelle the keys. I shook hands with the teenagers and said "Go on, get in your car!"

At first they didn't say a word and politely obeyed. Then the youngest said, "Excuse me, Miss Jane, I'll be seventeen in two weeks and I never thought I'd get a chance to drive. Thank you so much."

The older boy said, "Why would you do something like this?"

"We have a car," I said, "and you don't."

Along with a check to pay for the first year's insurance, we wished the Butts family good luck and much happiness in the future. I know it was meaningful for them, but it was the reality of actually seeing the gratitude in their eyes that meant the most to me and to all of the volunteers. I was so thankful for that happy opportunity. We had made a significant difference in that family's life.

A few days later, I got a call from a friend, who asked whether I had heard that Janet, a mutual friend, had breast cancer and no health insurance. I hadn't, and although we didn't have much money in our general account, we were able to pay one-thousand dollars toward a medical bill for her.

She wrote me this note:

> *Dear Jane,*
>
> *You leave me speechless. Your surprise gift came just as my medical bills are piling up and the collection agencies are calling at all hours.*
>
> *As you know, I am a single mother of two children. Prior to our divorce we were covered by my husbands insurance, but circumstances leave you with choices and insurance was not a priority.*
>
> *Believing that I was young and healthy I went back to work at a job that didn't offer insurance, but gave me the hours I needed to still take care of my kids.*
>
> *Then I discovered the lump. I'm only 48, how could it be cancer? Clearly I have made some wrong choices.*
>
> *Now that I've had the surgery and I'm going through radiation, I must say that everyone involved in my treatment has been wonderful, and somehow we'll get through this. Your gift has given me hope, and I thank you so much.*
>
> *... Janet*

ANOTHER PHONE CALL CAME from a woman who had made a donation for Angel, the Good Samaritan, a year earlier. She asked if we could help her seventy-six-year-old sister, who had a life-threatening oral infection. She needed thirteen-thousand dollars to pay for dental bills, and was living on her Social Security alone. I thanked the donor for remembering us and was delighted that we were able to help her sister with a small check, until we could raise some more money. She was extremely grateful, and when we did another fundraiser we were able to help her with a little more.

These stories are similar to what the Oprah recipients had done on her "Big Give" TV show. I was grateful to be able to help others as they had done. It was becoming crystal clear to me that this must be my calling.

WORD WAS SPREADING ABOUT THE GREAT WORK Giants of Generosity was performing, and soon the calls for help began to pour in. Over the course of the first three years of our existence, I built out the board of directors. I called on members of the local Rotary Clubs, Knights of Columbus, and church groups, and I spoke with everyone I had come in contact with about my plans. I was looking to find like-minded people who would consider joining our board.

We were developing a reputation and a much-needed track record. The kind of help we were offering to our clients attracted several loyal volunteers who believed in our mission. They liked the fact that we were helping less fortunate people right in our own neighborhoods.

By then, my freelance jobs had slowed again, and I reached a new crossroad. I connected with Jeff Brockman, the head of a networking group and a career transition consultant whom I had met while handing out flyers for our wine-sampling fundraiser in the fall of 2009. I explained that I had started a charity and that I was also looking for a graphics job. As it turned out, Jeff was holding a group-networking meeting at a local restaurant. He invited me to join them. It was a small group of men and me.

Jeff briefly told everyone that I had started a charity called Giants of Generosity, and that he believed in what I was doing. Then we each described where we were in our job search, and the type of work that we were looking for.

As the others discussed their backgrounds, one man in particular stood out to me. I don't know if it was what he said, or his body language that had attracted me to him. He seemed frightened or distressed but trying to maintain a macho, if lighthearted manner. There was an all-too-familiar angst about him, though, telling me he was precariously close to the edge. I asked him toward the end of the meeting if he would mind staying for a few minutes.

He said that he would.

I opened the conversation with, "Are you alright?"

He looked at me suspiciously. "What do you mean?"

"Is there anything I can do to help you?"

I had never met him before but still sensed his feelings of desperation, so I said, "If I were to give you some money, would that help?"

"What do you mean give me some money? I can't take your money, and I could never repay you," he said.

"Would a thousand dollars help?"

"A thousand bucks? Why would you do that? I can't take your money. I'm an actor, and I've been out of work for over a year. I could never pay you back," he said again.

"You don't have to pay me back. It would be a gift, and maybe you could pay-it-forward and help someone else when you get back on your feet."

He was stunned, but when I asked for his name, address, and email, he gave me the first two, saying, "I don't use email because I can't afford the service. Why are you doing this?"

"This is exactly why I started Giants, and you seem to be a perfect candidate. Do you mind telling me what led you to this point?"

He thought for a moment. "If this is for real, the thousand would be like manna from heaven and would likely save my life."

We cried and hugged as he revealed some very private information with me that day about betrayal, because he said, "I feel like you really care. I *need* someone to." I could relate, because I, too, needed someone to care about me.

He went on to say, "Prior to this meeting, I told myself, if something good doesn't come out of this networking thing,

I'm just going to pull the trigger."

There was no question in my mind as to why God placed me in that man's path that day.

There but for the grace of God, go I.

32

A CHILL IN THE NIGHT

OUR HELP DOESN'T ALWAYS STOP with a financial gift. Wherever possible we reach out to members of the community for assistance with other types of needs that our recipients may have.

When the storm clouds of life brought another violent outburst, with it came another major family crisis. Eamonn Radburn, a Ridgefield Park DPW worker, was electrocuted by a downed live power line while cleaning up debris in Haworth. Severely injured, he was rushed to the hospital.

"It felt like my left foot blew off, and there was a loud pop like popping a brown paper bag," he said. "I went down on one knee. It literally felt like a big hand had folded me in half. By the time the ambulance got there, it felt as if my other side had gotten folded back over again. I was just crunched, in a fetal position, and the pain was terrible."

He had third-degree burns on the soles of his feet, pain in his left arm and leg, and muscle spasms on the left side of his body. Doctors advised him that he might never fully recover. He would need extensive physical therapy, and he would be out of work for an extended and uncertain period of time.

Through the efforts of his community, more than thirty-three-thousand dollars was raised to help pay for the materials needed to retrofit his home, making it wheelchair-accessible. I received a call from Denise, the pharmacist who gave us our very first case, asking if we could help find contractors who would be willing to donate their services to build an extension on the Radburn home. This was no easy task, given the urgency, and the poor economy as we were in the midst of a recession, and the size of the job.

I didn't know where to begin, so I just started researching builders' names in the (now very obsolete) phone book, and expanded my search by Googling "contractors."

After leaving a hundred or so agonizingly long messages on contractors' voice-mails from the Tappan Zee Bridge to Newark, I went to bed frustrated, figuring it might be a lost cause. At eight the next morning, just as I was about to get out of bed, the phone rang.

"Good morning, Jane. I'm Tim Wallace, and I'm a member of (NARI), the National Association of the Remodeling Industry. I was at a board meeting of contractors last night, and I mentioned that you had called. Seven other men at the meeting said that they'd also heard from you. So I said, we'd better take a look at what she needs."

"Oh, *thank you*, Tim! Let me explain the situation." I then did, in detail.

He said, "Let me discuss the particulars with the other board members, and I'll get back to you."

When he called later that afternoon, he simply said, "We'll do your job, and I'll act as the general contractor."

Once again I was bowled over—and grateful for my perseverance.

What a gift it was to the family, and to all those who so generously donated money to help a neighbor in need.

Tim was able to call upon his fellow NARI members to get on board. Everything from the excavation and framing, to plumbing and electrical supplies, was donated. Painters, drywallers, and roofers also pitched in, offering their services. He also had supply houses donate Anderson windows, roofing materials, plywood, a hot water boiler, and new kitchen cabinets.

They broke ground early in October 2010 and added a thirty-one-foot extension to the Radburn home, estimated value is well over one-hundred-thirty-five-thousand dollars of donated and in-kind services.

Clearly, this was another example of God working through me as a vehicle of His love. Here's how I know that for sure. Three days after Tim's call to me, I awoke in a cold sweat. I couldn't quite grasp what I was feeling, but something was telling me to *stop the job*. Almost sick to my stomach, I called Tim.

"Please put everything on hold," I said. "I've had a very unsettling nightmare, and I woke up in a cold sweat. Something must be terribly wrong."

We had never met in person, and I was concerned about what Tim might think, but I asked him to give me a few days, and he agreed and asked to be kept in the loop.

That afternoon I went to see Eamonn to determine if there was something about his story at which I needed to take a closer look. We sat in his living room; I couldn't put my finger on anything that appeared to be out of the ordinary. I left there still feeling uncomfortable, though, and even more unsure of the meaning of the shakes I had from the dream. This certainly was a bigger case than Giants of Generosity had ever handled before, so I thought maybe I was just having cold feet.

That evening I got a call from Eamonn. He said, "Jane, you're not going to believe this. About an hour after you left, a quick and powerful storm blew into the area, and our big old maple tree in the backyard was struck by lightning and fell, just missing the house by about six inches."

I soon understood my chills and fever. There could be no other explanation but a warning from God. He was trying to alert me that a storm was coming. The tree, which looked perfectly healthy, had fallen on the exact area where the men were going to begin their excavation. I immediately called Tim to explain, and he drove right over to the house. He couldn't believe his eyes.

Here's a photo of Tim standing among the branches of the fallen tree. He looks about two feet tall with the monstrous old maple towering over him.

Before construction could resume, the tree needed to be cut up and hauled away. Another extraordinary gift from Tim and his contractors. A few days later, excavation would begin and the new extension added.

To complicate the problems the Radburns were already facing, they had three daughters, the youngest of whom had recently been diagnosed with a rare childhood neurological disease. They were very appreciative on many levels of the resources Giants of Generosity was able to provide to assist their family.

The donated plans had been drawn up, and construction finally got under way. They were to receive a new ground-floor bedroom and bathroom, plus a new laundry room. As work began connecting the new with the old, the kitchen ceiling unexpectedly fell onto the floor below, creating a mess in the older part of the home. Tim checked out the bathroom on the second floor, and he could see that the tub must have been leaking for quite some time causing the floor below it to collapse. Fortunately, no one had been injured there either.

Once again, his men stepped up, and renovated the upstairs bathroom. They went on to completely remodel the kitchen that had been damaged by the ceiling collapse. With contractors and suppliers from all over the county now participating, the entire kitchen was replaced, featuring all-new, donated top-of-the-line appliances to help the family.

Upon completion, all who participated were delighted and gratified by the opportunity to pitch in. We held a barbecue and ribbon-cutting ceremony at the house. The local papers covered the story. I still couldn't believe the uncanny stroke of luck that my cold sweat and my perseverance had provided.

33

THE MIDAS TOUCH

EVERYTHING'S HAPPENING SO QUICKLY, I thought, and we were getting some great newspaper coverage. Like a flower, Giants of Generosity was coming into full bloom. Among some of the slogans we came up with to describe our mission were: Join us in the joy of giving; We provide our recipients with financial aid, community resource referrals, moral support, and hope for the future; We are ordinary people dedicated to the betterment of other people's lives—a simple yet powerful concept.

Although our slogans may have changed over the years, our goal of helping others, and my passion for the blessing of being called to do this work, have remained steadfast. Every crisis solved has given me a great sense of accomplishment.

With each new case came a set of new challenging circumstances. Brain tumors have become an all-too-common diagnosis.

It's public knowledge that Beau Biden, former Vice President Biden's son, along with Senators Ted Kennedy and John McCain have died from this dreaded disease.

Giants of Generosity had been called upon to help in three cases of brain tumors. Two were cancerous and both of those patients lost their battles. The third was a young girl whose tumors were not malignant, and fortunately she has recovered nicely.

We began to receive calls for help from other organizations like the Community Resource Council of Hackensack, the United Water Foundation (now Suez) of Haworth, and the Center for Food Action. They each had clients who had needs that they themselves could not fill, so they reached out to Giants.

I had been gifted with a God-given knack for getting things done, and they'd heard that I seemed to have the Midas touch. Wherever possible, we were able to help their clients in addition to the ones that were coming our way directly through word of mouth. In return, these organizations and others would help the clients that we were unable to assist. Hundreds of families needed help with utility bills, past due rent payments or eviction notices, as well as medical bills.

One thing I know for sure is that we had the ability to quickly respond, unlike many other charities, easing the burdens of those who are facing desperate times.

As each new situation presented itself, the board and I would immediately discuss the circumstances and vet the client's story by validating their sources of income and reaching out to their doctors, landlords, utility companies, or social workers to verify the details. Then, if funds were available, a check would be cut and mailed directly to the doctor or service provider. No red tape *here!*

At ten one evening I got a call from a woman who was staying at the Clinton Inn. She introduced herself and said that she had seen my photo in *201 Magazine*, standing next to a personal friend of hers. She'd called the friend to ask how to get in touch with me.

Earlier that day, her home in Tenafly had burned to the ground and she and her family had lost almost everything. They'd run out with just the clothes on their backs. The Red Cross had put them up, but they needed clothes, shampoo, toothbrushes, deodorant, shaving cream, and so much more, and she wondered if we could help in some way.

This was a case that didn't need too much verifying and we had just done a fundraiser, so I told her I would meet her in the lobby of the Inn in fifteen minutes. She was stunned, but I was able to give her a check for five-hundred dollars to help them begin to rebuild their lives. She told me that even her family would not come to their rescue, an all-too-familiar tune. I was glad that we could help.

Being a hands-on, grassroots charity had its advantages as well as its disadvantages. I was becoming more visible in the community, and people could actually speak with me, the organization's founder, on the phone when they called, unlike most well-known national charities. They either felt reassured that their money would be handled properly, or, as I had heard through the grapevine, some doubted my "motives."

I had a friend tell me that her mother had said, "Why would you give money to Jane? She's probably paying her mortgage with it. Another person said, "You drive a nice car, why should we support you?"

I was appalled.

Apparently, they didn't understand that we do incur actual operating expenses like postage, printing, phone and Internet charges, and so forth. We've never paid rent or hired anyone to help me carry the load, and most of the funds we raised went directly to help our clients.

I was keenly aware that the IRS closely governs all 501(c)3s, and I certainly didn't want any problems with them. So for the first four years or so, my work with Giants of Generosity was totally on a volunteer basis. Not a single dollar found its way into my pocket.

I had researched every aspect of the information I could find on how to run a charity. I studied the regulations and frequently called the IRS to ask questions and confirm my understanding of the rules. There was no way that I would mishandle donations for fear of the consequences.

As I continued to convey what it was that we were attempting to do, I learned how to apply for grants from local corporations and family foundations, to help us financially in assisting our clients.

Eventually, as we organized more fundraisers and were able to acquire sponsorships, our board determined that it was time to hire an executive director. It was only logical to hire *me* (at a very modest salary), since I was the brains behind the operation and the first point of contact, running the organization from my living room.

I CONTINUED TO DEVOTE MY ENTIRE LIFE to Giants and to our clients, at the sacrifice of my personal life. I was still reeling from the loss of my family and needed the distraction as well as the sense of gratification I got from healing other people's wounds. I was also seeking love and acceptance from those we were able to help.

There had still been no contact with my family, or with Dom's, yet I hoped that they had heard of the good works that we were doing. I believe that Giants in its own way exonerates me, proving that, in caring for others as I do, I am not the monster that they have tried to portray.

HERE ARE SOME OF THE MORE MEMORABLE accounts of the many people we have helped.

Luis Torres called about his son Liam, age 7, who suffers from a severe case of cerebral palsy. As the boy was growing, Luis had tried raising funds to purchase a special electrical bed for Liam. It took almost three years for him to raise three-thousand dollars toward a nearly ten-thousand dollar KayserBetten bed. When I heard of the need, I contacted the bed company, explained the situation, and asked if they could help in some way by accepting just the three-thousand. Much to my surprise, the woman on the other end of the phone said, "That's an amazing story, and we'd like to become part of the solution. Yes, we'll accept the three-thousand and we'd like to donate the balance. If it would be convenient, we can deliver the new bed the day after tomorrow."

My spirit was filled to overflowing, and I couldn't wait to give Luis the great news. When I met Liam for the first time, my heart broke, and I had great difficulty holding back the tears. This sweet young boy was unable to speak and had to be on oxygen 24/7. He was wheelchair-bound, and his mom and dad had to carry him from room to room. I can't begin to comprehend the extraordinary love Luis and his wife have for their son.

The gift of the bed helps with Liam's care. He can be bathed in it as it raises and lowers, making it more comfortable for them all. The family is extremely grateful for the assistance. I am equally grateful, knowing that I have been chosen to help make this kind of gift possible.

I RECEIVED ANOTHER CALL, this time from Brian Carr, a board member, who said, "Jane, one of my co-workers, Andy Patel, was in a serious accident while on vacation. The snowmobile he was driving unexpectedly lunged forward, hitting a solid wall at great speed, and he suffered a traumatic brain injury. He was transported to a trauma center in Bangor, Maine, and has been in a coma for two months. It was similar to the accident that took the life of Sonny Bono.

"Andy has three teenage children, and he lost his wife last year. He'll be returning home this week, and his mother is flying in from India to care for him. Is there anything we can do to help?"

"Brian," I said, "can you find out what their most pressing needs are? This type of ongoing assistance might be more than we can handle, but let's see what we can do."

Within days of Andy's return home, I went with Brian and Caryn Starr-Gates, our board chair, to visit Andy. It was so sad to see this once-vibrant man unable to speak or make eye contact. We had the pleasure of meeting his mother, who was overwhelmed by our offer to do what we could. We told them we would help with some of his medical bills.

I felt that our gifts were insignificant, just a drop in the bucket given the severity of his accident. Andy has a very long road to recovery, but we hope that our financial aid eases the pain of the many complications that he has still to face.

A friend from Our Lady of Mt. Carmel Church decided to give me a call.

"Jane," she said, "I think you've heard of my son Patrick's accident. He was hit head-on at about sixty miles an hour on Route 287 when he was coming home from work.

"The young driver entered the highway via an off-ramp and was driving the wrong way on the divided highway. Before Patrick realized that this man was heading right for him, they collided driver-to-driver. Patrick's pelvis has been crushed, and his legs and ankles are severely broken. The other driver was killed. Soon afterwards, Patrick lost his job and his medical coverage. I've been trying to help him financially, but I'm running out of money myself," she explained.

I suggested, "Let's meet and put some photos and the story together, and see what we can do."

When we sent out the information to Patrick's family and friends, as well as to our church members, and everyone saw the gruesome pictures of the crash, it drove the story home. Money began to pour in to help pay for the many surgeries Patrick needed to rebuild his body. We were able to pay for his Cobra insurance until he was released from the hospital fifteen months later.

The following year we held a German Festival fundraiser at the Greek Orthodox Church in Tenafly, and Patrick was able to walk into the event on crutches to the rousing applause of the crowd.

34

HER NAME WAS SANDY

WHILE ENJOYING THE SUNSHINE on vacation in Florida, we were unexpectedly advised to prepare for the arrival of a major hurricane. Watching her path, I was concerned. I felt fortunate, though, when she had skirted past the East coast of Florida. She was heading right up the coastline, with her target set on New Jersey. There was no way anyone could have fathomed the damage she would leave in her wake.

Superstorm Sandy made landfall on October 29, 2012, striking near Atlantic City, with sustained winds of 80 miles per hour. The city's famous boardwalk was ripped apart, the streets flooded, and trees and power lines knocked down. The full moon made high tides higher than usual amplifying Sandy's storm surge. All along the Jersey shore and the southern coast of Long Island and much of New York City, people were stranded in their homes. One massive fire consumed a whole neighborhood in Queens, destroying more than eighty buildings.

Thousands of structures up and down the East Coast suffered severe damage, with some completely destroyed by the wind, rain, and storm surge. Nature in all its fury caused many people to lose their lives, and millions of others lost their livelihoods. It was the second-costliest hurricane on record in the United States up to that time.

Wall Street went dark. Hospital patients and tourists scrambled for safety. Skyscrapers in midtown Manhattan swayed and creaked in the wind. Seawater surged over the seawalls of Lower Manhattan streets, flooding them unlike anything in recorded history. The water filled subway tunnels and drowned out stations and electrical systems.

Nearly five million people in fifteen states were without electricity. Gas stations were closed. Airlines canceled thousands of flights around the world coming in or out of the Eastern hubs.

As soon as the airports reopened, I returned home.

The first call I received was from Bob Kutik, a former board member. He said, "Jane, my nephew Sean owns several restaurants and bars in New York City and Hoboken, and they have all been affected by the hurricane. Sean's partner, Michael Sinensky, lost his family's home in the storm. The Red Cross hasn't even gotten there yet, so Michael has set up a command post. They're out buying generators, wet vacs, mops, masks, shovels, and whatever else they can get their hands on to begin helping with the clean-up. They also have large donation pretzel jars set up in as many of their restaurants as are still open. They need a 501(c)3 to manage the funds for them. Will you consider doing that?"

Without hesitation, I said, "Yes, of course. Where can I meet with Sean or Michael?"

He gave me an address near Rockaway Beach, on the Long

Island coast, I immediately enlisted board member, Brian Carr, and we headed out to see the destruction for ourselves.

We were unprepared for what we came upon. The skies were ominous, but sunlight began to lick the blackened, angry clouds, offering rays of hope.

Right in the midst of the chaotic scene stood a two-story house that had been condemned, and there on the rickety porch stood three young men. As we approached, I said, "Hi, guys, I'm looking for Michael Sinensky."

The slender, dark-haired one said, "I'm Michael."

"Hey, I'm Jane Albanese from Giants of Generosity. *Wow, what a mess!"*

"You haven't seen anything yet," he said.

He introduced us to the other men and said, "Thanks for coming out so quickly. Let me give you a full tour of the area."

As we climbed into his Jeep, he said, "Can you imagine how long it would take me to set up a 501(c)3?"

"Yes, I can."

With a jolt, he looked at me and said, "Do you mean to tell me that *you are* Giants of Generosity?"

"That's right. I started Giants from scratch five years ago."

"That's impressive. Thanks again for helping us out. Let's have our lawyers get together and work out the details."

He drove us around the debris fields, and as we passed burned-out buildings one after the other, he drove onto the beach.

He explained, "The Atlantic Ocean met with Jamaica Bay, and the seawater completely swamped the peninsula with about twelve feet of water, coming up to the second floor of all of the structures in its path. The homes that partially remain along the beach had their first floors completely wiped away, and all that was left standing were second and third floors that cantilevered over thin air, with furniture, pianos, and fireplaces hanging off their edges."

The scene left us speechless. Other homes had shifted off of their foundations and were stacked up onto one another. People looked dazed as they wandered around the area, trying to comprehend what had happened. Some tried gathering whatever personal belongings they could that had remained of what used to be their homes; others simply stood there in tears and disbelief. We took many pictures, but they didn't nearly reflect the extent of the destruction that we had witnessed.

Still in a bit of shock, Michael and I hugged as we parted, and we knew that we would be in this together for the long haul.

No one knew at the time how complex our involvement would be, though. The infrastructure had been so severely damaged that everything appeared to be out of control.

Michael and his band of men worked tirelessly day and night to get a handle on what had to be done, and that condemned house indeed became the command post for the entire area. By word of mouth, he and his friends created a database of the names of all of the homeowners and their insurance company information, which then became the bible of necessary information needed to begin the rebirth of the Rockaways. The government, the Red Cross, the Robin Hood Foundation, and the St. Bernard Project, as well as many other organizations involved in the clean-up operation, all relied upon the information that had been gathered, organized, and computerized by the "Friends of Rockaway" team of volunteers.

Michael explained, "We have to raise money and rebuild. This is my neighborhood, where I have so many fond memories, and I'll do whatever I can to help. I want to hire unemployed contractors and retired military personnel to help with the rebuilding efforts. Hopefully a catastrophe of this magnitude happens only once in a lifetime."

"Mike, Giants of Generosity is committed to helping the victims of this storm in any way that we can. We'll act as fiscal sponsors for Friends of Rockaway. Under the circumstances, and as a courtesy to you, we'll reduce our customary administrative rate by more than half, to six percent, in order to expedite the receipt of funds. I think a separate Giants/Hurricane Sandy Relief Fund checking account should be opened in a local bank, with a branch that is convenient for you over here. That way you can make direct deposits."

"That sounds great. Do you have an accountant who can help?"

"Yes. I'll reach out to her as soon as I get back. What else do you think we'll need?"

"I guess we'll need some kind of insurance coverage. I'll check with my team and get back with you about that," he said.

Upon returning to the comfort of my home, I immediately contacted our attorney, who reached out to Michael's attorney, and within a week we had a client service agreement drawn up between Friends of Rockaway and Giants of Generosity.

My next call was to our board's treasurer, who was a CPA. As I presented the sketchy details of what Brian and I had witnessed and what we needed to do to help with the rebuilding efforts, she had many questions and concerns.

"How do we know who these workers are, and whether they are qualified? We'll need to get the names and contact information of anyone being hired, along with their Social Security numbers and phone numbers," she said. "We'll have to set up an account with Paychex."

Everything was happening very quickly, and there was no time to mess things up. Hundreds of workers had to be hired, and they needed to be insured. That, then, also became our responsibility. I contacted the Johl & Company Insurance Agency and told them the story. John Johl had been one of our founding board members. He and I have become good friends. Whenever I sought guidance, even after he retired and moved to Connecticut, I knew I could call upon him for sage advice and a good laugh.

I called Karen at the Johl agency.

"Karen, I need your help," I said. "Here's what's going on. Michael will be interviewing and hiring workers, and Giants will be managing all of the funds, at least initially. We'll need to be sure we have worker's comp and general liability insurance for everyone who sets foot into one of the damaged structures. God forbid someone should get hurt on the job. What if they were to take down the wrong wall or get sick from the mold that was quickly forming? Where do we begin?"

"We'll have to contact our different insurance carriers in New York, to see who will write the policies," Karen remarked. "Due to the chaos and size of the devastation, this could take some time."

"Can you get right on it, please?" I asked. "Time is not something that we have a lot of. So many people have lost their homes."

As Karen reached out to the different carriers, she was met with a great deal of resistance. The entire area was unstable. What we were asking for seemed to be an impossibility given that we weren't working with one construction company, but rather hundreds of men and women who needed the work, having lost their jobs and their homes because of the storm.

Weeks passed. Michael was completing the interviews, and he was understandably growing impatient, because without the insurance, the work could not begin.

"Jane, what's going on?" he asked. What's taking so long?"

"Michael, no one wants to take this on. They're afraid of the possible consequences, since the main substructures and everything else there is so volatile. They want to know who the general contractor will be."

"I have someone in mind," he said. "I'll get back to you."

Another week passed, and we were approaching a long weekend. On Friday morning, I sat watching TV, frustration burning under my collar, when I had a thought. I called Karen. It felt like our case was being put on the back burner, and I had to set a fire under her.

"Hi, Karen. Did you watch TV this morning with your cup of coffee?"

"Yes, I did," she replied.

"Karen, we have hundreds of families that don't even have a roof over their heads, and they're living in squalor. We need to get this insurance *now!*"

I couldn't blame her—she had not witnessed the destruction firsthand as Brian and I had—and so from the comfort of her home, she couldn't comprehend the urgency. She had made the calls and was waiting for the carriers to call back.

The devastation was something they had all seen on TV, but it hadn't personally touched their lives, and I'm sure it seemed as though it was in some far-off land.

The determination in my voice appeared to have ignited a spark in her. By four that same Friday afternoon, Karen advised me that we had, at last, received the coverage that we needed. Now Michael and his team of superheroes could begin the long and arduous work of cleaning up and rebuilding.

I called Michael immediately, "We got the coverage," I said, with great relief in my voice.

"Great job, Jane! Thanks! *Let's do this!*" he said.

The following day, the work began.

We forwarded the names and contact information of each

worker to our CPA and Paychex accounts were established—we were then off to the races. She did an outstanding job of keeping track of all of the details, and this coordinated effort greatly helped in re-establishing a sense of community in the Rockaways.

Astonishingly, Michael's first deposit into our account was ninety-five-thousand dollars, all from the pretzel jars he had placed in his restaurants.

I called upon Carole, a friend with bookkeeping experience, and we set up a Quickbooks program designed to keep the funds organized.

Michael's impressive talent for pulling people together to make it happen was something to be greatly admired. Even more striking to me, though, was the fact that *my little organization* had become an important part of the recovery efforts. Michael and I had great respect for each other, and together we got the job done.

He was coordinating all of the efforts in the cleanup operation, and meeting with the head organizers of all of the relief organizations. Friends of Rockaway had been assigned four hundred family homes and businesses in a certain zip code as their area to be gutted, mucked, and mold-remediated.

Giants of Generosity was designated as the depository for funds during the early relief efforts, and we were given the mandate to screen all of the requests for relief. We worked day and night in concert with Friends of Rockaway to accomplish everything that

Rockaway Beach, New York

needed to be done.

That entire year was dedicated to this process, and before all was said and done, another two-hundred-seventy-thousand dollars had been raised with the aid of grants from the Red Cross, the Robin Hood Foundation, the St. Bernard Project, the Religious Action Center of Reform Judaism, and KidCare, as well as private contributions from major donors.

A second annual Hurricane Sandy fundraiser called "Champions of Rockaway" was held at Hudson Terrace in New York City, which Michael owned, at 9 p.m. on Tuesday, November 18, 2014, in honor of all of the champions who had made the recovery effort possible.

The lovely Scarlett Johansson and her brother Hunter, who had worked for Michael in his restaurant operations, hosted the event.

Jamie Foxx & me

Academy Award-winning actor and singer Jamie Foxx topped off the evening with an intimate performance. He called me by name to join him on the stage to thank me for being the catalyst that had made everything possible. I felt greatly honored and enjoyed a big hug of gratitude from Jamie.

An additional seventy-six-thousand dollars was raised that evening, and this event was the culmination of our efforts in the recovery from Superstorm Sandy.

Eventually all of our operations were turned over to the St. Bernard Project, and they took it from there.

Michael has continued to be involved, and at last count he had raised more than *seven-million dollars* to help rebuild his hometown.

Great pride fills my heart as I think of the role that Giants of Generosity played by being in the right place at the right time, which helped to make it all happen.

35

A FOOD AND WINE SHOW

As I GOT BACK INTO A NORMAL ROUTINE, calls continued to come in for all kinds of help. One Sunday afternoon I met Paul Hellman, another friend from Our Lady of Mt. Carmel church, and he asked if I'd be interested in doing a Food and Wine Show as a fundraiser. He suggested that the Clinton Inn would be a perfect venue. I couldn't begin to imagine the details that kind of show would require, but Paul had some very good connections with Guy Mitchell, of the White House Chef's Tour. He also knew Maneet Chauhan, restaurateur and judge on

Maneet Chauhan & Guy Mitchell

the Food Network's *Chopped* program.

We thought about inviting all the local restaurants and wine vendors to display and sample their fare for the first two hours on the lower level of the Inn.

The weather was crisp and clear, and high cirrus clouds floated above as spring was ready to burst onto the scene. Daffodils danced in the breeze, and the delicate aroma of fresh blooming hyacinths filled the air. The guests could come right over from church and sample great tidbits from some of the best local eateries, while enjoying many varieties of wine, before adjourning upstairs to the Grand Ballroom of the Inn and a cooking demonstration by Maneet.

Maneet and Doug Singer, her manager, had met with Paul and me several months earlier to confirm how the performance would go. They also wanted to verify the legitimacy of our organization and hear about people we'd helped. They were all donating their time and talent. It was a great meeting, and we felt confident that we would put on a wonderful show.

We decided to make it a two-day fundraiser, at which Guy and Maneet would perform both days. Maneet would also do a book signing, and the staff at the Inn would duplicate the meal she had prepared and serve small samples to each of our audience members. This was becoming a major undertaking, and the timing of each segment had to be precise.

The event was to take place in March 2014. I knew that I would need some help for the six months of planning, and putting the many pieces together, so I hired an event planner. Christine Steigman and I had worked together many years earlier. She and I have the same work ethic and enjoy each other's company, and fortunately she also has youth on her side. When I told her I had Maneet Chauhan as our celebrity guest, Christine was very excited.

Guy and Maneet had completed a nationwide tour promoting

Paul Hellman's cutlery business, and they were a fine-tuned team.

I made sure we got coverage in all the local newspapers and magazines, while Christine began contacting as many local restaurants, and wine and spirit vendors, as she could, to explain the concept of the event and to ask for their participation.

Since Giants of Generosity did not have a congregation of people or a membership to draw upon, we had to rely on the general public to see our ads, flyers, and billboards. We could only hope that they would join us and attend the major event at the Clinton Inn. Tickets could be bought online, plus we had many walk-ins, all of whom seemed delightfully surprised at the magnitude of the event. It had the flair of a Manhattan affair.

We drew up contracts for each vendor to sign and continually kept on top of them to be sure they would come and share their favorite food samples with our guests.

I had invited local community leaders, many of our donors, and the sponsors as our guests, and lo and behold approximately two-hundred people showed up. As they arrived, a local seven-piece all-boy-band, looking to start their career at our social venue, filled the air with lively and inviting pop music, while a jazz combo entertained in the main ballroom. We had a custom stage built and set it up on risers so everyone could see Maneet as she cooked. Doug remained backstage and coordinated the timing of everyone's performance.

Guy Mitchell, who is a tall, distinguished-looking chef in his starched white jacket with its White House emblem stitched onto it, was the emcee. Everyone was seated in a theater-type setup facing the stage—and in walked Guy. With his boisterous voice he said, "Hi, everyone, welcome. My wife and I just landed on the roof with Marine One, coming in from Washington, D.C. …Well, no, actually my wife drove up on the Turnpike, but here we are and were ready to have a great event for Giants of Generosity.

"I'd like you all to meet Jane Albanese, the founder of this great organization. Jane, come up here and take a bow and say a few words."

"Thanks, Guy. Isn't it great to have Guy Mitchell here today? Thank you all for coming. I'd like to introduce you to one of our recipients. I'm sure you've heard of the Good Samaritan who ran from his home a few years ago to help a woman whose handbag was being stolen.

"Angel was pushed to the ground, hit his head on a parked car, and he broke his neck. He was paralyzed from his eyes down," I said, as tears trickled down my cheeks. By the grace of God, Angel surgically had his neck replaced with a titanium hinge, and he's here with us today. Please give a rousing round of applause for Angel Deida!"

Angel Deida & me

In that moment my heart swelled, as Angel stood up and, with great difficulty, walked toward me. There was a loud gasp from the audience as they stood up and broke into applause, giving Angel a standing ovation. As I write these words, I can still hardly hold myself together. Being part of this brave soul's journey is clearly among the highlights of my life.

Angel thanked me and Giants for helping him get through his trauma, adding, "If I could, I would do it all over again. God bless Giants of Generosity, and God bless America."

Before we took our seats, I said, "We have a great show planned for you, so sit back and enjoy." I turned the mic back over to Guy. He went on to talk about the nationwide tour he and Maneet had just completed, and then he introduced Maneet. She was dressed in a colorful, customary Indian sari, and she had a diamond piercing in her nose. She looked even more beautiful in person than she does on TV, with her shiny black hair and effervescent personality as she greeted the audience.

"Thank you, Jane, for inviting us here today," she said. "We're happy to support your incredible charity. Now, I'm going to prepare an Indian version of the good old American hamburger. Are you ready? Let's get started."

As Maneet began to prepare the ingredients, she told us of some of the backstage antics that take place on the *Chopped* program. She took some questions from the audience and, with a chuckle, said, "Some of the food we have to taste is not always so good, but we have to keep a smile on our faces and politely critique the meal."

She went on, "You can see this recipe in my latest cookbook, and when I'm finished, the staff of the Inn will serve you a sample. Please enjoy!"

Following the demonstrations and the tastings, the silent-auction winners were announced. Then, at the end of the evening, we gathered everything together and prepared to do it all over again the next afternoon.

This time, I introduced Edwina Manansala, Bong's wife. She spoke eloquently, thanking Giants for all we had done to help her family cope with the tragic accident that Bong had suffered.

Maneet and Guy were great sports. They stayed at the Inn that first night, as did Doug Singer. Just as we were concluding the second performance, I caught a glimpse of what appeared to be a giant-light-bulb moment as Doug Singer smacked his forehead and came running over to me saying, "Jane, it just occurred to me that you may be able to help a dear friend of mine. Her adult son, Brian, has brain cancer. They have just gotten him into a clinical trial in Los Angeles at Cedars Sinai Medical Center, but now they can't afford to get him and his wife, Stephanie, there for the treatments. They have to go back and forth five times. Do you think

Giants can help?"

"Doug, please give me a few days to see how we made out with this event, and let's plan on meeting with Brian's mother, Mia, sometime next week."

We did meet, and Mia, who happens to also be Greek, and I got along famously right off the bat. She made her plea for helping her son get to Los Angeles. After reviewing the details, Giants was able to help pay for the flights for both Brian and Stephanie, and thanks to my persistence we arranged for their car service, meals, and a hotel room right across from the hospital, all complimentary due to the graciousness of each vendor involved. Once they heard Brian's story, they wanted to help and they jumped through hoops to accommodate this family. I had to smile, because here again I threw my hands up in the air in praise, as I watched God perform His miracles.

Brian bravely faced the very painful treatments that were deemed to be a great success. He was in remission for several years upon his return, long enough for he and Stephanie to get pregnant with their precious little son, James.

36

YOU'RE GOING TO NEED AN ELEVATOR

A SOCIAL WORKER CALLED in the spring of 2015 to tell me about her client, Conrado. "He suffers from kidney failure and has to be taken three times a week by a medical transport van for his dialysis treatments. He and his mother live in a small private home in Paterson, and there are eight steps up to get into their home. He has to be carried up and down on a stretcher," she said. "Is there any way you could have a contractor build a ramp, so Conrado could go up and down in his wheelchair on his own?"

"I don't know," I said." Let me find out, and I'll get back to you. Please send me his contact info."

I reached out to Chris Caputo of G & L and Sons Construction to see if he would visit the home and determine whether a ramp would be feasible. Chris and his brother David had been in the group of men from NARI who volunteered to rebuild the Radburn home a few years earlier.

When Chris had arrived to analyze the situation, it was evident to him that a ramp wouldn't work, so he called me and said, "The stairs are too steep. If we were to put a ramp, he'd run right out into the street, so you're going to need an elevator."

My eyes nearly popped out of my head, "I'm going to need a *what?*"

"An elevator," he repeated.

"An *elevator*! Are you kidding? How the hell am I going to do that?"

Chris laughed, and then he recommended a company he had worked with in the past. He suggested that I give them a call. I took the information and buried my head in my hands as I said a quick prayer. I was convinced there was no way we could afford an elevator.

Calling the social worker back, I explained, "A ramp won't work for him. We'll need an elevator, so let me see what I can do."

Chris had sent me some photos of the steps that we were dealing with, and I could see what he meant. The thought of finding a solution confounded me; but as I quickly reviewed the many miraculous gifts that had been donated to help our clients in the past, my heart began to skip a beat with excitement.

I looked up the company that Chris had recommended and placed the call. When I had explained the situation, I asked, "Would you consider providing the elevator at your cost?"

The salesman took my contact information and said he'd get back to me, but he never did. So I let my fingers do the walking on Google, and began my search for other elevator companies.

My second call was to Handi-Lift, LLC, in Carlstadt, a stone's throw away from Paterson. I spoke with Luke, their sales manager, and explained who I was. "We have a client who needs to be transported to the hospital for dialysis three times a week and he has to be carried down his outside steps and then back up. Is there something you might be able to do to help us? He needs an elevator," I said, matter-of-factly.

Luke replied, "Can you send me some photos of the building?"

"Sure, I'll get them right off to you. What's your email?"

The very next day, he called to say, "We'd like to donate a fourteen-thousand dollar elevator for your client."

"Oh, my goodness! Are you serious?" I don't know why I was so shocked by their generosity—things like that just kept happening.

"Yes. James Boydston, the owner, is thrilled to be able to assist. We've been looking to help someone in need right here in our own neighborhood."

"That's *wonderful!* Thank you again. What's the next step?"

"Can you have your contractor call me? We'll have to see about getting the permits needed from the city, and that may take some time."

"Thanks again, Luke. I'll have him give you a call."

Within days the permits were in the works. Chris and his crew would pay for the electrical, Handi-Lift would donate and install the elevator, and Giants would pay to have the base of the sidewalk resurfaced and prepared for the elevator, something much more manageable financially for us.

My head was spinning. The gratitude I felt toward Chris and Handi-lift was immeasurable. In my eyes, it was yet another act of God.

When the leaves had turned to their autumn palette and there was a nip in the air, I met with Conrado and his mother to have our client-service agreement signed. His complexion was sallow and he was obviously quite ill. They expressed their deep appreciation of the gift. It was, indeed, a very heartwarming gesture.

The whole process took a couple of months of going back and

forth with plans and permits, but sure enough, an external elevator was installed and, as Conrado put it, "You've given me my freedom back. There are no words to express what that means to me. I can go to the library or the grocery store by myself now. Thank you so much. I will forever be indebted to you."

Upon completion, the spring blossoms were beginning to bloom, so we planned a ribbon-cutting ceremony and invited the mayor and many of the local newspapers to join us. It was bright and sunny, like the outlook for Conrado's future.

James Boydston and Luke were on hand for the happy occasion in support of all the efforts made on behalf of this *one* man in need. The owner of the factory even flew in from Vancouver, British Columbia for the ceremony. It was a beautiful thing to watch. To me, the generosity and graciousness of everyone involved was astounding.

37

The Most Stunning Call

One day as I was busy working on the bookkeeping and the filing, I decided to prepare a new design update for our website. It was a blustery winter morning. The ground was covered with a dingy-looking gray snow that had fallen the week before, now with blackened edges from the soot of the roadway. It appeared as though dusk was falling early, and everything seemed bleak. I had soft music playing in the background, and as I looked out the window again I wondered if the sun would ever return.

Spooked by the phone, I jumped, glad to know someone out there was thinking of me.

A frail voice on the other end said, "Is this Giants of Generosity?"

"Yes. My name is Jane. How can I help?"

"I got your number from a man at church, and he said that you might be able to assist me."

The woman sounded quite frazzled, so I turned the music down and, listening intently, I asked, "What's your name, and what's going on?"

"My name is Maddie."

"Hi, Maddie. How are you doing?"

She began to cry.

I said, "Can you tell me a little bit about what's happening and how I might help?"

"My ex-husband had been paying the rent and the utilities, but then he just stopped paying them and never told me. Yesterday, I got an eviction notice from the landlord, and PSE&G is going to turn off my power on Friday. I'm disabled and haven't been able to work for the last several years. What am I going to do? I have no place to go."

"Do you have any family or friends who can give you some moral support and perhaps help you get caught up on your past-due bills?"

She began to cry a little harder, so I tried to calm her.

"It's going to be okay," I said. "Please give me your full name and address, and let's see what we can do."

As I was filling out the intake form, she went on to say, "My mother lives on her Social Security, and she helps me whenever she can, but she has no room for me to live with her."

Soon her tears turned into inconsolable sobbing.

"Maddie, please try to calm down and keep your faith strong. It will all work out, I promise. How much do you owe?"

"I owe PSE&G $2,673.85, and my rent is past due for three months, totaling more than $3,600 including late fees. I've reached out to everyone I know."

I said, "Take a deep breath, and let's try to figure this out."

"It sounds like you're not going to help me either," she said.

"I didn't say that, I'm just trying to gather some information and see how we can best help. We don't have five or six-thousand dollars to give to you, but let me see what I can do. Give me all of the PSE&G information, and let me try to work with them."

"How's that going to help if I get evicted?"

"Let's take one step at a time," I said, as I could feel her beginning to panic.

"I'm going to be homeless, and I'm *so scared!*" she cried.

"Don't go there yet," I said. "If worse comes to worst, I can always put you up at the Clinton Inn in Tenafly for a while."

There was a sudden gasp and then silence.

"Maddie, are you there?"

"Yes, I'm here. What do you mean, the Clinton Inn?"

"If need be, I can arrange to have you stay there until we figure this all out. So please don't panic. I'm not going to let you be homeless."

"The Clinton Inn?" she repeated.

"Yes. My father used to own the Inn, and they occasionally work with us to accommodate some of our clients."

Again there was a strange silence.

Then she said, "Do you know someone named Tom Chagaris?"

"Yes, he's my brother. Why?" How did she know Tom? *Could Maddie be someone I had also known?* "How do you know him?" I asked eagerly.

After a long hesitation and some labored breathing, she explained, "He was married to my mother *forty-seven years ago*."

A chill shook my entire body as if an icicle had pierced the back of my neck. How had it happened that she found me?

"What? Do you mean to tell me that you're *that Maddie?*" When you first told me your name, I had a fleeting memory of a little girl I had known briefly many years ago named Maddie. It's an unusual name, but I didn't give it much more thought when you began to tell me your story. That Maddie was Tommy's three-year-old stepdaughter from his first wife."

"Yes, that's me. I'm fifty years old now, and life has been so cruel to me."

"Oh, my goodness! How did you find me?"

"I didn't. I didn't know it was you."

"Your mother and Tommy were only married for a short time," I said, "but I remember you." Many thoughts were racing through my head. "How's your mother?"

"My mom's okay, but she's also struggling. She remarried but then divorced again."

"Please give her my love."

"I will."

My heart skipped a beat, and I knew that Maddie was God-sent. This was *no* coincidence. I had to find a way to help her for sure.

"I remember my mother saying to me back then that Tommy had a really nice sister," she said. "That must be you."

"And I remember you. You always seemed to be very shy as you clung to your mother's leg whenever you came over to the house."

"I was very afraid of him," she said, and she began to sob. We both cried as I tried to console her.

We talked for a long while and she described her experiences with him. I felt a great sense of empathy for what she had been through. I could also relate to much of her distress. As we hung up I assured her that I would do whatever I could to help.

I started negotiating immediately with PSE&G and with her landlord. Once they understood that they were dealing with an official 501(c)3 charity, they worked with us, and Maddie was protected from eviction and from further power shut-offs.

OUR SIGNATURE EVENTS

IN MARCH OF 2015, IT WAS TIME for another fundraising event, and this time, our event planner, Christine and I had felt more confident as we planned the next Food and Wine Show. We seemed to have the routine down pat by then, although there were thousands of tiny little details. We called upon the Clinton Inn, and they offered us the entire ballroom space once again for our event.

To me, their kindness and respect were testament to the great man who had founded it—my dad Peter Chagaris. I could feel him walking the halls of the Inn with me as arrangements were made.

I wondered who we could get as our celebrity guest this time?

I had heard of Logan Guleff, a young man from Memphis, Tennessee, who at the ripe old age of twelve had won $100,000 on Gordon Ramsey's "MasterChef Junior" contest.

He shouldn't be that hard to find, I thought.

I found his Facebook page and an email address for him and decided I had nothing to lose by writing to him and explaining what I had in mind for the event. Within an hour I got an email back saying, "I'd love to do your show. Let me speak with my parents, and I'll get back with you."

What a charming and talented young man Logan turned out to be. We arranged for his flight to New York with his mother, and we put them up at the Inn.

Fundraisers serve an important, two-fold function: First, obviously, they raise funds in support of our mission; second, they draw attention to the work of the organization itself. We are a local, non-governmentally-supported charity with limited resources, and we have worked tirelessly to help raise awareness of the needs of our fellow citizens right here in our own backyard. By coming together as a community, we could make miracles like a donated elevator happen.

We'd got such great reviews for our first show that this type of event would become our signature fundraiser. I often heard comments about how we had pulled off such a great function.

While seeking publicity for the second show, I was in contact with Angela Thomas of Prana Marketing. She represented Lori Stokes, who at the time was the morning co-anchor with Ken Rosato on "Eyewitness News This Morning" on WABC-TV. Lori's visibility in the non-profit arena was well-documented, and with her bubbly personality she was in high demand. Over the years, I saw her eating at the Inn and other local restaurants—she lived nearby.

Angela was able to confirm Lori's appearance at our event, and that she would serve as a judge during the cooking competition between students from Eastwick College's culinary program. These students had competed internally for an opportunity to cook onstage at our show, and they were to be judged by Lori and two audience members who bid on their seats to become judges. The winner would take home a $500 scholarship.

Each student would concoct a dish of their choosing, with forty minutes to prepare, cook, and present it to the judges. We had a countdown clock just as they do on TV. It was all in great fun and added to the entertainment schedule of the Food and Wine Show.

The vendors, all of whom had donated their delicacies, were in place in the lower lobby along with the musicians as the day began. There was a great variety of tastings, from barbecue to egg foo young, buffalo wings to duck sliders, and for dessert, each guest had a choice of chocolate fondue from the Melting Pot, Ben and Jerry's ice cream, or delectable petit fours and cupcakes from many local bakeries.

Wine samplings were abundant, and there was a vodka-flowing ice sculpture. At the end of *that part* of the four-hour party and the feeding frenzy, our guests made their way up to the stage area of the main ballroom. They took their seats, which had been set up theater-style in anticipation of a very entertaining student cook-off and demonstration by Logan.

Once the timer was started, Doug Singer, who so wanted to be our emcee for this event, said, "I believe in this great organization and the amazing work that they do to help our friends in need. Please continue to support them."

Then Doug called up his friend Mia Wood, Brian's mother, to the microphone. She had been a producer for ABC News and was comfortable talking about her journey with her son's cancer battle. She expressed her deepest gratitude to me, and to Giants, for the support we had given her family. Mia briefly discussed how Dr. John S. Yu of Cedars Sinai Medical Center in Los Angeles had accepted Brian into his revolutionary new clinical trial. He had received a cutting-edge treatment called a dendritic cell vaccine ICT-107. It was proving to be helpful for many people with brain cancer. Mia reported that her son was doing remarkably well after receiving the treatments, and she was very confident that Brian would be cured. That part of the event brought tears to everyone's eyes, especially mine.

She gave the mic back to Doug, and he continued the show. "Without further ado, let's have a great big round of applause for Chef Logan, the winner of 'MasterChef Junior.'"

Logan took the stage in his white chef's jacket and his signature bow tie, and went on to prepare and explain his dish to the audience. Despite his youth, he had great stage presence and a wonderful sense of humor. He was tall and lanky for his age, with a full head of sandy blond hair, and a broad, toothy grin. He also had an uncanny command of a master chef's lingo. He was very impressive—and so adorable!

His entree was shrimp and scallops in a Champagne cream sauce (though he wasn't old enough to drink the Champagne, of course). He accompanied the main course with a vegetable medley and his southern specialty of hominy cheese grits. The aromas coming from the stage filled the air, and as the audience's taste buds tingled, they were captivated by his charisma.

It was an extremely successful event.

THE FOLLOWING YEAR WE HELD our third annual Food and Wine fundraiser. This time Christine, our event planner, was pregnant and would be in her seventh month as the event approached. Fortunately, most of the details were in place when she called me about a month before to say that she had the flu. She was the backbone of the entire event. I was, more or less, the headliner, showing up on the day all dressed up and ready to greet our more than two hundred guests, while Christine ran everything behind the scenes. I was deeply concerned that we wouldn't be able to pull it off without her.

She thought she'd be okay by the time of the event, but being pregnant, she was unable to take any medication, so she only got worse. We were all worried about the baby and kept them both in our prayers. (Thankfully, little Rebecca was born as scheduled and is now a bouncing, healthy, and happy child.)

We survived that day with a little help from one of Christine's co-workers, and aside from my frayed nerves, I don't think our guests even noticed. It takes many hands to pull off these events, even when everyone is in place.

That year's cooking show included two new students from Eastwick College. The main cooking competition, however, was between Carissa Lawson, the morning anchor of "News 12 New Jersey," and Sheryl Fody, who had been in the process of producing her own television show called "Consumer 411."

They each cooked a favorite dish as time ticked away, and once again audience members judged their dishes. Although both meals were excellent, Carissa walked away with an Oscar-type trophy. She was thrilled and offered great praise for the work of Giants of Generosity.

39

A HUGE CHALLENGE

ANOTHER CALL CAME IN and the voice on the other end said, "Ms. Albanese, this is Bianca Madzarova, from Senator Cory Booker's office in Newark."

I had taken one of our clients to the senator's office several years earlier to see if he could help with a difficult situation that was beyond our scope, and Bianca had remembered me.

"Would you consider taking a look at a client case we've been working on?" she asked. "There is a very large woman who is a victim of Superstorm Sandy, and she is in need of an oversized bariatric hospital bed. She lives in Monmouth County."

"Yes, of course," I replied. "How can I help?"

"While she was being evacuated during the storm, she fell and injured her ankle, more than two years ago now. Due to her excessive weight, she's been in and out of hospitals and nursing facilities ever since, and she has developed an extremely large and seriously infected, life-threatening, stage-three pressure ulcer, like a massive bedsore, on her backside. It's almost the size of a leg of lamb. The open wound is about six inches deep. In desperation, Angela and her husband John, who is her sole caregiver, have reached out to everyone, from Governor Chris Christie to Congressman Frank Pallone, before reaching out to Senator Booker.

"When she was finally released from the medical facilities, Medicare sent her home with a prescription for a *forty-eight-inch-wide* low-rise bariatric hospital bed with a true air-flow air mattress to help improve circulation. But the one they had sent was too high off the ground. Angela, who's only about five-feet tall and *very* large, couldn't get onto the bed, so they returned it to Medicare, expecting to have it replaced with a lower base.

"We have been in touch with Medicare, but all of our efforts have failed. Their policy states that a patient is only eligible for a replacement bed once every five years, and they refused to make an exception in this case, even though the error was on their part."

"Wow," I said. "That's hard to believe. Can you put me in touch with Angela? I'll do an intake form directly with her, and then see what I can do."

Bianca thanked me and said, "Please keep us informed of your progress. We'll work with you in any way that we can."

When I reached Angela by phone, she was extremely grateful that she was finally making progress, although I couldn't promise her a positive outcome.

I told her, "Now that I have the details, let me make some calls, and I'll get back to you."

"Oh, thank you. God bless you," she said. "I've been living on our love seat with my feet propped up on two hassocks for over seven months now, and all of my weight is on the open wound. It's extremely painful, and it's getting worse. I'm afraid that I'm going to die. Thank you for whatever you can do."

I began researching bariatric hospital bed manufacturers throughout the northeast, and started making the calls. I was astonished at the prices they were quoting, from seventeen to twenty-thousand dollars. I also contacted Medicare and explained the extenuating circumstances of Angela's story, but my plea also fell on deaf ears.

Finally, I reached Sizewise Healthcare Systems of Ellis, Kansas, and, upon hearing my plea, they agreed to discount the bed and the special mattress to thirty-four-hundred dollars, which was certainly more manageable for us.

"Angela, I've found a bed for you and you'll have it in about a week," I told her. "It has to be shipped from Kansas to a warehouse in New Jersey, and then it will be delivered to you. I'll be there when it arrives. I look forward to meeting you."

She began to cry and said, "Oh, that would be great! Thank you, Jane, *thank you*."

In speaking with Sizewise, I negotiated the terms of the agreement and, as in the past, they were compassionate and glad to be able to help.

Giants didn't have the money needed to pay for the bed in full, so I called several organizations in the Monmouth County area asking for their support. I was able to raise two-thousand-seven-hundred dollars of the three-thousand-four-hundred needed, and we were able to handle the rest.

Edie Sims, who was a Giants board member, and I, were excited for Angela and drove down the shore to their home. It was a cloud-less sunny day, and as we approached we could smell the salty sea air and hear the call of the seagulls. It was hard to imagine how Angela had been sitting on that enormously painful wound. She had lived and slept on her love seat twenty-four hours a day for seven months following her release from rehab.

When the Sizewise truck arrived, a cheer went up from all of us. As we made room in her living quarters, the deliverymen set up the bed, and then they departed.

Edie and I braced the bed from one side so it didn't slide as Angela labored trying to get onto it. Once she pulled herself up to the head with John's help, Angela had the biggest smile of gratitude on her face.

Moments like that make my job so rewarding.

We are happy to report that, four months later, Angela's wound began to heal, and she is on the road to recovery.

MOST OF OUR RECIPIENTS were unsuccessful in their own efforts to get the help they needed. By God's grace, we have been able to pull together resources like Angela's bed, as if pulling that famous rabbit out of the hat.

Over the years, we had developed a "Friends Helping Friends" arm of Giants, as crowd-funding sites like GoFundMe and Kickstarter became more popular. In contrast to those sites, contributions to us are not only tax-exempt for the donor, but the funds raised are also tax-free for the recipient. Additionally, there are distinct advantages of using a 501(c)3 charitable organization such as Giants, since we also advocate on behalf of the clients, reducing their financial obligations, and coordinating services with contractors and suppliers.

HERE'S THE KIND OF CALL I never like to receive: In a freak accident, forty-year-old Christine Danza slipped and fell in her kitchen, resulting in significant neck and spinal-cord injuries. She spent two-and-a-half months at the Kessler Rehabilitation Center as a quadriplegic, where she and her team of physicians and therapists have been working hard to help her regain some function.

Christine is continuing her therapy through Kessler's outpatient rehab program. She suffers from full-body muscle spasms and has very limited use of her legs and hands. She requires around-the-clock care to provide for her basic needs, and she is unable to care for her young children, Michael and Lia.

While we all remain positive and hopeful, there is the possibility that she may never regain full functional use of her limbs. We are confident that, if Christine's remarkable courage, strength, and determination alone could make her walk, she would already have *run out of Kessler* by now!

Giants acted as fiscal sponsors for a group of Friends Helping Friends, who pulled together a few intimate fundraisers to assist with her expenses. More than sixty-thousand dollars was raised on behalf of the Danza family.

Although Giants was not a faith-based organization, I often gave this stone angel to our recipients to comfort them.

40

Was It Happenstance or Heaven-Sent?

So much of what Giants has achieved over the first ten years of our history rings true with an uncanny sense of happenstance.

It was evident, however, that the success of Giants was not merely a stroke of luck. It had happened through the sheer grit, perseverance, and dedication to the organization that we were able to fulfill the immediate and desperate needs of so many families seeking relief from catastrophic circumstances.

The board of Giants all watched from afar as our clients had miraculous things happen in their lives. They would often attend the ribbon-cutting ceremonies and photo ops.

In spite of all of our efforts, though, it became clear that we needed assistance to bring in enough money and/or in-kind donations to help everyone who had reached out to us. That's when we brought on John Corcoran of D'Alessandro, Inc., a fundraising consulting firm, to join our team. Together, we reached out to corporations for sponsorships, family foundations, and to the philanthropic community at large, explaining the important mission of Giants of Generosity and our clients' needs. With John's help, we expanded our donor base and increased awareness of our grassroots organization.

Over the course of time, we have also created a Dream Team, consisting of men and women who believe in our mission and can lend their expertise, services, or donated products to help our recipients, without having to join the board or attend monthly meetings. This group of volunteers has become an invaluable part of the organization. They play important roles in solving many of our clients' problems.

I BELIEVE THAT OUR MANY TRIUMPHS have been heaven-sent, as witnessed in this next and final story.

One Sunday morning late in 2016, a member of the Knights of Columbus at the Church of the Presentation approached me and asked, "Have you heard about Carol Caneriato? She's fallen down her basement stairs, and she's in critical condition."

I immediately called her husband, Sal, to see if there was anything I could do to help.

He said, "Jane, just pray. She's in very bad shape." He could barely speak.

"I will Sal, I will."

As the details of her freak accident began to unfold, we were told that Carol might not make it. I felt so helpless.

I'll let Sal tell you the story:

"Days after Carol and I celebrated our fiftieth wedding anniversary, I was out playing tennis and returned home late in the afternoon. As I came through the garage door it looked as though Carol had thrown a large rug down the stairs. I went over to pick it up, and that's when I discovered that the heap on the ground *was my wife, Carol.*

"Oh, my God! She was lying face down in a pool of blood and vomit, and she was writhing in pain. How could this have happened? I realized that she must have lost her balance and fallen from the top of the stairs, landing directly on her face. I called the ambulance and tried to comfort her, but I was afraid to move her," he said. "And I prayed."

Every bone in her face, and both wrists were broken, as were most of her ribs, and she had also suffered a traumatic brain injury.

"The doctors told me," he went on, "that if she lives, she would most likely never fully recover."

I think Sal was still in shock as he told me the story.

After a long stay in the hospital and several surgeries, Carol was allowed to come home. Their bedrooms are on the second floor, so I knew that they would need at least a stair lift to assist her.

Once again I reached out to James Boydston to see if he could help. We measured the stairs, and within days of Carol's arrival, the donated stair-lift was installed. This was one small thing that we could do to help alleviate Sal's fears of bringing Carol home.

AS WE CELEBRATED THE FOURTH Food and Wine Show, which would also be in celebration of our tenth anniversary, Caryn Starr-Gates, our board chair, suggested that the board of directors honor me at the event, since I had been the brainchild of the organization and the force behind its growth.

I asked Sal if there was any chance he could come to the event as our esteemed guest. When I mentioned that I was being honored for my ten years of service, he said that he would make every effort to be there. Although Carol was still quite unsteady, she had been making remarkable progress and she didn't want to miss the event, so she and Sal both joined us.

Doug Singer was once again our emcee. When he introduced me, I told the audience what had happened to my friend Carol. Then, I called Sal up onstage and turned the mic over to him.

Almost unable to control his emotions, Sal cried as he reiterated the trauma of Carol's accident, thanking me and Giants for the help we had offered to the love of his life. Our audience was blown away by the fact that they were both there to share their story.

James, of Handi-Lift, was in the audience as well, and so I introduced them. It was an emotional testimonial to the kindness of others as love and gratitude filled the ballroom.

James, Sal, Carol & daughter Christine

Doug introduced Caryn Starr-Gates, who presented me with a beautiful crystal-star award for the creation of this one-of-a-kind organization and for my years of service.

Doug went on to welcome some friends and colleagues, who wanted to say a few words about what had been accomplished. My longtime friend John Barrett reminisced about the years we had known each other. He told a funny story about what we did when he and I were in our late teens and early twenties. Whenever there was a fire in Tenafly, we'd drop everything and chase the fire engines, and we'd meet each other at the site of the fire. I still wonder about the intrigue. John also went on to say how impressed he was with the organization that I had created from scratch, and how monumental our achievements had been over the years.

Then John Corcoran took the stage to say a few words about his belief in what Giants of Generosity had achieved, and about the respect he had for me and for our working relationship.

He then introduced John Johl, our founding board member, who told of the organization's many accomplishments. John continued to say a few words about our humble beginnings and how far we had come. "Jane has been an exceptional founder," he said. Her philosophy is *lead, follow, or get out of the way*. She has nearly single-handedly created a very unique and praiseworthy charitable organization that has helped many. I'm proud to have been a part of Giants of Generosity since its inception."

As John took his seat, the student chefs were ready to present their dishes to the judges, and again the winner received a $500 scholarship.

Doug then thanked everyone for coming, and the event concluded.

OVERWHELMED WITH EXHAUSTION from the months of planning that went into our fundraisers, I needed some downtime. So, with the tenth anniversary event in the can, I looked forward to getting some much-needed rest.

As splendid as our fundraisers have been, and as rewarding as the results of our efforts were, the very long hours had begun to take a personal toll on me.

You may recall that Carol Caneriato and Sue DeMartini were the first two people I told about starting Giants of Generosity. Ironically, Carol would also become the last client we would help before my retirement.

41

The Hour Had Arrived

Sister Elizabeth, of Our Lady of Victories in Harrington Park, called to advise me that my mother was in the Care One nursing facility in Cresskill. She would occasionally keep me up to date on how my mother was doing. I was grateful for that connection. She'd always say, "Your mother is amazing for her age."

I sensed an urgency to send her an Easter card. It read, "Mom, I've never stopped loving you, Jane."

I asked Sister Elizabeth to deliver it for me, and to read it to my mother, wanting to hear her reaction, but when she arrived Mom was in a deep sleep. She chose to read it to her anyway, thinking that maybe, somehow, she would hear that I was thinking of her and praying for her.

At the time of her call, I wasn't aware that Mom was nearing the end of her life, although I should have expected it. She had been in and out of Care One several times in the past.

It was just two weeks after our tenth-anniversary celebration when I checked my messages and heard, "Hi, Jane, it's Linda, your sister. Mom is in Care One, and she's calling your name. You need to get over here and see her. When you come, wear a mask, because she has a bad cold or the flu."

Having not heard from anyone in my family for more than sixteen years, I called Sister Elizabeth, who said, "Your mother's not doing well now, Jane. You have to go."

"I can't bear the thought of seeing my mother after all these years."

"You have to go," she said.

"I can't," I said softly, as tears of pain gushed from my soul.

She pleaded with me, "Please go. I'll meet you there."

I was torn about what to do and asked if she thought Linda would accept a phone call from me.

She called her to ask and discovered that she was out to dinner, and I then placed the call to Linda.

When she answered, it was quite clear that we were both uncomfortable. I loved my family, but their treatment of me so many years ago has never, even for a moment, left me.

Before I could ask how Mom was, Linda said, "Do you want to know what's going on?"

"Sure," I said, hoping that the call would at least be cordial. Trying to make conversation, I asked, "Who are you having dinner with?"

She barked, "What difference does that make? I'm with Bill, Tommy, and Nifty."

"It makes no difference," I said.

She went on to tell me that my mother had been in Care One for a month or so, and she provided more details. Then said, "Mom's calling for you."

So my mother *had heard* Sister Elizabeth.

How poignant!

"We're putting her in hospice care tomorrow," she added with a tiny crack in her voice.

From my experience with Dom, I knew exactly what that meant.

I VERY RELUCTANTLY WENT TO SEE HER. Sister Elizabeth met me there while Linda and Tommy were still at dinner; I certainly didn't need to see *them* at that moment.

Standing at her bedside, I rested my hand on her shoulder and said, "Mom, it's Jane, I'm here. Go in peace. I love you, Mom. God bless you." Her frail body felt like a hollow skeleton as she lay unconscious in the final moments of her life.

Trying to protect my heart, I had decided years earlier that I would not go to her funeral, knowing how torturous that would be. I had great respect for her even though she had hurt me deeply. I felt that my siblings had manipulated her, and I never wanted to see them again. I knew Mom never would have emptied my checking account on her own, leaving me stranded as she had.

Scarred by years of sorrow, I had never once dated or lived a life that was even vaguely similar to the fabulous one our family had known. I was unable to have children of my own, I was widowed, and no one in my family or Dom's would speak with me. So work was all I knew, and aside from going to church, it was all I did. I had to survive and maintain two homes, in case I had been removed from my mother's will again. Although I could no longer live there, my home in Florida needed to be protected. It was the ticket to my survival.

THE NEXT CALL FROM LINDA was on Thursday, April 6, 2017.

"Hi, Jane. Mom died ten minutes ago."

It was exactly three weeks after her 104th birthday.

"I'm sorry. I hope she can rest in peace now."

"Tommy was with her when she died, and I'm at the hairdresser having my hair colored. The service is at Barrett's Funeral Home on Monday."

Sister Elizabeth called to be sure that I had heard Mom died, and she insisted that I must go to her funeral. I struggled with the very painful decision, and the pressure from her only made it more difficult. I felt as though I was being treated like an irresponsible child.

I knew that Sister Elizabeth was unable to understand my experience with them, and that she only wanted me to do the "right" thing. There's not a vicious bone in my body, and all of my life, I have always tried to do the right thing. So I prayed about it, asking God to guide me and to give me the strength that I needed if I chose to go.

As I drove to Barrett's, I kept repeating, "I can do all things through Christ who strengthens me." *(Philippians 4:13)*

After taking a deep breath, I walked into the funeral home. Tommy was the first person I saw. The expression of shock on his face spoke volumes. We shook hands, and then he said, "Can I have a hug?" We hugged. It felt so unfamiliar.

It was my turn then to be shocked. He was warm and friendly, and although his eyes were deep set and he appeared weary, it was good to see him. Nifty, on the other hand, looked as pretty as ever, but she was cold and distant. I thought it would have been the other way around. Since they had moved to Arizona, it'd been something like twenty-five or thirty years since we'd seen each other.

As I approached my mother's casket, Linda came over and hugged and kissed me, followed by her friend Bill.

The next shock was seeing my mother lying there, *dressed in exactly the same sage green outfit I had worn* just days earlier, the day I had visited her in an unconscious state in the nursing home.

No one could have expected that. It felt as if I was seeing *myself* lying there in the coffin.

Friends and family members were gathering, and then Linda made the strangest announcement that I have ever heard to the other mourners.

She said, "Jane and Mom have been so close all of these years, and she even wore the same outfit Mom has on when she went to see her the other day. Jane and Dad were also close. Dad even died on Jane's birthday."

What? *"So close?"*

I stood there in disbelief, unable to speak. It seemed to me that it was Linda's conscience speaking. *Was she trying to save face?*

I looked around at the curious facial expressions of those who knew better, and it made me wonder what she had been smoking.

Among the floral arrangements was a display of family photos. As I walked over to look at them, Linda and Tommy joined me. We stood in chronological order, reminiscing.

Linda said, "This one is from their thirty-fifth anniversary."

"Forty-fifth," Tommy and I said in unison.

I pointed out a portrait of the three of us, reminding them of how we had fought when I wanted to have that photo taken. I felt an electric spark of love shooting between us, and we chuckled—*it felt like family*. I was amazed and pleasantly surprised.

Maybe they didn't hate me as much as I had thought all of these years.

When the service at the cemetery concluded, we went to the Inn for the repast. It was very awkward. I sat at a table with John Barrett, my cousin Arthur and his wife Lia, and, probably the most startling of all, Tommy's best childhood friend, Fred Orsato, whom he had also thrown away, and his wife Katie. It was good to see them.

Linda came over to our table and said that Mom had been crying out, "Help me, *help me*."

Linda asked, "Mom, what's wrong?"

"Help me find Jane." Mom had answered.

Hearing that shattered the very epicenter of my being, like a baseball bat smashing through the protective glass shell that had encased my heart. The sound of my pain was deafening within my core. Why hadn't they at least called me while she was still alert? I wondered if they would have bothered calling me at all, had I not sent the note.

As we parted that day, Linda said, "I'll call you."

Tommy and I hugged and he said, "Goodbye, take care."

THE ENCOUNTER HAD BEEN FAR LESS PAINFUL than I expected, but quite strange nevertheless.

In our grieving, I thought that maybe Linda *would call*, or that Tommy would email to see how I was coping with the loss of our mother. It had in fact, for me, been the third time that I had to say goodbye to her. Deep down, I guess I was still hoping for their love and concern for me, but it was not meant to be.

That experience, so different from what I had expected, gave me pause. I wondered if they even knew exactly what had happened on August 21, 2001, when my mother threw me out. They hadn't been there.

Who had told her to say what she had said? What had she told them afterwards about that horrible moment?

Could they possibly not have even realized the magnitude of the crushing blow that they had delivered?

During the wake, Linda had also made a comment that "I had put up a barrier." She seemed to imply that was why we had stayed apart. *What barrier was she talking about?* After the breakup in 2001, I had tried calling them repeatedly, even going to Linda's house over and over again, all in vain. I now had more questions without answers!

I began to consider that the years I had suffered at their hands had, perhaps in their minds, been *my choice*. But I knew better. They hadn't answered the door or tried to reach out to me, even in the aftermath of September 11. They hadn't been there for me when I desperately needed them. I had been clinging to life by a thread emotionally. Then, Linda had offered a glimmer of hope when she said, "I'll call you."

As time passed and I hadn't heard from her, I sent her a note that read: "Dear Linda, you said you would call. If you're interested in having a conversation, please let me know, Love, Jane."

She wrote back, "Jane, I'm not interested at this time. Linda."

I had hoped to ask her some questions about my mother's health. There was an incident, many years before, when I wanted to buy my mom a new bathrobe after I watched her coming down the stairs with one so soiled and too long for her that it was scary; I feared she would trip on it. A few weeks later, we were at the mall, passing the lingerie department, when I said, "Mom, look at this pretty pale blue robe. It's so soft, and this color looks great on you."

She began pulling her hair, screaming at the top of her lungs, "I don't want it, I don't want it, *I don't want it!*"

I was mortified by everyone looking at her and then at me. Embarrassed, I escorted her out of the store. Otherwise she had seemed perfectly normal. Looking back, however, I also recall that after she returned from Arizona and Tommy's sixtieth birthday, she would often say, "You don't even say hello to me when you get up in the morning."

"Yes, I do. I always say good morning, Mom, but you don't reply."

I attributed that to her hearing loss. While she was in Florida with me, I had taken her to an audiologist for hearing aids several times. I thought that maybe she didn't have them in when I came down in the morning.

As I described these incidents to my counselor at the time, he said, "It sounds like she has dementia."

I had suspected the bathrobe scene was a sign of dementia, but before I could check further, I was exiled from the family.

If my mother had been suffering from that horrid disease, I could understand why Tommy emphasized at the funeral how well Linda had taken care of her.

This would appear to change the whole picture—not the pain caused, but maybe the reason for it. I thought of reaching out to Tommy, but with Nifty's coolness and Linda's lack of interest in communicating, I hesitated.

For many years, I sent my mother Christmas and birthday cards, never once receiving one in return. When she broke her hip in a fall several years earlier, I mailed her a love letter expressing my gratitude to her and to my dad for the extraordinary upbringing they had given us. But I never received a response.

It became crystal clear that they didn't want me in their lives, so I finally, out of self-preservation, stopped trying to reach out.

I have been deprived of our entire family and of the love we once knew—leaving me feeling empty and undeserving. It has colored the entire second half of my life. I've struggled each day since just to pick myself up and make it through another day, alone. I will forever grieve the loss of the family that I had once loved.

UPON MEETING WITH MOM'S FINANCIAL PLANNER after the funeral, I discovered that my mother's will had, indeed, been altered once again. I'd trusted that her attorneys would uphold her wishes when I was asked to leave the room back in 2001 as she was questioned extensively to be sure *no one* was trying to sway her decision.

In the end, however, my share was no longer equal. Linda received forty-five percent, Tommy thirty-five percent, and fortunately, I was not left out, and I received twenty percent.

One could draw the conclusion that my expulsion from the family was almost solely based on the almighty dollar. How sad.

While meeting with the financial planner, I asked if he would reach out to Tommy to see if he would be willing to have a conversation.

A week or so later, Tommy called and said, "You've made a lot of bad choices in your life. I hope you will do better now."

I told him, "I'll try."

"Don't try, just do it." He said.

What choices was he referring to? He doesn't even know me.

I am exceptionally pleased with every choice I have ever made, and proudly stand behind each of them, given the circumstances. The Libran symbol is *the scales of justice*. I seek equality, harmony, and balance, therefore, I weigh every decision, and I truly believe that all of *my* choices have been divinely blessed.

I wish that I could have said to him in return, "What about the bad choices *you've* made?" But as I've mentioned in the past, I avoid confrontation at all costs, and this was just another example of that, so I didn't say what I had been thinking.

Tommy called once again, and then stopped calling right before the holidays. That's just the way it is, I suppose.

He never even asked me how I've been.

THE MOST ASTONISHING PART OF THIS JOURNEY is that, in an uncanny twist of fate, *my name* was the last word on my mother's lips before she died.

Emily Augusta Moseman Chagaris
1913 - 2017

42

THE FINISH LINE

I CAN HONESTLY SAY THAT I HAVE NO REGRETS. The knowledge that I have never deliberately done anything to hurt anyone else is *my badge of honor*. Perhaps, had our family tragedy not happened, I might never have come to rely on our Heavenly Father as my friend and my savior. I most likely would never have fully understood human suffering, and thereby, conceivably, might not have started Giants of Generosity as an extension of His healing hands.

Though I've had many challenges throughout my life, I find the challenge of forgiving is the most daunting. We must do it for our own sanity, releasing whatever lingering thoughts there might be of the pain or hatred that we've been harboring.

I have chosen to forgive my family and to move on, understanding fully that forgiveness, however, does not necessarily mean reconciliation. I have discovered that Linda and Tommy have not yet evolved to a place where that is possible.

A few years back, at the request of Monsignor Ed Ciuba, of the Church of the Presentation, I had the good fortune of spending a private weekend for one at a Catholic retreat house down the Jersey shore. I had been trying to determine if I was going in the right direction with Giants.

Sister Anne, a handsome, middle-aged nun with a deep dimple in her left cheek, played devil's advocate. She was an articulate, well-spoken psychologist who looked like she could have been a corporate executive, with a posture as straight as a darning needle. Her pale, steely blue eyes peered into my soul as she strategically inquired into every aspect of my life. She tried to dissuade me, knowing that I needed to earn a living while helping others, thinking that I might just be doing this work for the joy of giving. In order to get a sense of my true motives, she then asked me to write my *heart's desire* before the end of the weekend.

During my reflective time at the retreat house, I came upon their library. With my head cocked to the side, I reached for the first book that caught my eye with its brightly colored spine, standing upright in line with many others. It was entitled *If You Want to Walk on Water, You've Got to Get Out of the Boat,* by John Ortberg. I took that as a very positive sign!

Ya think?

Here's what I came up with for Sister Anne: "My heart's desire is to be loved and financially secure; to be known as someone who gets the job done, who lives by integrity, and who by her faith accomplishes the impossible."

Upon carefully reading my note, her eyes softened with a moist twinkle, and she said, "I think you are exactly where you are supposed to be."

That was really good to hear.

Ortberg's book merely confirmed Sister Anne's assessment.

It is my belief that great values create great character. What matters is the way you treat others, the behaviors you exhibit, and the way you carry yourself with the nobility of spirit.

I have always felt that I was destined for greatness. I trust that I have done my part; I know that I have done my best. These particular Giants have helped a few thousand people in need, and we've raised more than *1.2 million dollars* to help those in despair.

I believe that I have proven my worth.

Through my desire for self-improvement, I have acquired the capacity to visualize a blackboard in front of me, from which the blackness of the past has dropped away and the board becomes crystal clear. I have the chalk in my hand and the ability to write the next chapter of my life.

"While I have been under God's divine guidance, there is no doubt that He has answered my prayers. When I told Him that I was going to walk on water to Him, *I meant it,* and, astonishingly, I have remained buoyant."

And still, *only* my sandals are wet.

Thank You, Jesus

The Hamilton Collection proudly presents

Deliverance

from Mystic Warriors plate collection limited to a total of 28 firing days.

Plate No. 0529P

About the Author

D. Jane Albanese is an award-winning, self-motivated artist, entrepreneur, and author. She lives in Bergen County, New Jersey, just moments away from the critically acclaimed Clinton Inn Hotel and Event Center in Tenafly, formerly owned and operated by her family for nearly five decades.

At age twenty-one she was a debutante in the Hope Cotillion at the Waldorf Astoria. At twenty-eight she owned and managed the Linwood Plaza Travel Agency. Upon moving to Florida ten years later, she acquired her real estate license. Albanese went on to purchase Maple Ridge Gourmet Foods, a food distribution company that she converted into a gourmet food mail-order catalog business.

Finding herself at a crossroads after losing her husband, Dom, in 1994, Albanese returned to college to study graphic design. At age fifty-two she opened Graphic Designs by the Drummer's Wife, a freelance design studio, in loving memory of her late husband.

At age sixty-two she founded Giants of Generosity, Inc., a grassroots charitable organization. Through a family crisis she learned firsthand that life is fragile, and sudden catastrophes can easily cause great pain and upheaval. She then devoted twelve years of her life to helping people who were experiencing critical, life-altering situations of their own. She was the spokesperson for Giants of Generosity and the force behind its growth.

Albanese has been a nominee of the Russ Berrie, Making a Difference Award, and has been recognized by the New Jersey Association of Women Business Owners for her community service and for being a positive role model for women.

Upon her retirement from Giants of Generosity in 2018, she completed this memoir at age seventy-four.

What a life it has been!

Testimonials

"When you are in need of help and the circumstances look bleak and dire, that's when Jane and Giants of Generosity jump into action to take away the fear and darkness, giving you hope and faith. Jane is an angel and so special." — *Sal and Carol Canariato*

"It is not often in life that you come across someone with the ambition and drive of Jane Albanese. A stunning example of one person's success in not only overcoming obstacles in her own life, but shining that light, love and energy onto others who have faced the greatest challenges—for no other reason than a selfless desire to make their lives just a little better—an angel walking amongst us."

— *Doug Singer*

"Our heartfelt and sincere thanks to D. Jane Albanese and her wonderful organization, Giants of Generosity. They provided our family with an immeasurable service when our daughter Christine suffered a catastrophic accident that left her paralyzed. Giants administered the donated funds in an efficient and timely fashion, thus relieving us of this difficult burden.

Although, our beautiful daughter has passed, we will be forever grateful to Ms. Albanese. God bless!"

— *Robert Dominici, father of Christine Danza*

"After injuring my ankle I developed a very severe pressure ulcer in rehab and needed a special bariatric hospital bed with an air-flow mattress. Medicare sent the wrong bed, and would not replace it. Senator Cory Booker's office put us in touch with Giants of Generosity. Jane Albanese became our angel as she worked tirelessly to find a bed for me. Jane and her Giants are selfless, wonderful people! My pressure ulcers have closed, and I no longer have to worry about constant infections. Thank you Jane, you have saved my life." — *Angela Falber*